P9-CLY-902

The
Encyclopedia of
WISCONSIN

Second Edition

The Encyclopedia of

WISCONSIN

Second Edition

* * *

VOLUME

II

SOMERSET PUBLISHERS, INC.
P.O. BOX 160
ST. CLAIR SHORES, MI 48080

ISBN   0-403-09753-3

CONTENTS

VOLUME ONE

PREHISTORY AND ARCHEOLOGY *(cont.)*

HISTORY 53

VOLUME TWO

POLITICAL SECTION

- U.S. Senators and Representatives
- State Executive Offices
- State Legislative Offices

1

U.S. CONGRESSIONAL
Delegates, Representatives and Senators

TWENTY-FOURTH CONGRESS
MARCH 4, 1835, to MARCH 3, 1837

TERRITORY OF WISCONSIN
U.S. DELEGATE
George W. Jones, *Sinsinawa Mound*

TWENTY-FIFTH CONGRESS
MARCH 4, 1837, to MARCH 3, 1839

TERRITORY OF WISCONSIN
U.S. DELEGATE
George W. Jones, *Sinsinawa Mound*
James D. Doty, *Astor*

TWENTY-SIXTH CONGRESS
MARCH 4, 1839, to MARCH 3, 1841

TERRITORY OF WISCONSIN
U.S. DELEGATE
James D. Doty, *Ashton*

TWENTY-SEVENTH CONGRESS
MARCH 4, 1841, to MARCH 3, 1843

TERRITORY OF WISCONSIN
U.S. DELEGATE
Henry Dodge, *Dodgeville*

TWENTY-EIGHTH CONGRESS
MARCH 4, 1843, to MARCH 3, 1845

TERRITORY OF WISCONSIN
U.S. DELEGATE
Henry Dodge, *Dodgeville*

TWENTY-NINTH CONGRESS
MARCH 4, 1845, to MARCH 3, 1847

TERRITORY OF WISCONSIN
U.S. DELEGATE
Morgan L. Martin, *Green Bay*

THIRTIETH CONGRESS
MARCH 4, 1847, to MARCH 3, 1849

TERRITORY OF WISCONSIN
U.S. DELEGATE
John H. Tweedy, *Milwaukee*
Henry H. Sibley, *Mendota*

THIRTY-FIRST CONGRESS
MARCH 4, 1849, to MARCH 3, 1851

U.S. SENATORS
Henry Dodge, *Dodgeville*
Isaac P. Walker, *Milwaukee*
U.S. REPRESENTATIVES
Charles Durkee, *Kenosha*
Orsamus Cole, *Potosi*
James Duane Doty, *Menasha*

THIRTY-SECOND CONGRESS
MARCH 4, 1851, to MARCH 3, 1853

U.S. SENATORS
Henry Dodge, *Dodgeville*
Isaac P. Walker, *Milwaukee*
U.S. REPRESENTATIVES
Charles Durkee, *Kenosha*
Ben C. Eastman, *Platteville*
James Duane Doty, *Menasha*

THIRTY-THIRD CONGRESS
MARCH 4, 1853, to MARCH 3, 1855

U.S. SENATORS

Henry Dodge, *Dodgeville*
Isaac P. Walker, *Milwaukee*
U.S. REPRESENTATIVES
Daniel Wells, Jr., *Milwaukee*
Ben C. Eastman, *Platteville*
John B. Macy, *Fond du Lac*

THIRTY-FOURTH CONGRESS
MARCH 4, 1855, to MARCH 3, 1857

U.S. SENATORS
Henry Dodge, *Dodgeville*
Charles Durkee, *Kenosha*
U.S. REPRESENTATIVES
Daniel Wells, Jr., *Milwaukee*
Cadwallader C. Washburn, *Mineral Point*
Charles Billingshurst, *Juneau*

THIRTY-FIFTH CONGRESS
MARCH 4, 1857, to MARCH 3, 1859

U.S. SENATORS
Charles Durkee, *Kenosha*
James R. Doolittle, *Racine*
U.S. REPRESENTATIVES
John F. Potter, *East Troy*
Cadwallader C. Washburn, *Mineral Point*
Charles Billinghurst, *Juneau*

THIRTY-SIXTH CONGRESS
MARCH 4, 1859, to MARCH 3, 1861

U.S. SENATORS
Charles Durkee, *Kenosha*
James R. Doolittle, *Racine*
U.S. REPRESENTATIVES
John F. Potter, *East Troy*
Cadwallader C. Washburn, *La Crosse*
Charles H. Larrabee, *Horicon*

THIRTY-SEVENTH CONGRESS
MARCH 4, 1861, to MARCH 3, 1863

U.S. SENATORS

James R. Doolittle, *Racine*
Timothy O. Howe, *Green Bay*
U.S. REPRESENTATIVES
Luther Hanchett, *Plover*
Walter D. McIndoe, *Wausau*
John F. Potter, *East Troy*
A. Scott Sloan, *Beaver Dam*

THIRTY-EIGHTH CONGRESS
MARCH 4, 1863, to MARCH 3, 1865

U.S. SENATORS
James R. Doolittle, *Racine*
Timothy O. Howe, *Green Bay*
U.S. REPRESENTATIVES
James S. Brown, *Milwaukee*
Amasa Cobb, *Mineral Point*
Charles A. Eldredge, *Fond du Lac*
Walter D. McIndoe, *Wausau*
Ithamar C. Sloan, *Janesville*
Ezra Wheeler, *Berlin*

THIRTY-NINTH CONGRESS
MARCH 4, 1865, to MARCH 3, 1867

U.S. SENATORS
James R. Doolittle, *Racine*
Timothy O. Howe, *Green Bay*
U.S. REPRESENTATIVES
Halbert E. Paine, *Milwaukee*
Ithamar C. Sloan, *Janesville*
Amasa Cobb, *Mineral Point*
Charles A. Eldredge, *Fond du Lac*
Philetus Sawyer, *Oshkosh*
Walter D. McIndoe, *Wausau*

FORTIETH CONGRESS
MARCH 4, 1867, to MARCH 3, 1869

U.S. SENATORS
James R. Doolittle, *Racine*
Timothy O. Howe, *Green Bay*
U.S. REPRESENTATIVES
Halbert E. Paine, *Milwaukee*

Political Section

Benjamin F. Hopkins, *Madison*
Amasa Cobb, *Mineral Point*
Charles A. Eldredge, *Fond du Lac*
Philetus Sawyer, *Oshkosh*
Cadwallader C. Washburn, *La Crosse*

FORTY-FIRST CONGRESS
MARCH 4, 1869, to MARCH 3, 1871

U.S. SENATORS
Timothy O. Howe, *Green Bay*
Matthew H. Carpenter, *Milwaukee*
U.S. REPRESENTATIVES
Halbert E. Paine, *Milwaukee*
Benjamin F. Hopkins, *Madison*
David Atwood, *Madison*
Amasa Cobb, *Mineral Point*
Charles A. Eldredge, *Fond du Lac*
Philetus Sawyer, *Oshkosh*
Cadwallader C. Washburn, *La Crosse*

FORTY-SECOND CONGRESS
MARCH 4, 1871, to MARCH 3, 1873

U.S. SENATORS
Timothy O. Howe, *Green Bay*
Matthew H. Carpenter, *Milwaukee*
U.S. REPRESENTATIVES
Alexander Mitchell, *Milwaukee*
Gerry W. Hazelton, *Columbus*
J. Allen Barber, *Lancaster*
Charles A. Eldredge, *Fond du Lac*
Philetus Sawyer, *Oshkosh*
Jeremiah M. Rusk, *Viroqua*

FORTY-THIRD CONGRESS
MARCH 4, 1873, to MARCH 3, 1875

U.S. SENATORS
Timothy O. Howe, *Green Bay*
Matthew H. Carpenter, *Milwaukee*
U.S. REPRESENTATIVES
Charles G. Williams, *Janesville*
Gerry W. Hazelton, *Columbus*

J. Allen Barber, *Lancaster*
Alexander Mitchell, *Milwaukee*
Charles A. Eldredge, *Fond du Lac*
Philetus Sawyer, *Oshkosh*
Jeremiah M. Rusk, *Viroqua*
Alexander S. McDill, *Plover*

FORTY-FOURTH CONGRESS
MARCH 4, 1875, to MARCH 3, 1877

U.S. SENATORS
Timothy O. Howe, *Green Bay*
Angus Cameron, *La Crosse*
U.S. REPRESENTATIVES
Charles G. Williams, *Janesville*
Lucien B. Caswell, *Fort Atkinson*
Henry S. Magoon, *Darlington*
William P. Lynde, *Milwaukee*
Samuel D. Burchard, *Beaver Dam*
Alanson M. Kimball, *Pine River*
Jeremiah M. Rusk, *Viroqua*
George W. Cate, *Stevens Point*

FORTY-FIFTH CONGRESS
MARCH 4, 1877, to MARCH 3, 1879

U.S. SENATORS
Timothy O. Howe, *Green Bay*
Angus Cameron, *La Crosse*
U.S. REPRESENTATIVES
Charles G. Williams, *Janesville*
Lucien B. Caswell, *Fort Atkinson*
George C. Hazelton, *Boscobel*
William P. Lynde, *Milwaukee*
Edward S. Bragg, *Fond du Lac*
Gabriel Bouck, *Oshkosh*
Herman L. Humphrey, *Hudson*
Thaddeus C. Pound, *Chippewa Falls*

FORTY-SIXTH CONGRESS
MARCH 4, 1879, to MARCH 3, 1881

U.S. SENATORS
Angus Cameron, *La Crosse*

Matthew H. Carpenter, *Milwaukee*
U.S. REPRESENTATIVES
Charles G. Williams, *Janesville*
Lucien B. Caswell, *Fort Atkinson*
George C. Hazelton, *Boscobel*
Peter V. Deuster, *Milwaukee*
Edward S. Bragg, *Fond du Lac*
Gabriel Bouck, *Oshkosh*
Herman L. Humphrey, *Hudson*
Thaddeus C. Pound, *Chippewa Falls*

FORTY-SEVENTH CONGRESS
MARCH 4, 1881, to MARCH 3, 1883

U.S. SENATORS
Angus Cameron, *La Crosse*
Philetus Sawyer, *Oshkosh*
U.S. REPRESENTATIVES
Charles G. Williams, *Janesville*
Lucien B. Caswell, *Fort Atkinson*
George C. Hazelton, *Boscobel*
Peter V. Deuster, *Milwaukee*
Edward S. Bragg, *Fond du Lac*
Richard W. Guenther, *Oshkosh*
Herman L. Humphrey, *Hudson*
Thaddeus C. Pound, *Chippewa Falls*

FORTY-EIGHTH CONGRESS
MARCH 4, 1883, to MARCH 3, 1885

U.S. SENATORS
Angus Cameron, *La Crosse*
Philetus Sawyer, *Oshkosh*
U.S. REPRESENTATIVES
John Winans, *Janesville*
Daniel H. Sumner, *Waukesha*
Burr W. Jones, *Madison*
Peter V. Deuster, *Milwaukee*
Joseph Rankin, *Manitowoc*
Richard W. Guenther, *Oshkosh*
Gilbert M. Woodward, *La Crosse*
William T. Price, *Black River Falls*
Isaac Stephenson, *Marinette*

FORTY-NINTH CONGRESS
MARCH 4, 1885, to MARCH 3, 1887

U.S. SENATORS
Philetus Sawyer, *Oshkosh*
John C. Spooner, *Hudson*
U.S. REPRESENTATIVES
Lucien B. Caswell, *Fort Atkinson*
Edward S. Bragg, *Fond du Lac*
Robert M. La Follette, *Madison*
Isaac W. Van Schaick, *Milwaukee*
Joseph Rankin, *Manitowoc*
Thomas R. Hudd, *Green Bay*
Richard W. Guenther, *Oshkosh*
Ormsby B. Thomas, *Prairie du Chien*
William T. Price, *Black River Falls*
Hugh H. Price, *Black River Falls*
Isaac Stephenson, *Marinette*

FIFTIETH CONGRESS
MARCH 4, 1887, to MARCH 3, 1889

U.S. SENATORS
Philetus Sawyer, *Oshkosh*
John C. Spooner, *Hudson*
U.S. REPRESENTATIVES
Lucien B. Caswell, *Fort Atkinson*
Richard W. Guenther, *Oshkosh*
Robert M. La Follette, *Madison*
Henry Smith, *Milwaukee*
Thomas R. Hudd, *Green Bay*
Charles B. Clark, *Neenah*
Ormsby B. Thomas, *Prairie du Chien*
Nils P. Haugen, *River Falls*
Isaac Stephenson, *Marinette*

FIFTY-FIRST CONGRESS
MARCH 4, 1889, to MARCH 3, 1891

U.S. SENATORS
Philetus Sawyer, *Oshkosh*
John C. Spooner, *Hudson*
U.S. REPRESENTATIVES

Political Section

Lucien B. Caswell, *Fort Atkinson*
Charles Barwig, *Mayville*
Robert M. La Follette, *Madison*
Isaac W. Van Schaick, *Milwaukee*
George H. Brickner, *Sheboygan Falls*
Charles B. Clark, *Neenah*
Ormsby B. Thomas, *Prairie du Chien*
Nils P. Haugen, *River Falls*
Myron H. McCord, *Merrill*

FIFTY-SECOND CONGRESS
MARCH 4, 1891, to MARCH 3, 1893

U.S. SENATORS
Philetus Sawyer, *Oshkosh*
William F. Vilas, *Madison*
U.S. REPRESENTATIVES
Clinton Babbitt, *Beloit*
Charles Barwig, *Mayville*
Allen R. Bushnell, *Madison*
John L. Mitchell, *Milwaukee*
George H. Brickner, *Sheboygan Falls*
Lucas M. Miller, *Oshkosh*
Frank P. Coburn, *West Salem*
Nils P. Haugen, *River Falls*
Thomas Lynch, *Antigo*

FIFTY-THIRD CONGRESS
MARCH 4, 1893, to MARCH 3, 1895

U.S. SENATORS
William F. Vilas, *Madison*
John L. Mitchell, *Milwaukee*
U.S. REPRESENTATIVES
Henry Allen Cooper, *Racine*
Charles Barwig, *Mayville*
Joseph W. Babcock, *Necedah*
Peter J. Somers, *Milwaukee*
George H. Brickner, *Sheboygan Falls*
Owen A. Wells, *Fond du Lac*
George B. Shaw, *Eau Claire*
Michael Griffin, *Eau Claire*
Lyman E. Barnes, *Appleton*

Thomas Lynch, *Antigo*
Nils P. Haugen, *River Falls*

FIFTY-FOURTH CONGRESS
MARCH 4, 1895, to MARCH 3, 1897

U.S. SENATORS
William F. Vilas, *Madison*
John L. Mitchell, *Milwaukee*
U.S. REPRESENTATIVES
Henry Allen Cooper, *Racine*
Edward Sauerhering, *Mayville*
Joseph W. Babcock, *Necedah*
Theobald Otjen, *Milwaukee*
Samuel S. Barney, *West Bend*
Samuel A. Cook, *Neenah*
Michael Griffin, *Eau Claire*
Edward S. Minor, *Sturgeon Bay*
Alexander Stewart, *Wausau*
John J. Jenkins, *Chippewa Falls*

FIFTY-FIFTH CONGRESS
MARCH 4, 1897, to MARCH 3, 1899

U.S. SENATORS
John L. Mitchell, *Milwaukee*
John C. Spooner, *Madison*
U.S. REPRESENTATIVES
Henry Allen Cooper, *Racine*
Edward Sauerhering, *Mayville*
Joseph W. Babcock, *Necedah*
Theobald Otjen, *Milwaukee*
Samuel S. Barney, *West Bend*
James H. Davidson, *Oshkosh*
Michael Griffin, *Eau Claire*
Edward S. Minor, *Sturgeon Bay*
Alexander Stewart, *Wausau*
John J. Jenkins, *Chippewa Falls*

FIFTY-SIXTH CONGRESS
MARCH 4, 1899, to MARCH 3, 1901

U.S. SENATORS
John C. Spooner, *Madison*

Joseph V. Quarles, *Milwaukee*
U.S. REPRESENTATIVES
Henry Allen Cooper, *Racine*
Herman B. Dahle, *Mount Horeb*
Joseph W. Babcock, *Necedah*
Theobald Otjen, *Milwaukee*
Samuel S. Barney, *West Bend*
James H. Davidson, *Oshkosh*
John J. Esch, *La Crosse*
Edward S. Minor, *Sturgeon Bay*
Alexander Stewart, *Wausau*
John J. Jenkins, *Chippewa Falls*

FIFTY-SEVENTH CONGRESS
MARCH 4, 1901, to MARCH 3, 1903

U.S. SENATORS
John C. Spooner, *Madison*
Joseph V. Quarles, *Milwaukee*
U.S. REPRESENTATIVES
Henry Allen Cooper, *Racine*
Herman B. Dahle, *Mount Horeb*
Joseph W. Babcock, *Necedah*
Theobald Otjen, *Milwaukee*
Samuel S. Barney, *West Bend*
James H. Davidson, *Oshkosh*
John J. Esch, *La Crosse*
Edward S. Minor, *Sturgeon Bay*
Webster E. Brown, *Rhinelander*
John J. Jenkins, *Chippewa Falls*

FIFTY-EIGHTH CONGRESS
MARCH 4, 1903, to MARCH 3, 1905

U.S. SENATORS
John C. Spooner, *Madison*
Joseph V. Quarles, *Milwaukee*
U.S. REPRESENTATIVES
Henry Allen Cooper, *Racine*
Henry C. Adams, *Madison*
Joseph W. Babcock, *Necedah*
Theobald Otjen, *Milwaukee*
William H. Stafford, *Milwaukee*

Charles H. Weisse, *Sheboygan Falls*
John J. Esch, *La Crosse*
James H. Davidson, *Oshkosh*
Edward S. Minor, *Sturgeon Bay*
Webster E. Brown, *Rhinelander*
John J. Jenkins, *Chippewa Falls*

FIFTY-NINTH CONGRESS
MARCH 4, 1905, to MARCH 3, 1907

U.S. SENATORS
John C. Spooner, *Madison*
Robert M. La Follette, *Madison*
U.S. REPRESENTATIVES
Henry Allen Cooper, *Racine*
Henry C. Adams, *Madison*
John M. Nelson, *Madison*
Joseph W. Babcock, *Necedah*
Theobald Otjen, *Milwaukee*
William H. Stafford, *Milwaukee*
Charles H. Weisse, *Sheboygan Falls*
John J. Esch, *La Crosse*
James H. Davidson, *Oshkosh*
Edward S. Minor, *Sturgeon Bay*
Webster E. Brown, *Rhinelander*
John J. Jenkins, *Chippewa Falls*

SIXTIETH CONGRESS
MARCH 4, 1907, to MARCH 3, 1909

U.S. SENATORS
John C. Spooner, *Madison*
Isaac Stephenson, *Marinette*
Robert M. La Follette, *Madison*
U.S. REPRESENTATIVES
Henry Allen Cooper, *Racine*
John M. Nelson, *Madison*
James W. Murphy, *Platteville*
William J. Cary, *Milwaukee*
William H. Stafford, *Milwaukee*
Charles H. Weisse, *Sheboygan Falls*
John J. Esch, *La Crosse*
James H. Davidson, *Oshkosh*

Gustav Kustermann, *Green Bay*
Elmer A. Morse, *Antigo*
John J. Jenkins, *Chippewa Falls*

SIXTY-FIRST CONGRESS
MARCH 4, 1909, to MARCH 3, 1911

U.S. SENATORS
Robert M. La Follette, *Madison*
Isaac Stephenson, *Marinette*
U.S. REPRESENTATIVES
Henry Allen Cooper, *Racine*
John M. Nelson, *Madison*
Arthur W. Kopp, *Platteville*
William J. Cary, *Milwaukee*
William H. Stafford,*Milwaukee*
Charles H. Weisse, *Sheboygan Falls*
John J. Esch, *La Crosse*
James H. Davidson, *Oshkosh*
Gustav Kustermann, *Green Bay*
Elmer A. Morse, *Antigo*
Irvine L. Lenroot, *Superior*

SIXTY-SECOND CONGRESS
MARCH 4, 1911, to MARCH 3, 1913

U.S. SENATORS
Robert M. La Follette, *Madison*
Isaac Stephenson, *Marinette*
U.S. REPRESENTATIVES
Henry Allen Cooper, *Racine*
John M. Nelson, *Madison*
Arthur W. Kopp, *Platteville*
William J. Cary, *Milwaukee*
Victor L. Berger, *Milwaukee*
Michael E. Burke, *Beaver Dam*
John J. Esch, *La Crosse*
James H. Davidson, *Oshkosh*
Thomas F. Konop, *Kewaunee*
Elmer A. Morse, *Antigo*
Irvine L. Lenroot, *Superior*

SIXTY-THIRD CONGRESS
MARCH 4, 1913, to MARCH 3, 1915

U.S. SENATORS
Robert M. La Follette, *Madison*
Isaac Stephenson, *Marinette*
U.S. REPRESENTATIVES
Henry Allen Cooper, *Racine*
Michael E. Burke, *Beaver Dam*
John M. Nelson, *Madison*
William J. Cary, *Milwaukee*
William H. Stafford, *Milwaukee*
Michael K. Reilly, *Fond du Lac*
John J. Esch, *La Crosse*
Edward E. Browne, *Waupaca*
Thomas F. Konop, *Kewaunee*
James A. Frear, *Hudson*
Irvine L. Lenroot, *Superior*

SIXTY-FOURTH CONGRESS
MARCH 4, 1915, to March 3, 1917

U.S. SENATORS
Robert M. La Follette, *Madison*
Paul O. Husting, *Mayville*
U.S. REPRESENTATIVES
Henry Allen Cooper, *Racine*
Michael E. Burke, *Beaver Dam*
John M. Nelson, *Madison*
William J. Cary, *Milwaukee*
William H. Stafford, *Milwaukee*
Michael K. Reilly, *Fond du Lac*
John J. Esch, *La Crosse*
Edward E. Browne, *Waupaca*
Thomas F. Konop, *Green Bay*
James A. Frear, *Hudson*
Irvine L. Lenroot, *Superior*

SIXTY-FIFTH CONGRESS
MARCH 4, 1917, to MARCH 3, 1919

U.S. SENATORS
Robert M. La Follette, *Madison*

Paul O. Husting, *Mayville*
Irvine L. Lenroot, *Superior*
U.S. REPRESENTATIVES
Henry Allen Cooper, *Racine*
Edward Voigt, *Sheboygan*
John M. Nelson, *Madison*
William J. Cary, *Milwaukee*
William H. Stafford, *Milwaukee*
James H. Davidson, *Oshkosh*
Florian Lampert, *Oshkosh*
John J. Esch, *La Crosse*
Edward E. Browne, *Waupaca*
David G. Classon, *Oconto*
James A. Frear, *Hudson*
Irvine L. Lenroot, *Superior*
Adolphus P. Nelson, *Grantsburg*

SIXTY-SIXTH CONGRESS
MARCH 4, 1919, to MARCH 3, 1921

U.S. SENATORS
Robert M. La Follette, *Madison*
Irvine L. Lenroot, *Superior*
U.S. REPRESENTATIVES
Clifford E. Randall, *Kenosha*
Edward Voigt, *Sheboygan*
James G. Monahan, *Darlington*
John C. Kleczka, *Milwaukee*
Victor L. Berger, *Milwaukee*
Florian Lampert, *Oshkosh*
John J. Esch, *La Crosse*
Edward E. Browne, *Waupaca*
David G. Classon, *Oconto*
James A. Frear, *Hudson*
Adolphus P. Nelson, *Grantsburg*

SIXTY-SEVENTH CONGRESS
MARCH 4, 1921, to MARCH 3, 1923

U.S. SENATORS
Robert M. La Follette, *Madison*
Irvine L. Lenroot, *Superior*
U.S. REPRESENTATIVES

Henry Allen Cooper, *Racine*
Edward Voigt, *Sheboygan*
John M. Nelson, *Madison*
John C. Kleczka, *Milwaukee*
William H. Stafford, *Milwaukee*
Florian Lampert, *Oshkosh*
Joseph D. Beck, *Viroqua*
Edward E. Browne, *Waupaca*
David G. Classon, *Oconto*
James A. Frear, *Hudson*
Adolphus P. Nelson, *Grantsburg*

SIXTY-EIGHTH CONGRESS
MARCH 4, 1923, to MARCH 3, 1925

U.S. SENATORS
Robert M. La Follette, *Madison*
Irvine L. Lenroot, *Superior*
U.S. REPRESENTATIVES
Henry Allen Cooper, *Racine*
Edward Voigt, *Sheboygan*
John M. Nelson, *Madison*
John C. Schafer, *Milwaukee*
Victor L. Berger, *Milwaukee*
Florian Lampert, *Oshkosh*
Joseph D. Beck, *Viroqua*
Edward E. Browne, *Waupaca*
George J. Schneider, *Appleton*
James A. Frear, *Hudson*
Hubert H. Peavey, *Washburn*

SIXTY-NINTH CONGRESS
MARCH 4, 1925, to MARCH 3, 1927

U.S. SENATORS
Robert M. La Follette, *Madison*
Robert M. La Follette, Jr., *Madison*
Irvine L. Lenroot, *Superior*
U.S. REPRESENTATIVES
Henry Allen Cooper, *Racine*
Edward Voigt, *Sheboygan*
John M. Nelson, *Madison*
John C. Schafer, *Milwaukee*

Victor L. Berger, *Milwaukee*
Florian Lampert, *Oshkosh*
Joseph D. Beck, *Viroqua*
Edward E. Browne, *Waupaca*
George J. Schneider, *Appleton*
James A. Frear, *Hudson*
Hubert H. Peavey, *Washburn*

SEVENTIETH CONGRESS
MARCH 4, 1927, to MARCH 3, 1929

U.S. SENATORS
Robert M. La Follette, Jr., *Madison*
John J. Blaine, *Boscobel*
U.S. REPRESENTATIVES
Henry Allen Cooper, *Racine*
Charles A. Kading, *Watertown*
John M. Nelson, *Madison*
John C. Schafer, *Milwaukee*
Victor L. Berger, *Milwaukee*
Florian Lampert, *Oshkosh*
Joseph D. Beck, *Viroqua*
Edward E. Browne, *Waupaca*
George J. Schneider, *Appleton*
James A. Frear, *Hudson*
Hubert H. Peavey, *Washburn*

SEVENTY-FIRST CONGRESS
MARCH 4, 1929, to MARCH 3, 1931

U.S. SENATORS
Robert M. La Follette, Jr., *Madison*
John J. Blaine, *Boscobel*
U.S. REPRESENTATIVES
Henry Allen Cooper, *Racine*
Charles A. Kading, *Watertown*
John M. Nelson, *Madison*
John C. Schafer, *Milwaukee*
William H. Stafford, *Milwaukee*
Florian Lampert, *Oshkosh*
Michael K. Reilly, *Fond du Lac*
Merlin Hull, *Black River Falls*
Edward E. Browne, *Waupaca*

George J. Schneider, *Appleton*
James A. Frear, *Hudson*
Hubert H. Peavey, *Washburn*

SEVENTY-SECOND CONGRESS
MARCH 4, 1931, to MARCH 3, 1933

U.S. SENATORS
Robert M. La Follette, Jr., *Madison*
John J. Blaine, *Boscobel*
U.S. REPRESENTATIVES
Thomas R. Amlie, *Elkhorn*
Charles A. Kading, *Watertown*
John M. Nelson, *Madison*
John C. Schafer, *Milwaukee*
William H. Stafford, *Milwaukee*
Michael K. Reilly, *Fond du Lac*
Gardner R. Withrow, *La Crosse*
Gerald J. Boileau, *Wausau*
George J. Schneider, *Appleton*
James A. Frear, *Hudson*
Hubert H. Peavey, *Washburn*

SEVENTY-THIRD CONGRESS
MARCH 4, 1933, to JANUARY 3, 1935

U.S. SENATORS
Robert M. La Follette, Jr., *Madison*
F. Ryan Duffy, *Fond du Lac*
U.S. REPRESENTATIVES
George W. Blanchard, *Edgerton*
Charles W. Henney, *Portage*
Gardner R. Withrow, *La Crosse*
Raymond J. Cannon, *Milwaukee*
Thomas O'Malley, *Milwaukee*
Michael. K. Reilly, *Fond du Lac*
Gerald J. Boileau, *Wausau*
James F. Hughes, *De Pere*
James A. Frear, *Hudson*
Hubert H. Peavey, *Washburn*

SEVENTY-FOURTH CONGRESS
JANUARY 3, 1935, to JANUARY 3, 1937

U.S. SENATORS
Robert M. La Follette, Jr., *Madison*
F. Ryan Duffy, *Fond du Lac*
U.S. REPRESENTATIVES
Thomas R. Amlie, *Elkhorn*
Harry Sauthoff, *Madison*
Gardner R. Withrow, *La Crosse*
Raymond J. Cannon, *Milwaukee*
Thomas O'Malley, *Milwaukee*
Michael K. Reilly, *Fond du Lac*
Gerald J. Boileau, *Wausau*
George J. Schneider, *Appleton*
Merlin Hull, *Black River Falls*
Bernard J. Gehrmann, *Mellon, R.F.D.*

SEVENTY-FIFTH CONGRESS
JANUARY 3, 1937, to JANUARY 3, 1939

U.S. SENATORS
Robert M. La Follette, Jr., *Madison*
F. Ryan Duffy, *Fond du Lac*
U.S. REPRESENTATIVES
Thomas R. Amlie, *Elkhorn*
Harry Sauthoff, *Madison*
Gardner R. Withrow, *La Crosse*
Raymond J. Cannon, *Milwaukee*
Thomas O'Malley, *Milwaukee*
Michael K. Reilly, *FondduLac*
Gerald J. Boileau, *Wausau*
George J. Schneider, *Appleton*
Merlin Hull, *BlackRiver Falls*
Bernard J. Gehrmann, *Mellon, R.F.D.*

SEVENTY-SIXTH CONGRESS
JANUARY 3, 1939, to JANUARY 3, 1941

U.S. SENATORS
Robert M. La Follette, Jr., *Madison*
Alexander Wiley, *Chippewa Falls*
U.S. REPRESENTATIVES
Stephen Bolles, *Janesville*
Charles Hawks, Jr., *Horicon*
Harry W. Griswold, *West Salem*
John C. Schafer, *Milwaukee*

Lewis D. Thill, *Milwaukee*
Frank B. Keefe, *Oshkosh*
Reid F. Murray, *Waupaca*
Joshua L. Johns, *Appleton*
Merlin Hull, *Black River Falls*
Bernard J. Gehrmann, *Mellon, R.F.D.*

SEVENTY-SEVENTH CONGRESS
JANUARY 3, 1941, to JANUARY 3, 1943

U.S. SENATORS
Robert M. La Follette, Jr., *Madison*
Alexander Wiley, *Chippewa Falls*
U.S. REPRESENTATIVES
Stephen Bolles, *Janesville*
Lawrence H. Smith, *Racine*
Harry Sauthoff, *Madison*
William H. Stevenson, *La Crosse*
Thaddeus F. B. Wasielewski, *Milwaukee*
Lewis D. Thill, *Milwaukee*
Frank B. Keefe, *Oshkosh*
Reid F. Murray, *Ogdensburg*
Joshua L. Johns, *Appleton*
Merlin Hull, *Black River Falls*
Bernard J. Gehrmann, *Mellon, R.F.D.*

SEVENTY-EIGHTH CONGRESS
JANUARY 3, 1943, to JANUARY 3, 1945

U.S. SENATORS
Robert M. La Follette, Jr., *Madison*
Alexander Wiley, *Chippewa Falls*
U.S. REPRESENTATIVES
Lawrence H. Smith, *Racine*
Harry Sauthoff, *Madison*
William H. Stevenson, *La Crosse*
Thaddeus F. B. Wasielewski, *Milwaukee*
Howard J. McMurray, *Milwaukee*
Frank B. Keefe, *Oshkosh*
Reid F. Murray, *Ogdensburg*
LaVern R. Dilweg, *Green Bay*
Merlin Hull, *Black River Falls*
Alvin E. O'Konski, *Mercer*

Political Section

SEVENTY-NINTH CONGRESS
JANUARY 3, 1945, to JANUARY 3, 1947

U.S. SENATORS
Robert M. La Follette, Jr., *Madison*
Alexander Wiley, *Chippewa Falls*
U.S. REPRESENTATIVES
Lawrence H. Smith, *Racine*
Robert K. Henry, *Jefferson*
William H. Stevenson, *La Crosse*
Thaddeus F. B. Wasielewski, *Milwaukee*
Andrew J. Biemiller, *Milwaukee*
Frank B. Keefe, *Oshkosh*
Reid F. Murray, *Ogdensburg*
John W. Byrnes, *Green Bay*
Merlin Hull, *Black River Falls*
Alvin E. O'Konski, *Mercer*

EIGHTIETH CONGRESS
JANUARY 3, 1947, to JANUARY 3, 1949

U.S. SENATORS
Alexander Wiley, *Chippewa Falls*
Joseph R. McCarthy, *Appleton*
U.S. REPRESENTATIVES
Lawrence H. Smith, *Racine*
Glenn R. Davis, *Waukesha*
William H. Stevenson, *La Crosse*
John C. Brophy, *Milwaukee*
Charles J. Kersten, *Milwaukee*
Frank B. Keefe, *Oshkosh*
Reid F. Murray, *Ogdensburg*
John W. Byrnes, *Green Bay*
Merlin Hull, *Black River Falls*
Alvin E. O'Konski, *Mercer*

EIGHTY-FIRST CONGRESS
JANUARY 3, 1949, to JANUARY 3, 1951

U.S. SENATORS
Alexander Wiley, *Chippewa Falls*
Joseph R. McCarthy, *Appleton*
U.S. REPRESENTATIVES
Lawrence H. Smith, *Racine*
Glenn R. Davis, *Waukesha*
Gardner R. Withrow, *La Crosse*
Clement J. Zablocki, *Milwaukee*
Andrew J. Biemiller, *Milwaukee*
Frank B. Keefe, *Oshkosh*
Reid F. Murray, *Ogdensburg*
John W. Byrnes, *Green Bay*
Merlin Hull, *Black River Falls*
Alvin E. O'Konski, *Mercer*

EIGHTY-SECOND CONGRESS
JANUARY 3, 1951, to JANUARY 3, 1953

U.S. SENATORS
Alexander Wiley, *Chippewa Falls*
Joseph R. McCarthy, *Appleton*
U.S. REPRESENTATIVES
Lawrence H. Smith, *Racine*
Glenn R. Davis, *Waukesha*
Gardner R. Withrow, *La Crosse*
Clement J. Zablocki, *Milwaukee*
Charles J. Kersten, *Milwaukee*
William K. Van Pelt, *Fond du Lac*
Reid F. Murray, *Ogdensburg*
John W. Byrnes, *Green Bay*
Merlin Hull, *Black River Falls*
Alvin E. O'Konski, *Mercer*

EIGHTY-THIRD CONGRESS
JANUARY 3, 1953, to JANUARY 3, 1955

U.S. SENATORS
Alexander Wiley, *Chippewa Falls*
Joseph R. McCarthy, *Appleton*
U.S. REPRESENTATIVES
Lawrence H. Smith, *Racine*
Glenn R. Davis, *Waukesha*
Gardner R. Withrow, *La Crosse*
Clement J. Zablocki, *Milwaukee*
Charles J. Kersten, *Milwaukee*
William K. Van Pelt, *Fond du Lac*
Melvin R. Laird, *Marshfield*

13

John W. Byrnes, *Green Bay*
Merlin Hull, *Black River Falls*
Lester R. Johnson, *Black River Falls*
Alvin E. O'Konski, *Mercer*

EIGHTY-FOURTH CONGRESS
JANUARY 3, 1955, to JANUARY 3, 1957

U.S. SENATORS
Alexander Wiley, *Chippewa Falls*
Joseph R. McCarthy, *Appleton*
U.S. REPRESENTATIVES
Lawrence H. Smith, *Racine*
Glenn R. Davis, *Waukesha*
Gardner R. Withrow, *La Crosse*
Clement J. Zablocki, *Milwaukee*
Henry S. Reuss, *Milwaukee*
William K. Van Pelt, *Fond du Lac*
Melvin R. Laird, *Marshfield*
John W. Byrnes, *Green Bay*
Lester R. Johnson, *Black River Falls*
Alvin E. O'Konski, *Mercer*

EIGHTY-FIFTH CONGRESS
JANUARY 3, 1957, to JANUARY 3, 1959

U.S. SENATORS
Alexander Wiley, *Chippewa Falls*
Joseph R. McCarthy, *Appleton*
William Proxmire, *Madison*
U.S. REPRESENTATIVES
Lawrence H. Smith, *Racine*
Donald E. Tewes, *Waukesha*
Gardner R. Withrow, *La Crosse*
Clement J. Zablocki, *Milwaukee*
Henry S. Reuss, *Milwaukee*
William K. Van Pelt, *Fond du Lac*
Melvin R. Laird, *Marshfield*
John W. Byrnes, *Green Bay*
Lester R. Johnson, *Black River Falls*
Alvin E. O'Konski, *Mercer*

EIGHTY-SIXTH CONGRESS
JANUARY 3, 1959, to JANUARY 3, 1961

U.S. SENATORS
Alexander Wiley, *Chippewa·Falls*
William Proxmire, *Madison*
U.S. REPRESENTATIVES
Gerald T. Flynn, *Racine*
Robert W. Kastenmeier, *Watertown*
Gardner R. Withrow, *La Crosse*
Clement J. Zablocki, *Milwaukee*
Henry S. Reuss, *Milwaukee*
William K. Van Pelt, *Fond du Lac*
Melvin R. Laird, *Marshfield*
John W. Byrnes, *Green Bay*
Lester R. Johnson, *Black River Falls*
Alvin E. O'Konski, *Mercer*

EIGHTY-SEVENTH CONGRESS
JANUARY 3, 1961, to JANUARY 3, 1963

U.S. SENATORS
Alexander Wiley, *Chippewa Falls*
William Proxmire, *Madison*
U.S. REPRESENTATIVES
Henry C. Schadeberg, *Burlington*
Robert W. Kastenmeier, *Watertown*
Vernon W. Thomson, *Richland Center*
Clement J. Zablocki, *Milwaukee*
Henry S. Reuss, *Milwaukee*
William K. Van Pelt, *Fond du Lac*
Melvin R. Laird, *Marshfield*
John W. Byrnes, *Green Bay*
Lester R. Johnson, *Black River Falls*
Alvin E. O'Konski, *Mercer*

EIGHTY-EIGHTH CONGRESS
JANUARY 3, 1963, to JANUARY 3, 1965

U.S. SENATORS
William Proxmire, *Madison*
Gaylord A. Nelson, *Madison*
U.S. REPRESENTATIVES

Political Section

Henry C. Schadeberg, *Burlington*
Robert W. Kastenmeier, *Watertown*
Vernon W. Thomson, *Richland Center*
Clement J. Zablocki, *Milwaukee*
Henry S. Reuss, *Milwaukee*
William K. Van Pelt, *Fond du Lac*
Melvin R. Laird, *Marshfield*
John W. Byrnes, *Green Bay*
Lester R. Johnson, *Black River Falls*
Alvin E. O'Konski, *Mercer*

EIGHTY-EIGHTH CONGRESS
JANUARY 3, 1963, to JANUARY 3, 1965

U.S. SENATORS
William Proxmire, *Madison*
Gaylord A. Nelson, *Madison*
U.S. REPRESENTATIVES
Henry C. Schadeberg, *Burlington*
Robert W. Kastenmeier, *Watertown*
Vernon W. Thomson, *Richland Center*
Clement J. Zablocki, *Milwaukee*
Henry S. Reuss, *Milwaukee*
William K. Van Pelt, *Fond du Lac*
Melvin R. Laird, *Marshfield*
John W. Byrnes, *Green Bay*
Lester R. Johnson, *Black River Fall*
Alvin E. O'Konski, *Mercer*

EIGHTY-NINTH CONGRESS
JANUARY 3, 1965, to JANUARY 3, 1967

U.S. SENATORS
William Proxmire, *Madison*
Gaylord Nelson, *Madison*
U.S. REPRESENTATIVES
Lynn E. Stalbaum, *Racine*
Robert W. Kastenmeier, *Watertown*
Vernon W. Thomson, *Richland Center*
Clement J. Zablocki, *Milwaukee*
Henry S. Reuss, *Milwaukee*
John A. Race, *Fond du Lac*
Melvin R. Laird, *Marshfield*

John W. Byrnes, *Green Bay*
Glenn R. Davis, *New Berlin*
Alvin E. O'Konski, *Mercer*

NINETIETH CONGRESS
JANUARY 3, 1967, to JANUARY 3, 1969

U.S. SENATORS
William Proxmire, *Madison*
Gaylord Nelson, *Madison*
U.S. REPRESENTATIVES
Henry C. Schadeberg, *Burlington*
Robert W. Kastenmeier, *Watertown*
Vernon W. Thomson, *Richland Center*
Clement J. Zablocki, *Milwaukee*
Henry S. Reuss, *Milwaukee*
William A. Steiger, *Oshkosh*
Melvin R. Laird, *Marshfield*
John W. Byrnes, *Green Bay*
Glenn R. Davis, *New Berlin*
Alvin E. O'Konski, *Mercer*

NINETY-FIRST CONGRESS
JANUARY 3, 1969, to JANUARY 3, 1971

U.S. SENATORS
William Proxmire, *Madison*
Gaylord Nelson, *Madison*
U.S. REPRESENTATIVES
Henry C. Schadeberg, *Burlington*
Robert W. Kastenmeier, *Watertown*
Vernon W. Thomson, *Richland Center*
Clement J. Zablocki, *Milwaukee*
Henry S. Reuss, *Milwaukee*
William A. Steiger, *Oshkosh*
Melvin R. Laird, *Marshfield*
David R. Obey, *Wausau*
John W. Byrnes, *Green Bay*
Glenn R. Davis, *Waukesha*
Alvin E. O'Konski, *Rhinelander*

NINETY-SECOND CONGRESS
JANUARY 3, 1971, to JANUARY 3, 1973

U.S. SENATORS
William Proxmire, *Madison*
Gaylord Nelson, *Madison*
U.S. REPRESENTATIVES
Les Aspin, *Racine*
Robert W. Kastenmeier, *Watertown*
Vernon W. Thomson, *Richland Center*
Clement J. Zablocki, *Milwaukee*
Henry S. Reuss, *Milwaukee*
William A. Steiger, *Oshkosh*
David R. Obey, *Wausau*
John W. Byrnes, *Green Bay*
Glenn R. Davis, *New Berlin*
Alvin E. O'Konski, *Mercer*

NINETY-THIRD CONGRESS
JANUARY 3, 1973, to JANUARY 3, 1975

U.S. SENATORS
William Proxmire, *Madison*
Gaylord Nelson, *Madison*
U.S. REPRESENTATIVES
Les Aspin, *Racine*
Robert W. Kastenmeier, *Sun Prairie*
Vernon W. Thomson, *Richland Center*
Clement J. Zablocki, *Milwaukee*
Henry S. Reuss, *Milwaukee*
William A. Steiger, *Oshkosh*
David R. Obey, *Wausau*
Harold V. Froehlich, *Appleton*
Glenn R. Davis, *Waukesha*

NINETY-FOURTH CONGRESS
JANUARY 3, 1975, to JANUARY 3, 1977

U.S. SENATORS
William Proxmire, *Madison*
Gaylord Nelson, *Madison*
U.S. REPRESENTATIVES
Les Aspin, *Racine*
Robert W. Kastenmeier, *Sun Prairie*
Alvin Baldus, *Menomonie*
Clement J. Zablocki, *Milwaukee*
Henry S. Reuss, *Milwaukee*

William A. Steiger, *Oshkosh*
David R. Obey, *Wausau*
Robert J. Cornell, *DePere*
Robert W. Kasten, Jr., *Thiensville*

NINETY-FIFTH CONGRESS
JANUARY 3, 1977, to JANUARY 3, 1979

U.S. SENATORS
William Proxmire, *Madison*
Gaylord Nelson, *Madison*
U.S. REPRESENTATIVES
Les Aspin, *Racine*
Robert W. Kastenmeier, *Sun Prairie*
Alvin Baldus, *Menomonie*
Clement J. Zablocki, *Milwaukee*
Henry S. Reuss, *Milwaukee*
William A. Steiger, *Oshkosh*
David R. Obey, *Wausau*
Robert J. Cornell, *DePere*
Robert W. Kasten, Jr., *Brookfield*

NINETY-SIXTH CONGRESS
JANUARY 3, 1979, to JANUARY 3, 1981

U.S. SENATORS
William Proxmire, *Madison*
Gaylord Nelson, *Madison*
U.S. REPRESENTATIVES
Les Aspin, *Racine*
Robert W. Kastenmeier, *Sun Prairie*
Alvin Baldus, *Menomonie*
Clement J. Zablocki, *Milwaukee*
Henry S. Reuss, *Milwaukee*
Thomas E. Petri, *Fond du Lac*
David R. Obey, *Wausau*
Toby A. Roth, *Appleton*
F. James Sensenbrenner, Jr., *Shorewood*

NINETY-SEVENTH CONGRESS
JANUARY 3, 1981, to JANUARY 3, 1983

U.S. SENATORS
William Proxmire, *Madison*

Robert W. Kasten, Jr., *Milwaukee*
U.S. REPRESENTATIVES
Les Aspin, *Racine*
Robert W. Kastenmeier, *Sun Prairie*
Steven Gunderson, *Osseo*
Clement J. Zablocki, *Milwaukee*
Henry S. Reuss, *Milwaukee*
Thomas E. Petri, *Fond du Lac*
David R. Obey, *Wausau*
Toby A. Roth, *Appleton*
F. James Sensenbrenner, Jr., *Shorewood*

NINETY-EIGHTH CONGRESS
JANUARY 3, 1983, to JANUARY 3, 1985

U.S. SENATORS
William Proxmire, *Madison*
Robert W. Kasten, Jr., *Milwaukee*
U.S. REPRESENTATIVES
Les Aspin, *Racine*
Robert W. Kastenmeier, *Sun Prairie*
Steven Gunderson, *Osseo*
Clement J. Zablocki, *Milwaukee*
Gerald D. Kleczka, *Milwaukee*
Jim Moody, *Milwaukee*
Thomas E. Petri, *Fond du Lac*
David R. Obey, *Wausau*
Toby Roth, *Appleton*
F. James Sensenbrenner, Jr., *Shorewood*

NINETY-NINTH CONGRESS
JANUARY 3, 1985, to JANUARY 3, 1987

U.S. SENATORS
William Proxmire, *Madison*
Robert W. Kasten, Jr., *Milwaukee*
U.S. REPRESENTATIVES
Les Aspin, *East Troy*
Robert W. Kastenmeier, *Sun Prairie*
Steven Gunderson, *Osseo*
Gerald D. Kleczka, *Milwaukee*
Jim Moody, *Milwaukee*
Thomas E. Petri, *Fond du Lac*

David R. Obey, *Wausau*
Toby Roth, *Appleton*
F. James Sensenbrenner, Jr., *Menomonee Falls*

ONE HUNDREDTH CONGRESS
JANUARY 6, 1987, to JANUARY 3, 1989

U.S. SENATORS
William Proxmire, *Madison*
Robert W. Kasten, Jr., *Milwaukee*
U.S. REPRESENTATIVES
Les Aspin, *Racine*
Robert W. Kastenmeier, *Sun Prairie*
Steven Gunderson, *Osseo*
Gerald D. Kleczka, *Milwaukee*
Jim Moody, *Milwaukee*
Thomas E. Petri, *Fond du Lac*
David R. Obey, *Wausau*
Toby Roth, *Appleton*
F. James Sensenbrenner, Jr., *Menomonee Falls*

ONE HUNDRED-FIRST CONGRESS
JANUARY 3, 1989, to JANUARY 3, 1991

U.S. SENATORS
Robert W. Kasten, Jr., *Milwaukee*
Herbert H. Kohl, *Milwaukee*
U.S. REPRESENTATIVES
Les Aspin, *Racine*
Robert W. Kastenmeier, *Sun Prairie*
Steven Gunderson, *Osseo*
Gerald D. Kleczka, *Milwaukee*
Jim Moody, *Milwaukee*
Thomas E. Petri, *Fond du Lac*
David R. Obey, *Wausau*
Toby Roth, *Appleton*
F. James Sensenbrenner, Jr., *Shorewood*

ONE HUNDRED-SECOND CONGRESS
JANUARY 3, 1991, to JANUARY 3, 1993

U.S. SENATORS
Robert W. Kasten, Jr., *Milwaukee*
Herbert H. Kohl, *Milwaukee*

U.S. REPRESENTATIVES
Les Aspin, *East Troy*
Scott L. Klug, *Madison*
Steven Gunderson, *Osseo*
Gerald D. Kleczka, *Milwaukee*
Jim Moody, *Milwaukee*
Thomas E. Petri, *Fond du Lac*
David R. Obey, *Wausau*
Toby Roth, *Appleton*
F. James Sensenbrenner, Jr., *Menomonee Falls*

ONE HUNDRED-THIRD CONGRESS
JANUARY 3, 1993, to JANUARY 3, 1995

U.S. SENATORS
Herbert H. Kohl, *Milwaukee*
Russell D. Feingold, *Middleton*
U.S. REPRESENTATIVES
Peter W. Barca, *Kenosha*
Scott L. Klug, *Madison*
Steven Gunderson,*Osseo*
Gerald D. Kleczka, *Milwaukee*
Thomas M. Barrett, *Milwaukee*
Thomas E. Petri, *FondduLac*
David R. Obey, *Wausau*
Toby Roth, *Appleton*
F. James Sensenbrenner, Jr., *Menomonee Falls*

ONE HUNDRED-FOURTH CONGRESS
JANUARY 3, 1995, to JANUARY 3, 1997

U.S. SENATORS
Herbert H. Kohl, *Milwaukee*
Russell D. Feingold, *Middletown*
U.S. REPRESENTATIVES
Mark W. Neumann, *Janesville*
Scott L. Klug, *Madison*
Steven Gunderson, *Osseo*
Gerald D. Kleczka, *Milwaukee*
Thomas E. Petri, *Fond du Lac*
David R. Obey, *Wausau*
Toby Roth, *Appleton*
F. James Sensenbrenner, Jr., *Menomonee Falls*

ONE HUNDRED-FIFTH CONGRESS
JANUARY 3, 1997, to JANUARY 3, 1999

U.S. SENATORS
Herbert H. Kohl, *Milwaukee*
Russell D. Feingold, *Middleton*
U.S. REPRESENTATIVES
Mark W. Neumann, *Janesville*
Scott L. Klug, *Madison*
Ron Kind, *La Crosse*
Gerald D. Kleczka, *Milwaukee*
Thomas M. Barrett, *Milwaukee*
Thomas E. Petri, *Fond du Lac*
David R. Obey, *Wausau*
Jay Johnson, *New Franken*
F. James Sensenbrenner, Jr., *Menomonee Falls*

U.S. SENATORS

BLAINE, JOHN JAMES, (1875-1934) — U.S. Senator from Wisconsin; born on a farm in Wingville Township, Grant County, Wisconsin, May 4, 1875; attended the common schools; was graduated from the law department of Valparaiso (Indiana) University in 1896; was admitted to the bar in 1896 and commenced practice in Montford; moved to Boscobel in 1897 and continued the practice of law; mayor of Boscobel 1901-1904, 1906-1907; member of the Grant County Board of Supervisors 1901-1904; member, State senate 1909-1913; unsuccessful candidate for Governor in 1914; attorney general of the State of Wisconsin 1919-1921; Governor of Wisconsin 1921-1927; elected as a Republican to the United States Senate for the term beginning March 4, 1927, and served from March 4, 1927, to March 3, 1933; unsuccessful candidate for renomination in 1932; resumed the practice of law at Boscobel; appointed a director of the Reconstruction Finance Corporation in 1933 and served until his death in Boscobel, Wisconsin, April 16, 1934; interment in Hillside Cemetery.

CAMERON, ANGUS, (1826-1897) — U.S. Senator from Wisconsin; born in Caledonia, Livingston County, New York, July 4, 1826; attended the public schools and the Genesee Wesleyan Seminary, Lima, New York; taught school; studied law in Buffalo, New York; was graduated from the National Law School, Ballston Spa, New York, in 1853; was admitted to the bar the same year and commenced practice in Buffalo, New York; engaged in banking for a year; moved to La Crosse, Wisconsin, in 1857 and resumed the practice of law; member, State senate 1863-1864, 1871-1872; member, State assembly in 1866-1867, and served as speaker in 1867; regent of the University of Wisconsin 1866-1875; elected as a Republican to the United States Senate on February 3, 1875, and served from March 4, 1875, until March 3, 1881; was not a candidate for re-election in 1881; elected March 10, 1881, to fill the vacancy caused by the death of Matthew H. Carpenter and took his seat March 14, 1881, and served until March 3, 1885; was not a candidate for re-election; chairman, Committee on Claims (Forty-seventh and Forty-eighth Congresses); resumed the practice of law in La Crosse, Wisconsin, and died there March 30, 1897;interment in Oak Grove Cemetery.

CARPENTER, MATTHEW HALE, (1824-1881) — U.S. Senator from Wisconsin; born Decatur Merritt Hammond Carpenter in Moretown, Washington County, Vermont, December 22, 1824; attended the common schools; entered the United States Military Academy at West Point in 1843 and remained two years; studied law; was admitted to the bar in 1847 and practiced in Boston, Massachusetts; moved to Beloit, Wisconsin, in 1848 and became known as Matthew Hale Carpenter; district attorney of Rock County 1850-1854; moved to Milwaukee in 1858; until the commencement of the Civil War belonged to the Douglas wing of the Democratic Party; elected as a Republican to the United States Senate and served from March 4, 1869, to March 3, 1875; unsuccessful candidate for re-election in 1875; served as President pro tempore of the Senate during the Forty-third Congress; chairman, Committee on Enrolled Bills (Forty-second Congress), Committee to Audit and Control the Contingent Expense (Forty-second and Forty-third Congresses); resumed the practice of law in Washington and in Milwaukee; again elected as a Republican to the United States Senate and served from March 4, 1879, until his death in Washington, D.C., February 24, 1881; interment in Forest Home Cemetery, Milwaukee, Wisconsin.

DODGE, HENRY (1782-1867) — U.S. Delegate and a Senator from Wisconsin; born in Vincennes, Indiana, October 12, 1782; received a limited schooling; moved to Missouri in 1796 and settled at Ste. Genevieve; sheriff of Cape Girardeau County in 1808; moved to Galena, Illinois, and operated a lead mine; moved to Wisconsin in 1827, then part of Michigan Territory, and settled near the present site of Dodgeville; served in the Black Hawk and other Indian wars; was commissioned major of United States Rangers 1832; left the Army as colonel of the First United States Dragoons 1836; appointed Governor of the Territory of Wisconsin 1836-1841; elected as a Democratic Delegate to the Twenty-seventh and Twenty-eighth Congresses (March 4, 1841-March 3, 1845); was not a candidate for renomination in 1844, having again accepted the appointment of Governor of the Territory of Wisconsin, and served from 1845 until 1848; upon the admission of Wisconsin as a State into the Union in 1848 was elected as a Democrat to the United States Senate; reelected in 1851 and served from June 8, 1848, to March 3, 1857; chairman, Committee on Commerce (Thirty-fourth Congress); declined the appointment of Governor of Washington Territory by President Franklin Pierce in 1857; retired to private life; died in Burlington, Des Moines County, Iowa, June 19, 1867; interment in Aspen Grove Cemetery.

DOOLITTLE, JAMES ROOD, (1815-1897) — U.S. Senator from Wisconsin; born in Hampton, New York, January 3, 1815; attended the common schools and Middlebury (Vermont) Academy, and was graduated from Hobart College, Geneva, New York, in 1834; studied law; was admitted to the bar in 1837 and commenced practice in Rochester, New York; moved to Warsaw, New York, in 1841; district attorney of Wyoming County, New York, 1847-1850; moved to Racine, Wisconsin, in 1851; judge of the first judicial circuit of Wisconsin 1853-1856, when he resigned; the repeal of the Missouri Compromise caused him to leave the Democratic Party; elected as a Republican to the United States Senate in January 1857; reelected in 1863 and served from March 4, 1857, to March 3, 1869; chairman, Committee on Indian Affairs (Thirty-seventh through Thirty-ninth Congresses); left the Republican Party and was an unsuccessful candidate for Governor on the Democratic ticket in 1871; resumed the practice of law in Chicago, Illinois, but retained his residence in Racine, Wisconsin; trustee of the University of Chicago, serving one year as its president, and was for many years a professor in its law school; died in Edgewood, Providence, Rhode Island, July 23, 1897; interment in Mound Cemetery, Racine, Wisconsin.

DUFFY, FRANCIS RYAN, (1888-1979) — U.S. Senator from Wisconsin; born in Fond du Lac, Fond du Lac County, Wisconsin, June 23, 1888; attended the public schools; was graduated from the University of Wisconsin at Madison, in 1910 and from its law department in 1912; was admitted to the bar in 1912 and commenced practice in Fond du Lac, Wisconsin; during the First World War served in the United States Army 1917-1919, attaining the rank of major; resumed the practice of law in Fond du Lac, Wisconsin; elected as a Democrat to, the United States Senate and served from March 4, 1933, to January 3, 1939; unsuccessful candidate for re-election in 1938; again resumed the practice of law before becoming United States district judge for the eastern district of Wisconsin, serving from 1939 to 1949, when he qualified as a United States circuit judge of the court of appeals for the seventh circuit, becoming chief judge in 1954 and served until 1959; retired as a full-time member of the court in 1966 and assumed the status of senior judge and continued to hear cases for several more years; died in Milwaukee, Wisconsin, August 16, 1979; interment in Calvary Cemetery, Fond du Lac, Wisconsin.

DURKEE, CHARLES, (1805-1870) — U.S. Representative and a Senator from Wisconsin; born in Royalton, Windsor County, Vermont, December 10, 1805; attended the common schools and the Burlington (Vermont) Academy; engaged in mercantile pursuits; moved to Wisconsin in 1836 and was one of the founders of Southport, now Kenosha; engaged in agricultural pursuits and lumbering; member, Territorial legislature 1836-1838, 1847-1848; elected as a Free-Soiler to the Thirty-first and Thirty-second Congresses (March 4, 1849-March 3, 1853); delegate to the World's Peace Convention in Paris; elected as a Republican to the United States Senate and served from March 4, 1855, to March 3, 1861; Governor of Utah Territory from 1865 until failing health compelled him to resign; died in Omaha, Nebraska, January 14, 1870; interment in Green Ridge Cemetery, Kenosha, Wisconsin.

FEINGOLD, RUSSELL, (1953-) — U.S. Senator from Wisconsin; born in Janesville, Rock County, Wisconsin, March 2, 1953; graduated, Janesville Craig High School 1971; graduated, University of Wisconsin-Madison 1975; attended Magdalen College, Oxford, England, as a Rhodes Scholar and received a graduate degree in 1977; graduated, Harvard University Law School 1979; admitted to the Wisconsin bar in 1979 and practiced law in Madison, Wisconsin, 1979-1985; visiting professor, Beloit College 1985; member, Wisconsin State Senate 1983-1993; elected in 1992 as a Democrat to the United States Senate for the term ending January 3, 1999; reelected in 1998.

HOWE, TIMOTHY OTIS, (1816-1883) — U.S. Senator from Wisconsin; born in Livermore, Androscoggin County, Maine, February 24, 1816; attended the common schools and graduated from the Maine Wesleyan Seminary; studied law;

was admitted to the bar in 1839 and commenced practice in Readfield, Maine; moved to Wisconsin in 1845 and settled in Green Bay; judge of the circuit court and supreme court justice of Wisconsin 1850-1853, when he resigned; unsuccessful Republican candidate for the United States Senate in 1856; elected as a Republican to the United States Senate in 1860; reelected in 1866 and 1872 and served from March 4, 1861, to March 3, 1879; unsuccessful candidate for re-election; chairman, Committee on Enrolled Bills (Thirty-eighth and Thirty-ninth Congresses), Committee on Claims (Thirty-ninth through Forty-second Congresses), Committee on the Library (Thirty-ninth Congress, Forty-first Congress, Forty-third through Forty-fifth Congresses), Committee on Foreign Relations (Forty-second Congress); served as a commissioner for the purchase of the Black Hills territory from the Indians; delegate to the International Monetary Conference held at Paris in 1881; appointed Postmaster General in the Cabinet of President Chester Arthur in 1881, and served until his death in Kenosha, Wisconsin, on March 25, 1883; interment in Woodlawn Cemetery, Green Bay, Wisconsin.

HUSTING, PAUL OSCAR, (1866-1917) — U.S. Senator from Wisconsin; born in Fond du Lac, Fond du Lac County, Wisconsin, April 25, 1866; moved with his parents to Mayville, Wisconsin, in 1876; attended the public schools and the law school of the University of Wisconsin at Madison; was admitted to the bar in 1895 and commenced practice in Mayville, Wisconsin; district attorney of Dodge County 1902-1906; member, State senate 1907-1913; elected as a Democrat to the United States Senate in 1914 and served from March 4, 1915, until his accidental death while duck hunting on Rush Lake, near Picketts, Wisconsin, on October 21, 1917; chairman, Committee to Investigate Trespassers Upon Indian Land (Sixty-fourth and Sixty-fifth Congresses), Committee on Fisheries (Sixty-fifth Congress); interment in Graceland Cemetery, Mayville, Wisconsin.

KASTEN, ROBERT WALTER, JR., (1942-) — U.S. Representative and a Senator from Wisconsin; born in Milwaukee, Milwaukee County, Wisconsin, June 19, 1942; graduated, The Choate High School, Wallington, Connecticut, 1960; graduated, University of Arizona 1964; received a graduate degree from Columbia University Graduate School of Business, New York City, 1966; vice president of marketing and sales manager for a Wisconsin shoe manufacturing company; United States Air Force 1966-1968; Air National Guard 1968-1972; member, Wisconsin State senate 1972-1974; elected in 1974 as a Republican to the Ninety-fourth Congress; reelected to the Ninety-fifth Congress (January 3, 1975-January 3, 1979); was not a candidate for re-election in 1978; unsuccessful candidate for the Republican nomination for Governor of Wisconsin in 1978; elected as a Republican to the United States Senate in 1980 for the term commencing January 3, 1981; reelected in 1986 for the term ending January 3, 1993.

KOHL, HERBERT, (1935-) — U.S. Senator from Wisconsin; born in Milwaukee, Wisconsin, February 7, 1935; attended Milwaukee public schools; graduated from the University of Wisconsin, Madison, 1956; received M.B.A. degree from Harvard School of Business Administration 1958; United States Army Reserves 1958-1964; businessman, President of Kohl Corporation and owner of Milwaukee Bucks basketball team; Wisconsin State Democratic Party chairman 1975-1977; elected as a Democrat to the United States Senate in 1988; reelected in 1994 for the term commencing January 3, 1995.

LA FOLLETTE, ROBERT MARION, (1855-1925) — U.S. Representative and a Senator from Wisconsin; born in Primrose, Dane County, Wisconsin, June 14, 1855; graduated from the University of Wisconsin at Madison in 1879; studied law; was admitted to the bar in 1880 and commenced practice in Madison, Wisconsin; district attorney of Dane County 1880-1884; elected as a Republican to the Forty-ninth, Fiftieth, and Fifty-first Congresses (March 4, 1885-March 3, 1891); unsuccessful candidate for re-election in 1890 to the Fifty-second Congress; chairman, Committee on Expenditures in the Department of Agriculture (Fifty-first Congress); resumed the practice of law in Madison, Wisconsin; Governor of Wisconsin 1901-1906, when he resigned, having previously been elected Senator; elected as a Republican to the United States Senate on January 25, 1905, for the term beginning March 4, 1905, but did not assume these duties until later, preferring to continue as Governor; reelected in 1911, 1917, and 1923, and served from January 2, 1906, until his death; chairman, Committee on the Census (Sixty-first and Sixty-second Congress), Committee on Corporations Organized in the District of Columbia (Sixty-third through Sixty-fifth Congresses), Committee on Manufactures (Sixty-sixth through Sixty-eighth Congresses); one of the founders of the National Progressive Republican League and several times unsuccessfully sought the Republican and Progressive Party presidential nominations; died in Washington, D.C., June 18, 1925; interment in Forest Hill Cemetery, Madison, Wisconsin.

LA FOLLETTE,ROBERT MARION, JR., (1895-1953) — U.S. Senator from Wisconsin; born in Madison, Wisconsin, February 6, 1895; attended the public schools of Madison and Washington, D.C.; attended the University of Wisconsin at Madison 1913-1917; private secretary to his father 1919-1925; elected as a Republican to the United States Senate on September 29, 1925, to fill the vacancy caused by the death of his father, Robert M. La Follette; reelected as a Republican in 1928, and as a Progressive in 1934 and 1940, and served from September 30, 1925, to January 3, 1947; unsuccessful candidate for re-election as a Republican in 1946; chairman, Committee on Manufactures (Seventy-first and Seventy-second Congresses); a champion of organized labor, La Follette gained national prominence between 1936 and 1940 as chairman of a special Senate investigating committee, commonly called the La Follette Civil Liberties Committee, which exposed techniques used to prevent workers from organizing; author, economic-research consultant, and foreign aid advisor to the Truman administration; died in Washington, D.C., February 24, 1953, of a self-inflicted gunshot wound; interment in Forest Hill Cemetery, Madison, Wisconsin.

LENROOT, IRVINE LUTHER, (1869-1949) — U.S. Representative and a Senator from Wisconsin; born in Superior, Wisconsin, January 31, 1869; attended the common schools; worked as a logger and a court reporter; studied law; was admitted to the bar in 1898 and commenced practice in Superior, Wisconsin; member, State assembly 1901-1907, and served as speaker 1903-1907; elected as a Republican to the Sixty-first and to the four succeeding Congresses and served from March 4, 1909, until April 17, 1918, when he resigned, having been elected Senator; elected as a Republican to the United States Senate on April 2, 1918, to fill the vacancy caused by the death of Paul O. Husting; reelected in 1920 and served from April 18, 1918, to March 3, 1927; unsuccessful candidate for renomination in 1926; chairman, Committee on Railroads (Sixty-sixth Congress), Committee on Public Lands and Surveys (Sixty-eighth Congress), Committee on Public Buildings and Grounds (Sixty-ninth Congress); resumed the practice of law in Washington, D.C.; appointed judge of the United States Court of Customs and Patent Appeals by President Herbert Hoover in 1929, and served until his retirement in 1944; died in Washington, D,C., January 26, 1949; interment in Greenwood Cemetery, Superior, Wisconsin.

McCARTHY, JOSEPH RAYMOND, (1908-1957) — U.S. Senator from Wisconsin; born in Grand Chute, Outagamie County, Wisconsin, November 14, 1908; attended a one-room country school; worked on a farm; at the age of nineteen moved to Manawa, Wisconsin, and enrolled in a high school; while working in a grocery store and ushering at a theater in the evenings, completed a four-year course in one year; graduated from Marquette University at Milwaukee, Wisconsin, with a law degree in 1935; was admitted to the bar the same year; commenced practice in Waupaca, and in 1936 moved to Shawano, Wisconsin, and continued to practice law; elected circuit judge of the tenth judicial circuit of Wisconsin in 1939; while serving in this capacity enlisted in 1942 in the United States Marine Corps; resigned as a lieutenant in 1945; unsuccessful candidate for the Republican nomination for United States Senator in 1944 while in military service; reelected circuit judge of Wisconsin in 1945 while still in the Marine Corps; elected as a Republican to the United States Senate in 1946; reelected in 1952 and served from January 3, 1947, until his death in the naval hospital at Bethesda, Maryland, May 2, 1957; emerged from obscurity in the Senate in 1950 with exaggerated claims of Communists in the State Department, which rapidly grew into charges of Communist infiltration into all facets of American life; the term "McCarthyism" became synonymous with the charge of Communists in government; co-chairman, Joint Committee on the Library (Eighty-third Congress), chairman, Committee on Government Operations (Eighty-third Congress), Special Committee on Unemployment Problems (Eighty-sixth Congress); used his position as chairman of the Committee on Government Operations and its Permanent Subcommittee on Investigations to launch investigations designed to document charges of Communists in government; for his unscrupulous tactics, McCarthy was censured by the Senate on December 2, 1954, for behavior that was "contemptuous, contumacious, and denunciatory"; funeral services were held in the Chamber of the United States Senate; interment in St. Mary's Cemetery, Appleton, Wisconsin.

MITCHELL, JOHN LENDRUM, (1842-1904) — U.S. Representative and a Senator from Wisconsin; born in Milwaukee, Wisconsin, October 19, 1842; attended the common schools at Milwaukee, and the military academy at Hampton, Connecticut; studied in Dresden and Munich, Germany, and Geneva, Switzerland; returned to the United States in 1860; served in the Civil War, becoming first lieutenant and later chief of ordnance; resigned in 1864; engaged in agricultural pursuits near Milwaukee; member, State senate 1872-1873, 1875-1876; president of the Milwaukee Public School Board 1884-1885; member of the board of managers of the National Home for Disabled Volunteer Soldiers 1886-1892; president of the Milwaukee Gas Co. 1890-1892; elected as a Democrat to the Fifty-second and Fifty-third Congresses and served from March 4, 1891, until his resignation on March 3, 1893, before the beginning of the Congress, having been elected Senator; elected to the United States Senate and served from March 4, 1893, to March 3, 1899; was not a candidate for renomination in 1898; went to Europe in 1899 and studied at Grenoble University, Grenoble, France; returned to the United States in 1902; president of the Wisconsin State Agricultural Society and of numerous banking institutions; trustee, director, and patron of numerous public institutions; died in Milwaukee, Wisconsin, June 29, 1904; interment in Forest Home Cemetery.

NELSON, GAYLORD ANTON, (1916-) — U.S. Senator from Wisconsin; born in Clear Lake, Polk County, Wisconsin, June 4, 1916; attended the public schools of Clear Lake; graduated from the San Jose (California) State College in 1939 and from the University of Wisconsin Law School in 1942; was admitted to the Wisconsin bar the same year; during the Second World War served as a lieutenant in the United States Army for four years, serving overseas in the Okinawa campaign; engaged in the practice of law in Madison, Wisconsin, in 1946; elected to the State senate in 1948, 1952, and 1956, and served as Democratic floor leader for eight years; Governor of Wisconsin 1959-1962; elected as a

Democrat to the United States Senate in November 1962 for the term commencing January 3, 1963; subsequently served out his term as Governor until January 7, 1963, and commenced term in Senate on January 8, 1963; reelected in 1968, and again in 1974, serving from January 8, 1963, to January 3, 1981; unsuccessful candidate for re-election in 1980; chairman, Select Committee on Small Business (Ninety-third through Ninety-sixth Congresses), Special Committee on Official Conduct (Ninety-fifth Congress); founder of Earth Day 1970; counselor, The Wilderness Society, Washington, D.C.; is a resident of Kensington, Maryland.

PROXMIRE, WILLIAM, (1915-) — U.S. Senator from Wisconsin; born in Lake Forest, Lake County, Illinois, November 11, 1915; attended the public schools of Lake Forest and the Hill School Pottstown, Pennsylvania; graduated, Yale University 1938, Harvard Business School 1940, and Harvard Graduate School of Arts and Sciences 1948; during the Second World War served in the Military Intelligence Service 1941-1946, member, Wisconsin State assembly 1951-1952; businessman; unsuccessful Democratic candidate for Governor of Wisconsin in 1952, 1954, and 1956; elected as a Democrat to the United States Senate in 1957 to fill the vacancy caused by the death of Joseph R. McCarthy and served from August 28, 1957, to January 3, 1959; reelected in 1958, 1964, 1970, 1976, and again in 1982 for the term ending Jaunary 3, 1989; chairman, Committee on Banking, Housing, and Urban Affairs (Ninety-fourth, Ninety-fifth, Ninety-sixth, and One hundredth Congresses); not a candidate for re-election in 1988; is a resident of Washington, D.C.

QUARLES, JOSEPH VERY, (1843-1911) — U.S. Senator from Wisconsin; born in Southport (now Kenosha), Kenosha County, Wisconsin, December 16, 1843; attended the common schools and the University of Michigan at Ann Arbor; during the Civil War served in the Union Army in the Thirty-ninth Regiment, Wisconsin Volunteers, and was mustered out as first lieutenant; graduated from the University of Michigan in 1866 and from its law department in 1867; was admitted to the bar in 1868 and commenced practice in Kenosha; district attorney for Kenosha County 1870-1876; mayor of Kenosha 1876; member, State assembly 1879; member, State senate 1880-1882; moved to Racine, Wisconsin, and six years later made Milwaukee his home; elected as a Republican to the

United States Senate and served from March 4, 1899, to March 3, 1905; was not a candidate for re-election in 1905; chairman, Committee on Transportation Routes to the Seaboard (Fifty-sixth Congress), Committee on the Census (Fifty-seventh and Fifty-eighth Congresses); appointed United States district judge for the eastern district of Wisconsin by President Theodore Roosevelt in 1905, and served until his death in Milwaukee, Wisconsin, October 7, 1911; interment in the City Cemetery, Kenosha, Wisconsin.

SAWYER, PHILETUS, (1816-1900) — U.S. Representative and a Senator from Wisconsin; born in Whiting, Rutland County, Vermont, September 22, 1816; moved with his parents to Crown Point, New York, in 1817; attended the common schools; moved to Fond du Lac County, Wisconsin, in 1847 and engaged in the lumber business; member, Wisconsin assembly 1857, 1861; mayor of Oshkosh 1863-1864; elected as a Republican to the Thirty-ninth and to the four succeeding Congresses (March 4, 1865-March 3, 1875); declined to be a candidate for renomination in 1874; chairman, Committee on Public Expenditures (Forty-second Congress), Committee on Pacific Railroads (Forty-third Congress); elected as a Republican to the United States Senate in 1881; reelected in 1887 and served from March 4, 1881, to March 3, 1893; was not a candidate for re-election; chairman, Committee on Railroads (Forty-eighth and Forty-ninth Congresses), Committee on Post Office and Post Roads (Fiftieth through Fifty-second Congresses); resumed his former business pursuits; died in Oshkosh, Winnebago County, Wisconsin, March 29, 1900; interment in the family vault at Riverside, Oshkosh.

SPOONER, JOHN COIT, (1843-1919) — U.S. Senator from Wisconsin; born in Lawrenceburg, Dearborn County, Indiana, January 6, 1843; moved to Wisconsin with his parents, who settled in Madison in 1859; attended the common schools and graduated from the University of Wisconsin at Madison, in 1864; during the Civil War enlisted as a private and was brevetted major at the close of the war; private and military secretary to the Governor of Wisconsin; studied law; was admitted to the bar in 1867 and served as assistant attorney general of the State until 1870; moved to Hudson, Wisconsin, and practiced law 1870-1884; member, State assembly 1872; member of the board of regents of Wisconsin University;

29

elected as a Republican to the United States Senate and served from March 4, 1885, to March 3, 1891; unsuccessful candidate for re-election; chairman, Committee on Claims (Forty-ninth through Fifty-first Congresses); unsuccessful Republican candidate for governor of Wisconsin in 1892; moved to Madison in 1893; again elected to the United States Senate in 1897; reelected in 1903 and served from March 4, 1897, until his resignation, effective April 30, 1907; chairman, Committee on Relations with Canada (Fifty-fifth Congress), Committee on Rules (Fifty-fifth through Fifty-ninth Congresses); engaged in the practice of law in New York City; declined the positions of Secretary of the Interior and Attorney General in the Cabinet of President William McKinley in 1898 and 1901; declined the position of Secretary of State in the Cabinet of President William Howard Taft; practiced law in New York City; died in New York City, June 11, 1919; interment in Forest Hill Cemetery, Madison, Wisconsin.

STEPHENSON, ISAAC, (1829-1918) — U.S. Representative and a Senator from Wisconsin; born in Yorkton near Fredericton, in York County, New Brunswick, Canada, June 18, 1829; attended the common schools; settled in Marinette, Wisconsin, in 1858 and engaged in the lumber business; held various local offices; member, Wisconsin State assembly 1866, 1868; founder and president of the Stephenson Banking Co. in 1873; elected as a Republican to the Forty-eighth, Forty-ninth, and Fiftieth Congresses (March 4, 1883-March 3, 1889); was not a candidate for renomination in 1888; resumed the lumber business in Marinette, Wisconsin; elected in 1907 as a Republican to the United States Senate to fill the vacancy caused by the resignation of John C. Spooner; reelected in 1909 and served from May 17, 1907, to March 3, 1915; chairman, Committee on Expenditures in the Department of Agriculture (Sixty-first Congress), Committee on Enrolled Bills (Sixty-second Congress), Committee to Investigate Trespassers Upon Indian Lands (Sixty-third Congress); died in Marinette, Wisconsin, on March 15, 1918; interment in Forest Home Cemetery.

VILAS, WILLIAM FREEMAN, (1840-1908) — U.S. Senator from Wisconsin; born in Chelsea, Orange County, Vermont, July 9, 1840; moved with his parents to Madison, Dane County, Wisconsin, in 1851; attended the common schools; graduated from the University of Wisconsin at Madison in

1858 and from the law department of the University of Albany, New York, in 1860; was admitted to the bar and commenced practice in Madison, Wisconsin, in 1860; enlisted in the Union Army during the Civil War; captain of Company A, Twenty-third Regiment, Wisconsin Volunteer Infantry, and afterward major and lieutenant colonel of the regiment; professor of law at the University of Wisconsin; regent of the university 1880-1885; one of three revisers appointed by the Wisconsin Supreme Court in 1875 to prepare a revised body of the statute law; member, State assembly 1885; Postmaster General of the United States in the Cabinet of President Grover Cleveland 1885-1888, when he became Secretary of the Interior of the United States, and served until March 1889; elected as a Democrat to the United States Senate in 1891, and served from March 4, 1891, to March 3, 1897; unsuccessful candidate for renomination in 1896; chairman, Committee on Post Office and Post Roads (Fifty-third Congress); regent of the University of Wisconsin 1898-1905; resumed the practice of law; member of the commission to provide for the construction of the State capitol in 1907; died in Madison, Wisconsin, August 27, 1908; interment in Forest Hill Cemetery.

WALKER, ISAAC PIGEON, (1815-1872) — U.S. Senator from Wisconsin; born near Wheeling, Virginia (now West Virginia), November 2, 1815; moved to Danville, Illinois, in early youth; attended the common schools; was employed as a clerk in a store; studied law; was admitted to the bar in 1834 and commenced practice in Springfield; served one term in the State house of representatives; presidential elector on the Democratic ticket in 1840; moved to Wisconsin Territory in 1841, settled in Milwaukee, and continued the practice of law; member, Territorial legislature 1847-1848; upon the admission of Wisconsin as a State into the Union was elected as a Democrat to the United States Senate; reelected in 1849 and served from June 8, 1848, to March 3, 1855; chairman, Committee to Audit and Control the Contingent Expense (Thirtieth Congress), Committee on Revolutionary Claims (Thirty-first through Thirty-third Congresses), Committee on Agriculture (Thirty-second Congress), Committee on Indian Affairs (Thirty-second Congress); engaged in agricultural pursuits in Waukesha County; returned to Milwaukee and resumed the practice of law; died there March 29, 1872; interment in Forest Home Cemetery.

WILEY, ALEXANDER, (1884-1967) — U.S. Senator from Wisconsin; born in Chippewa Falls, Chippewa County, Wisconsin, May 26, 1884; attended the public schools, Augsburg College, Minneapolis, Minnesota, and the University of Michigan at Ann Arbor; graduated from the law department of the University of Wisconsin at Madison in 1907; was admitted to the bar the same year and commenced practice in Chippewa Falls, Wisconsin; district attorney of Chippewa County 1909-1915; unsuccessful Republican candidate for governor in 1936; engaged in agricultural pursuits and banking; elected as a Republican to the United States Senate in 1938; reelected in 1944, 1950, and again in 1956, and served from January 3, 1939, to January 3, 1963; unsuccessful candidate for re-election in 1962; chairman, Committee on the Judiciary (Eightieth Congress), Committee on Foreign Relations (Eighty-third Congress), resided in Washington, D.C., until a few days before his death, May 26, 1967, at High Oaks Christian Science Church Sanitarium in Germantown, Pennsylvania; interment in Forest Hill Cemetery, Chippewa Falls, Wisconsin.

STATE EXECUTIVE OFFICE

GOVERNOR
State Capitol, P.O. Box 7863, Madison, WI 53707-7863
Fax: (608) 267-8983   TTY: (608) 267-5163
Mail to: wiscgov@mail.state.wi.us
Internet: http://www.wisgov.state.wi.us

Governor *Tommy G. Thompson* (R) . . . . . . (608) 266-1212

MILWAUKEE OFFICE
819 N. Sixth St., Rm. 560
Milwaukee, WI 53203
Fax: (414) 227-4500

Director (Vacant) . . . . (414) 227-4344

NORTHERN OFFICE
Rt. 8, Box 8071, Hayward, WI 54843
Fax: (715) 634-4636

Director *Mary Moser*. . . . . (715) 634-3531

WASHINGTON OFFICE
444 N. Capitol St., NW, Ste. 613
Washington, DC 20001
Fax: (202) 624-5871

Director (Vacant) . . . . (202) 624-5870

LIEUTENANT GOVERNOR
22 E. State Capitol
Madison, WI 53702
Fax: (608) 267-3571   Mail to: ltgov@mail.state.wi.us
(Area Code 608)
Lieutenant Governor *Scott McCallum* (R) 266-3516

SECRETARY OF STATE
30 W. Mifflin, 10th Fl., P.O. Box 7848
Madison, WI 53707-7848
Information: (608) 266-8888   Fax: (608) 266-3159

Secretary of State *Doug La Follette* **(D)** **266-8888**

ATTORNEY GENERAL (JUSTICE DEPARTMENT)
P.O. Box 7857, Madison, WI 53707-7857
Information: (608) 266-1221   Fax: (608) 267-2779

Attorney General *James E. Doyle* **(D)** **266-1221**

STATE TREASURER
P.O. Box 7871, Madison, WI 53707
Information: (608) 266-1714   Fax: (608) 266-2647
Internet: http://badger.state.wi.us/agencies/ost

Treasurer *Jack Voight* **(R)** **266-1714**

PUBLIC DEFENDER
P.O. Box 7923
Madison, WI 53707-7923
Information: (608) 266-0087   Fax: (608) 267-0584

State Public Defender *Nicholas L. Chiarkas.* **266-0087**

ADMINISTRATION DEPARTMENT
101 E. Wilson St., P.O. Box 7869
Madison, WI 53707-7869
Information: (608) 266-2309   Fax: (608) 264 9500
TTY: (608) 267-9629

Secretary *Mark D. Bugher.* **266-1741**

GAMING DIVISION
2005 W. Beltline Hwy., #201
Madison, WI 53708-8979
Fax: (608) 270-2564

Administrator *F. Scott Scepaniak.* **270-2555**

Political Section

TAX APPEALS COMMISSION
101 E. Wilson St., 6th Fl.
Madison, WI 53702

Chair *Mark E. Musolf.* 266-7763

CLAIMS BOARD
101 E. Wilson St., 10th Fl.
Madison, WI 53702
Information: (608) 266-1743

Secretary *Edward Main.* 266-2765

PUBLIC RECORDS BOARD
4622 University Ave., Rm. 10A
Madison, WI 53702

Chair *Sharon Halverson.* 266-2996

**AGRICULTURE, TRADE AND CONSUMER
PROTECTION DEPARTMENT**
2811 Agriculture Dr., P.O. Box 8911
Madison, WI 53708-8911
Fax: (608) 224-5045   TTY: (608) 224-5058
(Area Code 608)
Secretary *Ben Brancel.* **224-5012**

COMMERCE DEPARTMENT
P.O. Box 7970, Madison, WI 53707
Information: (608) 266-1018   Fax: (608) 267-0436
Internet: http://badger.state.wi.us/agencies/commerce

Secretary *William J. McCoshen.* **266-8976**

CORRECTIONS DEPARTMENT
149 E. Wilson St., P.O. Box 7925
Madison WI 53707-7925
Information: (608) 266-2471   Fax: (608) 267-3661
TTY: (608) 267-1746

Secretary *Michael J. Sullivan* **266-4548**

ADULT INSTITUTIONS DIVISION
Purchasing Fax: (608) 246-5648

Administrator *Dick Verhagen*. 266-6604

COMMUNITY CORRECTIONS DIVISION
Administrator *William Grosshans*. 266-3834

JUVENILE CORRECTIONS DIVISION
Information: (608) 266-9342   Fax: (608) 267-3693

Administrator *Eurial Jordan*. 267-3715

PROGRAM PLANNING AND MOVEMENT DIVISION
Administrator *Pamela J. Brandon*. 267-9073

PAROLE COMMISSION
Information: (608) 266-2957

Chairman *John Husz*. 266-1119

EMPLOYEE TRUST FUNDS DEPARTMENT
801 W. Badger Rd., P.O. Box 7931
Madison, WI 53707-7931
Information: (608) 266-0407   Fax: (608) 267-0633
TTY: (608) 267-0676
Internet: http://www.badger.state.wi.us/agencies/etf

Secretary *Eric Stanchfield*. 266-0301

EMPLOYMENT RELATIONS DEPARTMENT
137 E. Wilson St., P.O. Box 7855
Madison, WI 53707-7855
Information: (608) 266-9820   Fax: (608) 267-1020
TTY: (608) 267-1004
Mail to: derdas@mail.state.wi.us

Secretary *Jon E. Litscher*. 266-9820

FINANCIAL INSTITUTIONS DEPARTMENT
345 W. Washington Ave., P.O. Box 8861
Madison, WI 53708-8861
Information: (608) 264-7800   Fax: (608) 261-4334

Secretary *Richard L. Dean*. 265-7800

CREDIT UNIONS OFFICE
P.O. Box 14137, Madison, WI 53714-0137

Director *Ginger Larson*. 266-8893

ADMINISTRATIVE SERVICES AND TECHNOLOGY
DIVISION
P.O. Box 7876, Madison, WI 53707-7876

Administrator *Jacquelyn V. Rader*. 267-1707

BANKING DIVISION
P.O. Box 7876, Madison, WI 53707-7876

Administrator *Michael J. Mach* 266-0451

CORPORATE AND CONSUMER SERVICES DIVISION
P.O. Box 7846, Madison, WI 53707-7846

Administrator *Todd Hunter*. 266-5130

SAVINGS INSTITUTIONS DIVISION
P.O. Box 8306, Madison, WI 53708-8306
Information: (608) 242-2180   Fax: (608) 242-2187

Administrator *Thomas M. Boykoff*. 261-4338

SECURITIES DIVISION
P.O. Box 1768, Madison, WI 53701-1768
Information: (608) 266-3431   Fax: (608) 256-1259

Administrator *Patricia D. Struck*. 266-3432

HEALTH AND FAMILY SERVICES DEPARTMENT
P.O. Box 7850, Madison, WI 53707-7850
Information: (608) 266-3681   Fax: (608) 266-7882
TTY: (608) 266-3683

Secretary *Joe Leean*. 266-9622

CARE AND TREATMENT FACILITIES DIVISION
Information: (608) 266-8740   Fax: (608) 266-2579

Administrator *Thomas E. Alt* 266-8740

CHILDREN AND FAMILY SERVICES DIVISION
Information: (608) 267-3905   Fax: (608) 264-9832

Administrator *Susan N. Dreyfus*. 267-9685

HEALTH DIVISION
Information: (608) 266-1511   Fax: (608) 267-2832

Administrator *John Chapin*. 266-1511

MANAGEMENT AND TECHNOLOGY DIVISION
Information: (608) 266-1865   Fax: (608) 267-2147

Administrator *Mike Hughes*. 266-6954

SUPPORTIVE LIVING DIVISION
Information: (608) 266-2701   Fax: (608) 264-9832

Administrator *Sinikka McCabe*. 266-0554

STRATEGIC FINANCE OFFICE
Information: (608) 266-3816   Fax: (608) 267-0358

Administrator *Chuck Wilhelm*. 266-8402

MILITARY AFFAIRS DEPARTMENT
2400 Wright St., P.O. Box 2572
Madison, WI 53704-2572
Information: (608) 242-3000   Fax: (608) 242-3111

Adjutant General
  Maj. Gen. James G. Blaney. . . . .
242-3001

NATURAL RESOURCES DEPARTMENT
P.O. Box 7921, Madison, WI 53707
Information: (608) 266-2121   Fax: (608) 266-6983
TTY: (608) 267-6897
Internet: http://www.dnr.state.wi.us/

Secretary *George Meyer.* **266-2121**

ADMINISTRATION AND TECHNOLOGY DIVISION
Administrator *Franc Fennessy.* 264-6133

AIR AND WASTE DIVISION
Administrator *Jay Hochmuth.* 267-9521

CUSTOMER ASSISTANCE AND EXTERNAL RELATIONS
DIVISION
Administrator *Craig Karr.* 266-5896

ENFORCEMENT AND SCIENCE DIVISION
Administrator *Dave Meier.* 266-0015

LAND DIVISION
Administrator *Steve Miller.* 266-5782

WATER DIVISION
Administrator *Susan Sylvester.* 266-1099

PUBLIC INSTRUCTION DEPARTMENT
P.O. Box 7841, Madison, WI 53707-7841
Information: (608) 266-3390   Fax: (608) 267-1052
TTY: (608) 267-2427   Toll Free: (800) 441-4563
Internet: http://www.state.wi.us/agencies/dpi

State Superintendent *John T. Benson* **(I).** **266-1771**
FINANCE AND MANAGEMENT DIVISION
Assistant Superintendent *Faye Stark.* 266-3903

LEARNING SUPPORT: EQUITY AND ADVOCACY
DIVISION
Assistant Superintendent *Juanita Pawlisch.* 266-1649

LEARNING SUPPORT: INSTRUCTIONAL SERVICES
DIVISION
Assistant Superintendent *John Fortier.* 266-3361

LIBRARIES AND COMMUNITY LEARNING DIVISION
Interim Assistant Superintendent
   Carolyn Folke. 266-7049

DEAF AND EDUCATIONAL SERVICES CENTER FOR THE
HEARING IMPAIRED, SCHOOL FOR THE
309 W. Walworth, Ave.
Delavan, WI 53115-1099
TTY: (414) 728-7120

Superintendent *Alex Slappey.* . . . . (414) 728-7120

VISUALLY HANDICAPPED AND EDUCATIONAL
SERVICES CENTER FOR THE VISUALLY IMPAIRED,
SCHOOL FOR THE
1700 W. State St., Janesville, WI 53546-5399
                                                      (Area Code
608)
Superintendent *Gordon Schuetz.* 758-6127

REGULATION AND LICENSING DEPARTMENT
P.O. Box 8935, Madison, WI 53708-8935
Information: (608) 266-2112   Fax: (608) 267-0644
TTY: (608) 267-2416

Secretary *Marlene A. Cummings.* **266-8609**

REVENUE DEPARTMENT
P.O. Box 8933, Madison, WI 53708-8933
Information: (608) 266-1611   Fax: (608) 266-5718
TTY: (608) 266-1612

Secretary *Cate Zeuske* **266-6466**

TOURISM DEPARTMENT
P.O. Box 7976, Madison, WI 53707-7976
Information: (608) 266-2161   Fax: (608) 266-3403
TTY: (608) 267-0756   Toll Free: (800) 432-8747
Mail to: tourinfo@tourism.state.wi.us

Secretary *Richard Speros* **266-2345**

TRANSPORTATION DEPARTMENT
P.O. Box 7910, Madison, WI 53707-7910
Information: (608) 266-1113   Fax: (608) 266-9912

Secretary *Charles H. Thompson* **266-1113**

VETERANS AFFAIRS DEPARTMENT
P.O. Box 7843, Madison, WI 53707
Information: (608) 266-1311   Fax: (608) 267-0403
Mail to: wdva@mail.state.wi.us

Secretary *Raymond G. Boland* **266-1315**

WORKFORCE DEVELOPMENT DEPARTMENT
P.O. Box 7946, Madison, WI 53707
Information: (608) 266-3131   Fax: (608) 266-1784
TTY: (608) 267-0477   Internet: http://www.dwd.state.wi.us/

Secretary *Linda Stewart* **266-7552**

ADMINISTRATIVE SERVICES DIVISION
Fax: (608) 267-7952

Administrator *Orlando Canto* 266-1024

CONNECTING EDUCATION AND WORK DIVISION
Fax: (608) 261-6698

Director *Vicki J. Poole*. 264-6808

ECONOMIC SUPPORT DIVISION
Fax: (608) 261-6376

Administrator *J. Jean Rogers* 266-3035

EQUAL RIGHTS DIVISION
Fax: (608) 267-4592

Administrator *J. Sheehan Donoghue* 266-0946

UNEMPLOYMENT INSURANCE DIVISION
Fax: (608) 267-0593

Administrator *Maureen A. Hlavacek* 266-7074

VOCATIONAL REHABILITATION DIVISION
Fax: (608) 267-5680

Administrator *Judy J. Norman-Nunnery* 243-5603

WORKER'S COMPENSATION DIVISION
Fax: (608) 267-0394

Administrator *Gregory Krohm* 266-6841

WORKFORCE EXCELLENCE DIVISION
Fax: (608) 267-2392

Administrator *June M. Suhling* 266-2439

LEGISLATIVE AUDIT BUREAU
131 W. Wilson St., Ste. 402
Madison, WI 53703
Fax: (608) 267-0410

State Auditor *Dale Cattanach* 266-2818

REVISOR OF STATUTES BUREAU
131 W. Wilson St., Ste. 800
Madison, WI 53703-3233
Information: (608) 266-2011   Fax: (608) 264-6978

Revisor of Statutes *Bruce Munson* 267-3536

BUILDING COMMISSION
P.O. Box 7866, Madison, WI 53707
Information: (608) 266-1855   Fax: (608) 267-2710
TTY: (608) 267-9629

Chairman *Gov. Tommy G. Thompson* 266-1212

EMPLOYMENT RELATIONS COMMISSION
P.O. Box 7870, Madison, WI 53707-7870
Fax: (608) 266-6930

Chairman *James R. Meier* 266-1381

INSURANCE COMMISSION
P.O. Box 7873, Madison, WI 53707-7873
Information: (608) 266-3585   or   (800) 236-8517
Fax: (608) 266-9935   TTY: (800) 947-3529
Mail to: ocioci@mail.state.wi.us
Internet: http://badger.state.wi.us/agencies/oci/oci_home.htm

Commissioner (Acting) *Randy Blumer* 266-0102

LABOR AND INDUSTRY REVIEW COMMISSION
P.O. Box 8126, Madison, WI 53708-8126
Information: (608) 266-9850   Fax: (608) 267-4409

Chairman *Pamela I. Anderson* 266-9850

PERSONNEL COMMISSION
131 W. Wilson St., Ste. 1004
Madison, WI 53703
Information: (608) 266-1995

Chairperson *Laurie R. McCallum* 266-9571

PUBLIC SERVICE COMMISSION
P.O. Box 7854, Madison, WI 53707-7854
Information: (608) 266-5481   Fax: (608) 266-3957
TTY: (608) 267-1479   Mail to: pscres@psc.state.wi.us
Internet: http://badger.state.wi.us/agencies/psc
Commissioners Fax: (608) 266-1401

Chairman *Cheryl L. Parrino* 267-7897

HOUSING AND ECONOMIC DEVELOPMENT AUTHORITY
P.O. Box 1728, Madison, WI 53701-1728
Information: (608) 266-7884   Fax: (608) 267-1099
TTY: (800) 943-9430   Mail to: wheda@mail.state.wi.us

Executive Director *Fritz Ruf* 266-2893

AGING AND LONG TERM CARE, BOARD ON
214 N. Hamilton St., Madison, WI 53703
Information: (608) 266-8944   Fax: (608) 261-6570
TTY: (608) 266-8944

Executive Director *George F. Potaracke* 266-8945

ARTS BOARD
101 E. Wilson St., 1st Fl., Madison, WI 53702
Information: (608) 266-0190   Fax: (608) 267-0380
TTY: (608) 267-9629

Executive Director *George Tzougros* 267-2006

EDUCATIONAL COMMUNICATIONS BOARD
3319 W. Beltline Hwy.
Madison, WI 53713-4296
Information: (608) 264-9600   Fax: (608) 264-9664
TTY: (608) 264-9710   Mail to: ecbweb@mail.state.wi.us

Executive Director *Thomas L. Fletemeyer* 264-9676

Political Section

ELECTIONS BOARD
P.O. Box 2973, Madison, WI 53701-2973
Information: (608) 266-8005   Fax: (608) 267-0500

Executive Director *Kevin J. Kennedy* 266-8005

ETHICS BOARD
44 E. Mifflin St., Ste. 601
Madison, WI 53703-2800
Information: (608) 266-8123   Fax: (608) 264-9309
Mail to: ethics@mail.state.wi.us

Executive Director *R. Roth Judd* 266-8123

HIGHER EDUCATIONAL AIDS BOARD
131 W. Wilson St., P.O. Box 7885
Madison, WI 53707
Fax: (608) 267-2808

Executive Secretary *Valorie T. Olson* 267-2206

INVESTMENT BOARD
P.O. Box 7842, Madison, WI 53707
Information: (608) 266-2381   Fax: (608) 266-2436
Mail to: info@swib.ccmail.compuserve.com

Executive Director *Patricia Lipton* 266-9451

TECHNICAL COLLEGE SYSTEM BOARD
310 Price Pl., P.O. Box 7874
Madison, WI 53707-7874
Information: (608) 266-1770   Fax: (608) 266-1285
TTY: (608) 267-2483   Internet: http://www.tec.wi.us

Director *Edward Chin* 266-1770

WOMEN'S COUNCIL
16 N. Carroll St., Ste. 720, Madison, WI 53703
Fax: (608) 266-5046

45

Executive Director *Eileen D. Mershart* **266-2219**

HISTORICAL SOCIETY
816 State St., Madison, WI 53706
Information: (608) 264-6400   Fax: (608) 264-6433

Director *George L. Vogt* **264-6441**

GEOLOGICAL AND NATURAL HISTORY SURVEY
3817 Mineral Point Rd., Madison, WI 53705
Information: (608) 262-1705   Fax: (608) 262-8086

Director *James M. Robertson* **263-7384**

STATE LEGISLATIVE OFFICES

WISCONSIN LEGISLATURE
Fax: (608) 266-7038
Bill Status: (608) 266-1803

WISCONSIN SENATE
P.O. Box 7882, Madison, WI 53707-7882
Information: (608) 266-2517   TTY: (800) 228-2115

President of the Senate
Fred A. Risser **(D)** . . . . **(608) 266-1627**

SENATORS

PARTY AFFILIATION STATISTICS
Democrats: 16, Republicans: 16, Vacancies: 1

Robert M. Breske (D) District 12 - Florence, Forest, Langlade, Lincoln, Marathon, Marinette, Menominee, Oconto,
Oneida, Portage, Shawano, Vilas, Waupaca
8800 Hwy. 29, Eland, WI 54427

Brian B. Burke (D) District 3 - Milwaukee
2029 N. St., Milwaukee, WI 53208-1747

Charles J. Chvala (D) District 16 - Columbia, Dane, Green,
Rock
One Coach House Dr., Madison, WI 53714

Alice Clausing (D) District 10 - Burnett, Dunn, Pierce, Polk,
St. Croix
1314 Wilson Ave., Menomonee, WI 54751

Robert L. Cowles (R) District 2 - Brown, Oconto, Outagamie,
Shawano
300 W. St. Joseph St., Apt. 23, Green Bay, WI 54301

Alberta Darling (R) District 8 - Milwaukee, Ozaukee, Washington, Waukesha
1325 W. Dean Rd., River Hills, WI 53217

Russell S. Decker (D) District 29 - Marathon, Price, Ruck, Taylor
5106 Apache St., Schofield, WI 54476

Gary F. Drzewiecki (R) District 30 - Brown, Marinette, Oconto
419 Washington St., Pulaski, WI 54162

Michael G. Ellis (R) District 19 - Outagamie, Winnebago
101 W. Canal St., Neenah, WI 54956

Margaret A. Farrow (R) District 33 - Milwaukee, Waukesha
14905 Watertown Plank Rd., Elm Grove, WI 53122

Scott Fitzergerald (R) District 13 - Columbia, Dane Dodge, Jefferson, Rock, Waukesha
105 Leonard Ave., Juneau, WI 53039

Gary R. George (D) District 6 - Milwaukee
4011 W. Capitol Dr., Milwaukee, WI 53216

Richard A. Grobschmidt (D) District 7 - Milwaukee
1513 Mackinac Ave., South Milwaukee, WI 53172

Joanne B. Huelsman (R) District 11 - Jefferson, Rock, Walworth, Washington, Waukesha
235 W. Broadway, Ste. 210, Waukesha, WI 53186-4382

Robert Jauch (D) District 25 - Ashland, Barron, Bayfield, Douglas, Iron, Polk, Sawyer, Washburn
5271 S. Maple Dr., Poplar, WI 54864

Alan J. Lasee (R) District 1 - Brown, Calumet, Door, Fond Du Lac, Kewaunee, Manitowoc, Outagamie, Winnebago
2259 Lasee Rd., De Pere, WI 54115

Political Section

Rodney C. Moen (D) District 31 - Buffalo, Eau Claire, Jackson, Monroe, Pepin, Trempeauleau
P.O. Box 215, Whitehall, WI 54773-0215

Gwendolynne S. Moore (D) District 4 - Milwaukee
4043 N. 19th St., Milwaukee, WI 53209

Mary E. Panzer (R) District 20 - Dodge, Fond Du Lac, Ozaukee, Sheboygan, Washington
635 Tamarack Dr., West, West Bend, WI 53095

Kimberly M. Plache (D) District 21 - Racine
2614 - 17th St., Racine, WI 53405

Calvin Potter (D) District 9 - Calumet, Manitowoc, Sheboygan
808 Green Tree Rd., Kohler, WI 53044

Fred A. Risser (D) District 26 – Dane
5008 Risser Rd., Madison, WI 53705

Carol A. Roessler (R) District 18 - Dodge, Fond Du Lac, Winnebago
1506 Jackson St., Oshkosh, WI 54901

Peggy A. Rosenzweig (R) District 5 - Milwaukee, Waukesha
6236 Upper Pkwy., North, Wauwatosa, WI 53213

Brian D. Rude (R) District 32 - Crawford, La Crosse, Monroe, Richland, Vernon
115 Fifth Ave. South, #414, La Crosse, WI 54601-4018

Dale W. Schultz (R) District 17 - Grant, Iowa, Juneau, Lafayette, Richland, Sauk
515 N. Central Ave., Richland Center, WI 53581

Kevin Shibilski (R) District 24 - Adams, Portage, Waushara, Wood
457 W. Scenic Circle, Stevens Point, WI 54481

Timothy L. Weeden (R) District 15 - Rock, Walworth
2263 Cobblestone Ct., Beloit, WI 53511

Robert T. Welch (R) District 14 - Adams, Columbia, Fond Du Lac, Green, Marquette, Outagamie, Sauk, Waupaca, Waushara, Winnebago
P.O. Box 523, Redgranite, WI 54970

Joseph S. Wineke (D) District 27 - Dane, Green, Rock
412 Edward St., Verona, WI 53593

Robert W. Wirch (D) District 22 - Kenosha, Racine, Walworth
3007 Springbrook Rd., Kenosha, WI 53142

David A. Zien (R) District 23 – Barron, Chippewa, Clark, Dunn, Eau Claire, Marathon, Wood
21 E. Columbia St., Chippewa Falls, WI 54729

SENATE STANDING COMMITTEES

AGRIGULTURE AND ENVIRONMENTAL RESOURCES
Chairman *Alice Clausing* (D-10)

ECONOMIC DEVELOPMENT, HOUSING AND GOVERNMENT OPERATIONS
Chairman *Gwendolynne S. Moore* (D-4)

EDUCATION
Chairman *Calvin Potter* (D-9)

HEALTH, HUMAN SERVICES, AGING, CORRECTIONS, VETERANS AND MILITARY AFFAIRS
Chairman *Rodney C. Moen* (D-31)

INSURANCE, TOURISM AND RURAL AFFAIRS
Chairman *Roger M. Breske* (D-12)

JUDICIARY, CAMPAIGN FINANCE REFORM AND CONSUMER AFFAIRS
Chairman *Robert W. Wirch* (D-22)

LABOR, TRANSPORTATION AND FINANCIAL INSTITU-
TIONS
Chairman *Kimberly M. Plache* (D-21)

SENATE ORGANIZATION
Chairman *Charles J. Chvala* (D-16)

UTILITY REGULATION
Chairman *Rodney C. Moen* (D-31)

WISCONSIN STATE ASSEMBLY
P.O. Box: 8952, Madison, WI 5370
Information: (608) 266-1501   Fax: (608) 266-7038

Speaker of the Assembly
Scott R. Jensen **(R)** . . . . **(608) 264-6970**

REPRESENTATIVES

PARTY AFFILIATION STATISTICS
Democrats: 46, Republicans: 52, Vacancies: 1

John H. Ainsworth (R) District 6 - Oconto, Outagamie,
Shawano
W. 6382 Waukechon, Shawano, WI 54166

Sheryl K. Albers (R) District 50 - Juneau, Richland, Sauk
S6896 Seeley Creek Rd., Logansville, WI 53943

Tammy Baldwin (D) District 78 - Dane
525 Riverside Dr., Madison, WI 53704

James R. Baumgart (D) District 26 - Sheboygan
1337A Carl Ave., Sheboygan, WI 53081

Spencer Black (D) District 77 - Dane
5742 Alder Pl., Madison, WI 53705

Peter E. Bock (D) District 7 - Milwaukee
4710 W. Bluemound Rd., Milwaukee, WI 53208

Frank Boyle (D) District 73 - Bayfield, Douglas, Washburn
4900 E. Tri-Lakes Rd., Superior, WI 54880

David A. Brandemuehl (R) District 49 - Grant, Iowa, Lafayette
13081 Pine Rd., Fennimore, WI 53809-9619

Timothy Carpenter (D) District 9 - Milwaukee
2957 S. 38th St., Milwaukee, WI 53215

G. Spencer Coggs (D) District 17 - Milwaukee
3732 N. 40th St., Milwaukee, WI 53216

David A. Cullen (D) District 13 - Milwaukee, Waukesha
2845 N. 68th St., Milwaukee, WI 53210

John P. Dobyns (R) District 52 - Fond Du Lac
N7566 Sandy Beach Rd., Fond Du Lac, WI 54935

Robert M. Dueholm (D) District 28 - Burnett, Polk, St. Croix
904 State Rd. 48, P.O. Box 260, Luck, WI 54853

Marc C. Duff (R) District 98 - Milwaukee, Waukesha
1811 S. Elm Grove Rd., New Berlin, WI 53151

Steven M. Foti (R) District 38 - Dodge, Jefferson, Waukesha
1117 Dickens Dr., Oconomowoc, WI 53066

Stephen J. Freese (R) District 51 - Grant, Iowa, Lafayette, Sauk
310 E. North St., Dodgeville, WI 53533

John G. Gard (R) District 89 - Brown, Marinette, Oconto
481 Aubin St., P.O. Box 119, Peshtigo, 54157

Robert G. Goetsch (R) District 39 - Columbia, Dodge
Rt. 1, N6485 High Point Rd., Juneau, WI 53039

Mark A. Green (R) District 4 - Brown
2152 Gloucester Dr., Green Bay, WI 54304

Political Section

Barbara Gronemus (D) District 91 - Buffalo, Jackson, Pepin, Trempeauleau
36301 West St., P.O. Box 676, Whitehall, WI 54773-0676

Glenn Grothman (R) District 59 - Fond Du Lac, Ozaukee, Sheboygan, Washington
111 S. Sixth Ave., West Bend, WI 53095

Scott L. Gunderson (R) District 83 - Milwaukee, Racine, Walworth, Waukesha
P.O. Box 7, Waterford, WI 53185

Eugene Hahn (R) District 47 - Columbia, Dane
W3198 Old County Hwy. B, Cambria, WI 53923

Joseph W. Handrick (R) District 34 - Oneida, Vilas
8768 Handrick Dr., Minocqua, WI 54548

Doris J. Hanson (D) District 48 - Dane
4101 Monona Dr., Unit 304, Monona, WI 53716

Sheila E. Harsdorf (R) District 30 - Pierce, St. Croix
N6627 County Rd. "E", River Falls, WI 54022

Donald W. Hasenohrl (D) District 70 - Portage, Wood
9516 Bluff Dr., Pittsville, WI 54466

Tom Hebl (D) District 46 - Dane, Green, Rock
306 Windsor St., Sun Prairie, WI 53590

Timothy T. Hoven (R) District 60 - Ozaukee, Washington
204 S. Webster St., Port Washington, WI 53074

Gregory B. Huber (D) District 85 - Marathon
406 S. Ninth Ave., Wausau, WI 54401

Mary Hubler (D) District 75 - Barron, Polk, Washburn
1966 21-7/8 St., (Hawthorne Ln.), Rice Lake, WI 54868

Michael D. Huebsch (R) District 94 - La Crosse, Monroe
419 W. Franklin, West Salem, WI 54669

David E. Hutchison (R) District 1 - Brown, Door, Kewaunee
N8915 State Rd. 57, Luxemburg, WI 54217

Scott R. Jensen (R) District 32 - Waukesha
850 S. Springdale Rd., Waukesha, WI 53186-1402

Suzanne Jeskewitz (R) District 24 - Washington, Waukesha
N80 W15239 Hilltop Dr., Menomonee Falls, WI 53051

DuWayne G. Johnsrud (R) District 96 - Crawford, Richland, Vernon
Rt. 1, Box 91A, Ducharme Ridge, Eastman, WI 54626

Dean R. Kaufert (R) District 55 - Winnebago,
1360 Alpine Ln., Neenah, WI 54956

Neal J. Kedzie (R) District 43 - Rock, Walworth
N7661 Hwy. 12, Elkhorn, WI 53121

Carol R. Kelso (R) District 88 - Brown
416 E. LeCapitaine Cir., Green Bay, WI 54302

Judith A. Klusman (R) District 56 - Outagamie, Winnebago
7539 Green Meadow Rd., Oshkosh, WI 54904

Robin G. Kreibich (R) District 93 - Eau Claire
3437 Nimitz St., Eaus Claire, WI 54701

James E. Kreuser (D) District 64 - Kenosha
3313 - 24th Ave., Kenosha, WI 53140

Shirley I. Krug (D) District 12 - Milwaukee
6105 W. Hope Ave., Milwaukee, WI 53216

Margaret Ann "Peggy" Krusick (D) District 97 - Milwaukee
3426 S. 69th St., Milwaukee, WI 53219

Walter J. Kunicki (D) District 8 - Milwaukee
1550 S. Fourth St., Milwaukee, WI 53204

John La Fave (D) District 23 - Milwaukee, Ozaukee
5901 W. Brown Deer Rd., Brown Deer, WI 53223-2531

Bonnie L. Ladwig (R) District 63 - Racine
4616 Marcia Dr., Racine, WI 53405

Frank G. Lasee (R) District 2 - Brown, Manitowac
1735 Keehan Ln., Bellevue, WI 54311

Mary A. Lazich (R) District 84 - Milwaukee, Waukesha
4405 S. 129th St., New Berlin, WI 53151

John W. Lehman (D) District 62 - Racine
2421 James Blvd., Racine, WI 53403-3144

Michael A. Lehman (R) District 58 - Dodge, Ozaukee, Washington
1317 Honeysuckle Rd., Hartford, WI 53027

Barbara J. Linton (D) District 74 - Ashland, Bayfield, Iron, Sawyer
Rt. 1, Box 299 - Bass Lake Rd., Highbridge, WI 54846

William D. Lorge (R) District 40 - Outagamie, Waupaca
Rt. 1, P.O. Box 47, Bear Creek, WI 54922

Mark Meyer (D) District 95 - La Crosse
920 S. 16th St., La Crosse, WI 54601

Johnnie Morris-Tatum (D) District 11 - Milwaukee
3711 W. Douglas Ave., Milwaukee, WI 53209

William M. Murat (D) District 71 - Portage, Waushara
3401 Harmony Ln., P.O. Box 111, Stevens Point, WI 54481

Terry M. Musser (R) District 92 - Eau Claire, Jackson, Monroe
W13550 Murray Rd., Black River Falls, WI 54615

Stephen L. Nass (R) District 31 - Jefferson, Rock, Walworth, Waukesha
W8948 Willis Ray Rd., Whitewater, WI 53190

Barbara Notestein (D) District 19 - Milwaukee
2971 N. Stowell St., Milwaukee, WI 53211-3350

Luther S. Olsen (R) District 41 - Fond Du Lac, Green, Waushara, Winnebago
N2021 Hwy. 49, Berlin, WI 54923

Alvin R. Ott (R) District 3 - Brown, Calumet, Fond Du Lac, Outagamie, Winnebago
P.O. Box 112, Forest Junction, WI 54123-0112

Clifford Otte (R) District 27 - Calumet, Sheboygan
N5385 Bridgewood Rd., Sheboygan Falls, WI 53085

Thomas D. Ourada (R) District 35 - Langlade, Lincoln, Marathon, Shawano
425 Dorr St., Antigo, WI 54409

Carol Owens (R) District 53 - Dodge, Fond Du Lac, Winnebago
144 County Rd. C, Oshkosh, WI 54904

Jeffrey Plale (D) District 21 - Milwaukee
1404 - 18th Ave., South Milwaukee, WI 53172

Joe Plouf (D) District 29 - Dunn, Pierce, St. Croix
1421 Messenger St., Menomonee, WI 54751

Cloyd Porter (R) District 66 - Kenosha, Racine, Walworth
28322 Durand Ave., Burlington, WI 53105

Rosemary Potter (D) District 20 - Milwaukee
3113 S. Pennsylvania Ave., Milwaukee, WI 53207

Michael Powers (R) District 80 - Green, Rock
N6772 Attica Rd., Albany, WI 53502

Martin L. Reynolds (D) District 87 - Price, Rusk, Taylor
219 W. Second St., North, Ladysmith, WI 54848

Antonio R. Riley (D) District 18 - Milwaukee
1132 N. 22nd St., Milwaukee, WI 53233

Judith Biros Robson (D) District 45 - Rock
2411 E. Ridge Rd., Beloit, WI 53511

Political Section

John J. Ryba (D) District 90 - Brown
714 Wilson Ave., Green Bay, WI 54303

Chuck Schafer (R) District 68 - Chippewa, Eau Claire
19697 - 53rd Ave., Chippewa Falls, WI 54729

Marlin D. Schneider (D) District 72 - Adams, Portage, Wood
3820 Southbrook Ln., Wisconsin Rapids, WI 54494

Lorraine M. Seratti (R) District 36 - Florence, Forest, Lan-
glade, Marathon, Marinette, Menominee, Oconto, Portage,
Shawano, Waupaca
Spread Eagle, HC - 2, Box 588, Florence, WI 54121

Richard A. Skindrud (R) District 79 - Dane, Green
1261 LaFollette Rd., Mount Horeb, WI 53572

Joan Wade Spillner (R) District 42 - Adams, Columbia,
Marquette, Sauk
N5095 Town Hall Rd., Montello, WI 53949

Thomas J. Springer (D) District 86 - Marathon
701 - 16th St., Mosinee, WI 54455

Tony Staskunas (D) District 15 - Milwaukee
2010 S. 103rd Ct., West Allis, WI 53227

John P. Steinbrink (D) District 65 - Kenosha
8602 - 88th Ave., Kenosha, WI 53142

Tom Sykora (R) District 67 - Barron, Chippewa, Dunn
10688 State Hwy. 178, Chippewa Falls, WI 54729

David M. Travis (D) District 81 - Dane
4229 Mandrake Rd., Madison, WI 53704

Robert L. Turner (D) District 61 - Racine
36 McKinley Ave., Racine, WI 53404

Gregg Underheim (R) District 54 - Winnebago
1652 Beech St.. Oshkosh, WI 54901

Frank H. Urban (R) District 99 - Waukesha
3645 Emberwood Dr., Brookfield, WI 53045

William N. Vander Loop (D) District 5 - Brown, Outagamie
1908 Parkwood Dr., Kaukauna, WI 54130

Daniel P. Vrakas (R) District 33 - Washington, Waukesha
N45 W28912 E. Capitol Dr., Hartland, WI 53029

Scott K. Walker (R) District 14 - Milkwaukee
2334 N. 73rd St., Wauwatosa, WI 53213

David W. Ward (R) District 37 - Columbia, Dane, Dodge,
Jefferson, Rock
N3401 Hwy. G, Fort Atkinson, WI 53538

Sheldon A. Wasserman (D) District 22 - Milwaukee, Ozaukee
3487 N. Lake Dr., Milwaukee, WI 53211

Steve Wieckert (R) District 57 - Outagamie
3038 N. Ballard Rd., #214, Appleton, WI 54911

Annette P. Williams (D) District 10 - Milwaukee
3927 N. 16th St., Milwaukee, WI 53206

Wayne W. Wood (D) District 44 - Rock
2429 Rockport Rd., Janesville, WI 53545

Leon D. Young (D) District 16 - Milwaukee
2351 N. Richards St., Milwaukee, WI 53212

Rebecca Young (D) District 76 - Dane
639 Crandall St., Madison, WI 53711

Robert F. Ziegelbauer (D) District 5 - Calumnet, Manitowoc
P.O. Box 325, Manitowoc, WI 54221-0325

Robert K. Zukowski (R) District 69 - Clark, Eau Claire,
Marathon, Wood
W9884 County Rd. MM, Thorp, WI 54771-8106

ASSEMBLY STANDING COMMITTEES

AGING AND LONG-TERM CARE
Chairman *Robert K. Zukowski* (R-69)

AGRICULTURE
Chairman *Alvin R. Ott* (R-3)

ASSEMBLY ORGANIZATION
Chairman *Scott R. Jensen* (R-32)

CAMPAIGN FINANCE REFORM
Chairman *Joseph W. Handrick* (R-34)

CHILDREN AND FAMILIES
Chairman *Michael D. Heubsch* (R-94)

COLLEGES AND UNIVERSITIES
Chairman *Robin G. Kreibich* (R-93)

CONSUMER AFFAIRS
Chairman *Clifford Otte* (R-27)

CORRECTIONS FACILITIES
Chairman *Scott K. Walker* (R-14)

CRIMINAL JUSTICE AND CORRECTIONS
Chairman *Robert G. Goetsch* (R-39)

EDUCATION
Chairman *Luther S. Olsen* (R-41)

ELECTIONS AND CONSTITUTIONAL LAW
Chairman *Scott K. Walker* (R-14)

ENVIRONMENT
Chairman *Marc C. Duff* (R-98)

FINANCIAL INSTITUTIONS
Chairman *David W. Ward* (R-37

GOVERNMENT OPERATIONS
Chairman *John P. Dobyns* (R-52)

HEALTH
Chairman *Gregg Underheim* (R-54)

HIGHWAYS AND TRANSPORTATION
Chairman *David A. Brandemuehl* (R-49)

HOUSING
Chairman *Carol Owens* (R-53)

INCOME TAX REVIEW
Chairman *Frank G. Lasee* (R-2)

INSURANCE, SECURITIES AND CORPORATE POLICY
Chairman *William D. Lorge* (R-40)

JUDICIARY
Chairman *Mark A. Green* (R-4)

LABOR AND EMPLOYMENT
Chairman *Daniel P. Vrakas* (R-33)

LAND USE
Chairman *Michael Powers* (R-80)

MANAGED CARE
Chairman *John G. Gard* (R-89)

MANDATES
Chairman *Stephen L. Nass* (R-31)

NATURAL RESOURCES
Chairman *DuWayne G. Johnsrud* (R-96)

RULES
Chairman *Steven M. Foti* (R-38)

RURAL AFFAIRS
Chairman *John H. Ainsworth* (R-6)

Political Section

SMALL BUSINESS AND ECONOMIC DEVELOPMENT
Chairman *Lorraine M. Seratti* (R-36)

STATE AFFAIRS
Chairman *Richard A. Skindrud* (R-79)

STATE-FEDERAL RELATIONS
Chairman *Gregg Underheim* (R-54)

TOURISM AND RECREATION
Chairman *Eugene Hahn* (R-47)

URBAN AND LOCAL AFFAIRS
Chairman *Scott L. Gunderson* (R-83)

UTILITIES OVERSIGHT
Chairman *Timothy T. Hoven* (R-60)

VETERANS AND MILITARY AFFAIRS
Chairman *Terry M. Musser* (R-92)

WAYS AND MEANS
Chairman *Michael A. Lehman* (R-58)

WISCONSIN WORKS OVERSIGHT
Chairman *John G. Gard* (R-89)

WORKING FAMILIES
Chairman *Carol R. Kelso* (R-88)

JOINT STANDING COMMITTEES

JOINT ADMINISTRATIVE RULES REVIEW
Co-Chairman *Sen. Richard A. Grobschmidt* (D-7)
Co-Chairman *Rep. Glenn Grothman* (R-59)

JOINT AUDIT
Co-Chairman *Sen. Robert W. Wirch* (D-22)
Co-Chairman *Rep. Mary A. Lazich* (R-84)

JOINT EMPLOYMENT RELATIONS
Co-Chairman *Sen. Fred A. Risser* (D-26)
Co-Chairman *Rep. Scott R. Jensen* (R032)

JOINT FINANCE
Co-Chairman *Sen Brian B. Burke* (D-3)
Co-Chairman *Rep. John G. Gard* (R-89)

JOINT INFORMATION POLICY
Co-Chairman *Sen. Robert Jauch* (D-25)
Co-Chairman *Rep. David E. Hutchison* (R-1)

JOINT LEGISLATIVE ORGANIZATION
Co-Chairman *Sen. Fred A. Risser* (D-26)
Co-Chairman *Rep. Scott R. Jenson* (R-32)

JOINT RETIREMENT SYSTEMS
Co-Chairman *Richard A. Grobschmidt* (D-7)
Co-Chairman *Judith A. Klusman* (R-56)

JOINT TAX EXEMPTIONS
Co-Chairman *Sen. Robert S. Wineke* (D-27)
Co-Chairman *Rep. Frank H. Urban* (R-99)

DIRECTORY
OF
STATE SERVICES

DIRECTORY OF STATE SERVICES

OFFICE OF THE GOVERNOR
PO Box 7863
Madison, WI 53707-7863
Fax: 608-267-8983
Governor: 608-266-1212

Washington, DC Office
444 N. Capitol St. Ste. 613
Washington, DC 20001

OFFICE OF THE LIEUTENANT GOVERNOR
22 E. State Capitol
Madison, WI 53702
Fax: 608-267-3571
Lieutenant Governor: 608-266-3516

ATTORNEY GENERAL (JUSTICE DEPARTMENT)
PO Box 7857
Madison, WI 53707-7857
Fax: 608-267-2223
Attorney General: 608-266-1221

SECRETARY OF STATE
PO Box 7848
Madison, WI 53707-7848
Fax: 608-267-6813
Secretary of State: 608-266-8888

The Encyclopedia of Wisconsin

TREASURER
PO Box 7871
Madison, WI 53707
Fax: 608-266-2647
Treasurer: 608-266-1714

ADMINISTRATION DEPARTMENT
PO Box 7864
Madison, WI 53707-7864
Fax: 608-267-3842
Secretary: 608-266-1714

Claims Board
101 S. Wilson St.
Madison, WI 53702
Fax: 608-267-3842
Secretary: 608-266-2765

Revisor of Statutes Bureau
131 W. Wilson St. Ste. 800
Madison, WI 53703-3233
Fax: 608-267-0410
Revisor of Statutes: 608-267-3536

Sentencing Commission
PO Box 8457
Madison, WI 53708-8457
Fax: 608-261-8141
Executive Director: 608-267-2437

Tax Appeals Commission
101 E. Wilson St.
Madison, WI 53702
Chairman: 608-266-1391

AGRICULTURE, TRADE AND CONSUMER PROTECTION DEPARTMENT
PO Box 8911
Madison, WI 53708
Fax: 608-224-5045
Secretary: 608-224-5012

Central Animal Health Laboratory
6101 Mineral Point Rd.
Madison, WI 53705
Fax: 608-267-0636
Director: 608-266-2465

CORRECTIONS DEPARTMENT
PO Box 7925
Madison, WI 53707-7925
Fax: 608-267-3661
Secretary: 608-266-4548

DEVELOPMENT DEPARTMENT
PO Box 7970
Madison, WI 53707
Fax: 608-267-0436
Secretary: 608-266-7088

EMPLOYMENT RELATIONS DEPARTMENT
PO Box 7855
Madison, WI 53707-7855

Fax: 608-267-1020
Secretary: 608-266-9820

EMPLOYEE TRUST FUNDS DEPARTMENT
201 E. Washington, Rm. 171
Madison, WI 53702
Fax: 608-267-0633
Secretary: 608-266-1071

HEALTH AND SOCIAL SERVICES DEPARTMENT
PO Box 7850
Madison, WI 53707-7850
Fax: 608-266-7882
Secretary: 608-266-9622

Care and Treatment Facilities Division
PO Box 7850
Madison, WI 53707-7850
Fax: 608-266-2579

Community Services Division
PO Box 7850
Madison, WI 53707-7850
Fax: 608-266-2579
Administrator: 608-266-0554

Economic Support Division
PO Box 7850
Madison, WI 53707-7850
Fax: 608-261-6376
Administrator: 608-266-3035

Health Division
PO Box 7850
Madison, WI 53707-7850
Fax: 608-267-2832
Administrator: 608-266-1511

Management Services Division
PO Box 7850
Madison, WI 53707-7850
Fax: 608-267-2147
Administrator: 608-266-6954

Vocational Rehabilitation Division
PO Box 7850
Madison, WI 53707-7850
Fax: 608-267-3657
Administrator: 608-266-5466

INDUSTRY, LABOR AND HUMAN RELATIONS DEPARTMENT
PO Box 7946
Madison, WI 53707
Fax: 608-266-1784
Secretary: 608-266-7552

MILITARY AFFAIRS DEPARTMENT
PO Box 8111
Madison, WI 53708-8111
Fax: 608-242-3111
Adjutant General: 608-242-3001

NATURAL RESOURCES DEPARTMENT
PO Box 7921
Madison, WI 53707
Fax: 608-266-6983
Secretary: 608-266-2121

PUBLIC INSTRUCTION DEPARTMENT
PO Box 7841
Madison, WI 53707-7841
Fax: 608-267-1052
State Superintendent: 608-266-1771

Learning Support Instructional Services Division
PO Box 7841
Madison, WI 53707-7841
Fax: 608-267-1052
Assistant Superintendent: 608-266-3361

Management and Budget Division
PO Box 7841
Madison, WI 53707-7841
Fax: 608-267-1052
Assistant Superintendent: 608-266-3903

School Financial Resources and Management Services Division
PO Box 7841
Madison, WI 53707-7841
Fax: 608-267-1052
Assistant Superintendent: 608-266-3851

School for the Deaf and Hearing Impaired
309 W. Walwroth Ave.
Delavan, WI 53115
Fax: 414-728-7160
Superintendent: 414-728-7120

School for the Visually Handicapped
1700 W. State St.
Janesville, WI 53545
Fax:608-758-6161
Superintendent: 608-755-2950

REGULATION AND LICENSING DEPARTMENT
PO Box 8935
Madison, WI 53708-8935
Fax: 608-267-0644
Secretary: 608-266-8609

REVENUE DEPARTMENT
PO Box 8933
Madison, WI 53708
Fax: 608-266-5718
Secretary: 608-266-1611

TRANSPORTATION DEPARTMENT
PO Box 7910
Madison, WI 53707-7910
Fax: 608-266-9912
Secretary: 608-266-1113

VETERANS AFFAIRS DEPARTMENT
PO Box 7843
Madison, WI 53707

Fax: 608-267-0403
Secretary: 608-266-1315

AGING AND LONG TERM CARE BOARD
214 N. Hamilton St.
Madison, WI 53707
Fax: 608-261-6570
Executive Director: 608-266-8944

ARTS BOARD
101 E. Wilson St., 1st Fl.
Madison, WI 53702
Fax: 608-267-0380
Executive Director: 608-266-0190

BANKING COMMISSION
PO Box 7876
Madison, WI 53707-7876
Fax: 608-267-6889
Commissioner: 608-266-1621

BUILDING COMMISSION
PO Box 7866
Madison, WI 53707
Fax: 608-267-2710
Chairman: 266-1031

CREDIT UNIONS COMMISSIONER
101 E. Wilson St., 4th Fl.
Madison, WI 53702
Fax: 608-267-0479
Commissioner: 608-266-0438

EDUCATIONAL COMMUNICATIONS BOARD
3319 Beltine Hwy.
Madison, WI 53713-4296
Fax: 608-264-9622
Executive Director: 608-264-9697

ELECTIONS BOARD
132 E. Wilson St., 3rd Fl.
Madison, WI 53702
Fax: 608-267-0500
Chairman: 608-266-8087

EMPLOYMENT RELATIONS COMMISSION
PO Box 7870
Madison, WI 53707-7870
Fax: 608-266-6930
Chairman: 608-266-1381

ETHICS BOARD
44 E. Mifflin St., Ste. 601
Madison, WI 53703-2800
Fax: 608-264-9309
Executive Director: 608-266-8123

GAMING COMMISSION
PO Box 8979
Madison, WI 53708-8979
Fax: 608-267-4879
Chairman: 608-264-6607

HEALTH EDUCATIONAL FACILITIES AUTHORITY
18000 W. Sarah Ln., Ste. 140
Brookfield, WI 53045-5843

Fax: 414-792-0649
Executive Director: 414-792-0466

HIGHER EDUCATIONAL AIDS BOARD
PO Box 7885
Madison, WI 53707
Fax: 608-267-2808
Executive Secretary: 608-267-2208

HISTORICAL SOCIETY
816 State St.
Madison, WI 53706
Fax: 608-264-6404
Director: 608-264-6400

HOUSING AND ECONOMIC DEVELOPMENT AUTHORITY
PO Box 1728
Madison, WI 53701-1728
Fax: 608-267-1099
Executive Director: 608-266-7884

INSURANCE COMMISSION
PO Box 7873
Madison, WI 53707-7873
Fax: 608-266-9935
Commissioner: 608-266-3585

JUDICIAL COMMISSION
110 E. Main St., Ste. 606
Madison, WI 53703
Fax: 608-266-8647
Executive Director: 608-266-7637

JUDICIAL COUNCIL
25 W. Main St., Rm. 777
Madison, WI 53703
Fax: 608-267-4507
Executive Secretary: 608-266-1319

LABOR AND INDUSTRY REVIEW COMMISSION
PO Box 8126
Madison, WI 53708
Fax: 608-267-4409
Chairman: 608-266-9850

LEGISLATIVE AUDIT BUREAU
131 W. Wilson St., Ste. 402
Madison, WI 53703
Fax: 608-267-0410
State Auditor: 608-266-2818

PERSONNEL COMMISSION
131 W. Wilson St., Rm. 1004
Madison, WI 53702
Chairperson: 608-266-1995

PUBLIC DEFENDER
PO Box 7923
Madison, WI 53707
Fax: 608-267-0584
State Public Defender: 608-266-0087

PUBLIC SERVICE COMMISSION
PO Box 7854
Madison, WI 53707-7854
Fax: 608-266-1401
Chairman: 608-267-7897

SAVINGS & LOAN COMMISSION
4785 Hayes Rd., Ste. 202
Madison, WI 53704-7365
Fax: 608-242-2187
Commissioner: 608-242-2180

SECURITIES COMMISSION
PO Box 1768
Madison, WI 53701
Fax: 608-256-1259
Commissioner: 608-266-3431

STATE FAIR
PO Box 14990
West Allis, WI 53214-0990
Fax: 414-266-7007
Director: 414-266-7000

TECHNICAL COLLEGE SYSTEM
PO Box 7874
Madison, WI 53707-7874
Fax: 608-266-1285
Director: 608-266-1207

WISCONSIN LISTING FROM

The National Register of Historic Places

Guide to Criteria for Selection

The quality of significance in American history, architecture, archeology, engineering, and culture is present in districts, sites, buildings, structures, and objects that possess integrity of location, design, setting, materials, workmanship, feeling, and association, and:

A. that are associated with events that have made a significant contribution to the broad patterns of our history; or

B. that are associated with the lives of persons significant in our past; or

C. that embody the distinctive characteristics of a type, period, or method of construction, or that represent the work of a master, or that possess high artistic values, or that represent a significant and distinguishable entity whose components may lack individual distinction; or

D. that have yielded, or may be likely to yield, information important in prehistory or history.

Criteria considerations:

a. a religious property deriving primary significance from architectural or artistic distinction or historical importance; or

b. a building or structure removed from its original location but which is significant primarily for architectural value, or which is the surviving structure most importantly associated with a historic person or event; or

c. a birthplace or grave of a historical figure of outstanding importance if there is no other appropriate site or building directly associated with his productive life; or

d. a cemetery that derives its primary significance from graves of persons of transcendent importance, from age, from distinctive design features, or from association with historic events; or

e. a reconstructed building when accurately executed in a suitable environment and presented in a dignified manner as part of a restoration master plan, and when no other building or structure with the same association has survived; or

f. a property primarily commemorative in intent if design, age, tradition, or symbolic value has invested it with its own historical significance; or

g. a property achieving significance within the past 50 years if it is of exceptional importance.

ENTRY REFERENCES

(NHL) indicates National Historic Landmark. Eight-character number at the end of each entry is the computer reference number for obtaining detailed information from The National Park Service.

ENTRY INFORMATION

Each entry gives the following data:

1. property name as recorded in the National Register;
2. name of multiple property submission of nominations that include the property, if applicable; (MPS = Multiple Property Submission; MRA = Multiple Resource Area; TR = Thematic Resource); (Multiple property nominations were created to facilitate the nomination of groups of related properties in a defined area.)
3. address, if applicable;
4. town or vicinity;
5. date the property was listed in the National Register;
6. National Register criterion(ia) for which the property was accepted (upper case letter designation); (A,B,C,D,);
7. Criteria exception(s), if applicable (lower case designation); (a,b,c,d,e,f,g);
8. identification of National Historic Landmarks, if applicable (NPS or NHL);
9. computer reference number for the property.

Detailed information is available from:

National Register
Inter-agency Resource Division
800 North Capitol
Ste. 250
Washington, D.C. 20002

WISCONSIN
HISTORIC PLACES

ADAMS COUNTY

Adams County Courthouse, County Courthouse of Wisconsin TR, 402 Main St., Friendship, 3/09/82, C, 82000627
Roche-a-Cri Petroglyphs, Friendship vicinity, 5/11/81, C, D, 81000031

ASHLAND COUNTY

Apostle Islands Lighthouses, N. and E. of Bayfield on Michigan, Raspberry, Outer, Sand and Devils Islands, Bayfield vicinity, 3/08/77, A, NPS, 77000145
Ashland County Courthouse, County Courthouses of Wisconsin TR, 201 W. 2nd St., Ashland, 3/09/82, C, 82000628
Ashland Middle School, Wildhagen, Henry, Schools of Ashland TR, 1000 Ellis Ave., Ashland, 7/17/80, C, 80000101
Bass Island Brownstone Company Quarry, N of La Pointe on Basswood Island, La Pointe vicinity, 3/29/78, A, NPS, 78000075
Beaser School, Wildhagen, Henry, Schools of Ashland TR, 612 Beaser Ave., Ashland, 7/17/80, C, 80000102
Ellis School, Wildhagen, Henry, Schools of Ashland TR, 310 Stuntz Ave., Ashland, 7/17/80, C, 80000103
Hadland Fishing Camp, N of La Pointe on Rocky Island, La Points vicinity, 8/18/77, A, b, g, NPS, 77000146
LUCERNE (Shipwreck), Address Restricted, La Pointe vicinity, 12/18/91, A, C, D, 91001775
La Pointe Indian Cemetery, S. Old Main St., La Pointe, 8/03/77, A, D, a, d, 77000028
La Pointe Light Station, U.S. Coast Guard Lighthouses and Light Stations on the Great Lakes TR, Long Island in Chequamagon Bay, Bayfield vicinity, 8/04/83, A, C, 83003366
Manitou Camp, Manitou Island, Apostle Islands National Lakeshore, 1/19/83, A, C, b, NPS, 83003367

Marina Site, Address Restricted, La Pointe vicinity, 12/22/78, A, D, d, 78000076

Marion Park Pavilion, Marion Park, Glidden vicinity, 6/04/81, A, C, 81000032

Mellen City Hall, Bennett and Main Sts., Ashland, 9/21/79, A, 79000341

Morty Site (47AS40), Address Restricted, Bayfield vicinity, 6/13/88, D, NPS, 88000145

NOQUEBAY (Schooner-Barge) Shipwreck Site, Great Lakes Shipwrecks of Wisconsin MPS, Address Restricted, La Pointe, 6/04/92, C, D, 92000593

Old Ashland Post Office, 601 West Second St., Ashland, 1/21/74, C, 74000054

P-Flat Site (47AS47), Address Restricted, Bayfield vicinity, 9/19/88, D, NPS, 88000144

R. G. STEWART (Shipwreck), Address Restricted, La Pointe vicinity, 12/27/91, D, 91001850

Security Savings Bank, 212-214 W. 2nd St., Ashland, 12/27/74, C, 74000055

Soo Line Depot, Third Ave. W. at Fourth St., Ashland, 11/03/88, A, C, 88002177

Trout Point Logging Camp, Address Restricted, Bayfield vicinity, 12/16/88, D, NPS, 88002756

Union Depot, 417 Chapple Ave., Ashland, 3/23/79, A, C, 79000058

West Second Street Historic District, W. 2nd St. from Ellis Ave. to 6th Ave., Ashland, 2/02/84, A, C, 84003619

Wheeler Hall, Northland College, 1411 Ellis Ave., Ashland, 9/13/77, A, 77000029

Wilmarth School, Wildhagen, Henry, Schools of Ashland TR, 913 3rd Ave. W., Ashland, 7/17/80, C, 80000104

BARRON COUNTY

Barron County Pipestone Quarry, E of Rice Lake, Rice Lake vicinity, 12/22/78, E, 78000077

Cumberland Public Library, Public Library Facilities of Wisconsin MPS, 1305 Second Ave., Cumberland, 6/25/92, A, C, 92000804

Rice Lake Mounds (47BN90), Rice Lake, 9/07/79, D, 79000059

ZCBJ Hall, 320 W. 3rd St., Haugen, 4/11/75, A, 85000768

Historic Places

BAYFIELD COUNTY

Bank of Washburn, Bayfield St. and Central Ave., Washburn, 1/17/80, C, 80000105

Bayfield County Courthouse, 117 E. 5th St., Washburn, 1/17/75, C, 75000060

Bayfield Fish Hatchery, WI 13, Salmo vicinity, 7/22/81, A, C, 81000033

Bayfield Historic District, WI J and WI 13, Bayfield, 11/25/80, A, C, 80000106

Booth Cooperage, 1 East Washington St., Bayfield, 8/13/76, A, 76000049

Boutin, Frank, Jr., House, 7 Rice St., Hayfield, 12/27/74, C, 74000056

Christ Episcopal Church, 121-125 North 3rd. St., Hayfield, 12/27/74, C, a, 74000057

Hokenson Fishing Dock, N of Bayfield at Little Sand Bay, Bayfield vicinity, 6/18/76, A, NPS, 76000050

Island Lake Camp, Island Lake Rd., Drummond vicinity, 3/12/82, A, B, 82000629

OTTAWA (Tug) Shipwreck Site, Great Lakes Shipwreck Sites of Wisconsin MPS, Address Restricted, Russell, 6/08/92, A, C, 92000594

Old Bayfield County Courthouse, Washington St. between 4th and 5th Sts., Bayfield, 12/27/74, C, 74000058

Pureair Sanatorium, S. of Bayfield, Bayfield vicinity, 8/20/81, A, 81000034

SEVONA (Bulk Carrier) Shipwreck Site, Great Lakes Shipwrecks of Wisconsin MPS, Address Restricted, Bayfield vicinity, 4/09/93, C, D, 93000229

Sevona Cabin, N. of Bayfield on Sand Island, Bayfield vicinity, 9/29/76, B, C, NPS, 76000051

Shaw Farm, Sand Island, Bayfield vicinity, 6/18/76, A, NPS. 76000052

Washburn Public Library, Washington Ave. and W. 3rd St., Washburn, 3/01/84, C, 84003621

BROWN COUNTY

Astor Historic District, WI 57, Green Bay, 2/27/80, A, C, 80000107

Baird Law Office, 2640 South Webster Avenue, Green Bay, 10/15/70, A, C, b, 70000025

Brown County Courthouse, 100 S. Jefferson St., Green Bay, 1/01/76, C, 76000053

Cotton House, 2640 South Webster Ave., Green Bay, 4/28/70, C, b, 70000026

Fisk, Joel S, House, 123 N. Oakland Ave., Green Bay, 8/11/78, C, 78000420

Fort Howard Hospital, 2640 S. Webster Ave., Green Bay, 7/22/79, A, C, b, 71001075

Fort Howard Officers' Quarters, 2640 S. Webster Ave., Green Bay, 7/22/79, A, C, b, 72001548

Fort Howard Ward Building, 2640 S. Webster Ave., Green Bay, 7/22/79, A, b, 72001547

Hazelwood, 1008 S. Monroe Ave., Green Bay, 4/28/70, A, C, 70000027

Henry House, 1749 Riverside Dr., Suamico, 1/31/80, A, C, 80000108

Kellogg Public Library and Neville Public Museum, 125 S. Jefferson St., Green Bay, 6/09/81, A, C, 81000035

Lawton, C, A., Company, 233 N. Broadway, De Pere, 1/30/92, A, C, 91001985

Main Hall, Third St. and College Ave., De Pere, 10/28/88, A, C, a, 88002001

Mueller-Wright House, Washington and Mueller Sts., Wrightstown, 3/29/78, B, C, 78000078

North Broadway Street Historic District, Broadway, Ridgeway Blvd., Morris, Fulton, Franklin, Cass, Front, and Wisconsin Sts., De Pere, 9/08/83, B, C, 83003368

Oakland–Dousman Historic District, Roughly bounded by Dousman St., Oakland Ave., Shawano Ave., Antoinette and Francis Sts., Green Bay, 4/27/88, B, C, 88000455

Tank Cottage, 2640 South Webster Avenue, Green Bay, 4/28/70, A, C, b, 70000028

Wisconsin State Reformatory, SE corner of Riverside Dr. and SR 172, Allouez, 5/03/90, A, C, 90000641

BUFFALO COUNTY

Alma Historic District, Alma MRA, Roughly bounded by RR tracks, 2nd, Swift, and Cedar Sts., Alma, 5/13/82, A, B, C, 82000631

Berni, Jacob, House, Alma MRA, 911 Riverview Dr., Alma, 5/13/82, C, 82000632

Burlington Hotel, Alma MRA, 809 N. Main St., Alma, 5/13/82, C, 82000633

Fugina House, 348 S. Main St., Fountain City, 5/08/79, B, C, 79000061

Laue, Frederick, House, 1111 S. Main St., Alma, 5/14/79, A, C, 79000062

Laue, Frederick, Jr., House, Alma MRA, 1109 S. Main St., Alma, 5/13/82, C, 82000634

Senn, John L, House, Alma MRA, 811 S. 2nd St., Alma, 5/13/82, C, 82000635

Sherman House, 301 S. Main St., Alma, 8/14/79, B, C, 79000063

Steiner, John, Store, Alma MRA, 1101 S. Main St., Alma, 5/13/82, C, 82000636

Tenny, Dr. J. T., House, Alma MRA, 305 N. 2111 St., Alma, 5/13/82, C, 82000637

Tester and Polin General Merchandise Store, 215 N. Main St., Alma, 5/14/79, A, B, C, 79000164

Walser, Ulrich, House, Alma MRA, 711 N. 2nd St., Alma, 5/13/82, C, 82000638

BURNETT COUNTY

Altern Site, Address Restricted, Hertel vicinity, 3/31/80, D, 80000391

Burnett County Abstract Company, 214 N. Oak St., Grantsburg, 5/07/80, A, C, 80000109

Ebert Mound Group (47BT28), Yellow Lake vicinity, 7/09/82, D, 82000639

Fickle Site (47BT25), Address Restricted, Siren vicinity, 1/26/90, D, 89002310

Jacobson House and Mill Site, E of Grantsburg on SR M, Grantsburg vicinity, 4/22/80, B, 80000110

Northwest and XY Company Trading Post Sites, Address Restricted, Webster vicinity, 2/15/74, D, 74000059

Sandrock Cliffs, Address Restricted, Grantsburg vicinity, 5/01/90, D, NPS, 90000632

Yellow River Swamp Site (47BT36), Address Restricted, Webster vicinity, 2/28/85, D, 85000405

CALUMET COUNTY

Aebischer Site (47CT30), Address Restricted, Chilton vicinity, 10/10/85, D, 85003136

Calumet County Courthouse, County Courthouses of Wisconsin TR, 206 Court St., Chilton, 3/09/82, C, 82000640

Haese Memorial Village Historic District, Milwaukee and Randolph Sts., Forest Junction, 3/02/82, A, B, C, 82000641

Ridge Group, Address Restricted, Chilton vicinity, 12/08/78, D, 78000079

Stockridge Indian Cemetery, N of Stockridge off WI 55, Stockbridge vicinity, 10/22/80, A, d, 80000111

CHIPPEWA COUNTY

Cook-Rutledge House, 509 W. Grand Ave., Chippewa Falls, 8/07/74, A, C, 74000060

Cornell Pulpwood Stacker, Cornell Mill Yard Park, Cornell, 12/23/93, A, C, 93001425

Marsh Rainbow Arch Bridge, Spring St., Chippewa Falls, 6/25/82, C, 82000642

McDonell High School, Notre Dame Parish TR, 3 S. High St., Chippewa Falls, 10/06/82, C, 82001840

Moon, D. R., Memorial Library, E. Fourth Ave., Stanley, 12/02/85, A, C, 85003096

Notre Dame Church and Goldsmith Memorial Chapel, Notre Dame Parish TR, 117 Allen St., Chippewa Falls, 4/07/83, C, a, 83003369

Roe, L. I., House, 410 N. Franklin St., Stanley, 8/27/80, B, 80000112

Sheeley House, 236 W. River St., Chippewa Falls, 9/05/85, A, C, 85001949

ZCBJ Hall, WI 277 mi. N of Cadott, Arthur, 6/25/92, A, 92000812

CLARK COUNTY

Clark County Jail, 215 E. 5th St., Neillsville, 12/08/78, A, C, 78000080

Schofield, Robert, House, 303 W. Schofield Ave., Greenwood, 9/09/82, B, C, 82000643

COLUMBIA COUNTY

Belimont Hotel, 120 N. Main St., Pardeeville, 11/04/93, C, 93001170

Bennett, H. H., Studio, 215 Broadway, Wisconsin Dells, 10/08/76, A, B, 76000054

Bowman House, 714 Broadway St., Wisconsin Dells, 4/03/86, C, 86000621

Chadbourn, F. A., House, 314 S. Charles St., Columbus, 12/28/90, C, 90001961

Columbus City Hall, 105 N. Dickason St., Columbus, 9/04/79, A, C, 79000065

Columbus Downtown Historic District, Roughly bounded by Mill, Water and Harrison Sts. and Dickason Blvd., Columbus, 3/05/92, A, C, 92000113

Columbus Public Library, Public Library Facilities of Wisconsin MPS, 112 S. Dickason Blvd., Columbus, 11/15/90 A, C, 90001704

Cox, Angie Williams, Library, Public Library Facilities of Wisconsin MPS, 129 N. Main St., Pardeeville, 11/15/90, A, B, 90001703

Durward's Glen, NE of Merrimac off WI 78, Merrimac vicinity, 11/07/78, A, C, 78000081

Farmers and Merchants Union Bank, 159 W. James St., Columbus, 10/18/72, C, NHL, 72000044

Fort Winnebago Site, Address Restricted, Portage vicinity, 5/17/79, D, 79000066

Fort Winnebago Surgeon's Quarters, 0.1 mi. & of corporate city limits on WI 33, Portage vicinity, 10/28/70, A, 70000029

Fox-Wisconsin Portage Site, Address Restricted, Portage vicinity, 3/14/73, A, 73000074

Gale, Zona, House, 506 W. Edgewater St., Portage, 10/24/80, B, C, 80000113

Holsten Family Farmstead, W. 1391 Weiner Rd., Columbia, 9/08/92, A, C, 92001189

Kilbourn Public Library, 429 Broadway, Wisconsin Dells, 12/27/74, C, 74000061

Kurth, John H., and Company Office Building, 729-733 Park Ave., Columbus, 12/02/93, A, C, 93001359

Lewis, Gov. James T., House, 711 W. James St., Columbus, 4/09/82, B, C, 82000644

McNeil, Henry, House, 505 E. Cook St., Portage, 7/08/93, C, b, 93000545

Merrimac Ferry, WI 113 at the Wisconsin River, Merrimac, 12/31/74, A, 74100330

Nashold 20-Sided Barn, Trunk Z, 0.4 mi. E of WI 146, Fall River vicinity, 2/11/88, A, C, 88000091

Old Indian Agency House, NE end of old Agency House Rd. (Rte.1) near NE city limits, Portage, 2/01/72, A, B, C, 72000045

Pardeeville Presbyterian Church, 105 S. Main St., Pardeeville, 1/15/80, C, a, 80000114

Portage Canal, Between Fox and Wisconsin Rivers, Portage, 8/26/77, A, 77000030

Society Hill Historic District, Roughly bounded by W. Wisconsin, Cass and W. Emmett Sts., and MacFarlane Rd., Portage, 3/05/92, C, a, 92000112

Wawbeek-Horace A, J. Upham House, WI 13, Wisconsin Dells, 6/19/85, A, C, 85001355

Weber, Jacob, House, 825 Oak St., Wisconsin Dells, 1/20/78, B, C, 78000083

CRAWFORD COUNTY

Astor Fur Warehouse, Water St., St. Feriole Island, Prairie du Chien, 10/15/66, A, NHL, 66000800

Brisbois, Michael, House, Water St., St. Feriole Island, Prairie du Chien, 10/15/66, A, C, NHL, 66000801

Crawford County Courthouse, County Courthouses of Wisconsin TR, 220 N. Beaumont Rd., Prairie du Chien, 3/09/82, A, C, 82000645

Dousman Hotel, Fisher St. and River Rd., Prairie du Chien, 10/15/66, A, C, NHL, 66000122

Foley Mound Group, Address Restricted, Lynxville vicinity, 7/15/74, D, 74000062

Folsom, W.H.C,, House, 109 Blackhawk Ave., Prairie du Chien, 12/06/84, A, C, 84000602

Fort Crawford Military Hospital, Rice Street and South Beaumont Rd., Prairie du Chien, 10/15/66, A, NHL, 66000121

Old Rock School, S. Marquette Rd. at Parrish St., Prairie du Chien, 12/01/83, A, C, 83004265

Olson Mound Group, Address Restricted, Seneca vicinity, 2/12/74, D, 74000063

Pedretti III, Address Restricted, Prairie du Chien vicinity, 12/18/78, D, 78000084

Powers, Strange, House, 338 N. Main St., Prairie du Chien, 8/27/79, C, 79000067

Reed, Alfred, Mound Group (47Cr311), Address Restricted, Prairie du Chien vicinity, 9/07/82, D, 82000646

Rolette House, NE corner of N. Water and Fisher Sts., Prairie do Chien, 2/01/72, B, 72000046

Villa Louis, Villa Rd. and Bolvin St., Prairie du Chien, 10/15/66, B, C, NHL, 66000123

Wall-Smethurst Mound Group, Address Restricted, Lynxville vicinity, 6/13/74, D, 74000064

DANE COUNTY

Agricultural Chemistry Building, 420 Hewnry Mall, University of Wisconsin campus, Madison, 6/19/85, A, C, 85001356

Agricultural Dean's House, 10 Babcock Dr., Madison, 9/20/84, A, B, C, 84003627

Agricultural Engineering Building, 460 Henry Mall, University of Wisconsin Campus, Madison, 6/27/85, A, C, 85001404

Agricultural Heating Station, 1535 Observatory Dr., Univ. at WI, Madison, 3/14/85, C, 85000570

Agriculture Hall, 1450 Linden Dr., University of Wisconsin campus, Madison, 3/14/85, A, C, 85000571

American Exchange Bank, 1 N. Pinckney St., Madison, 8/18/80, A, C, 80000115

Badger State Shoe Company, 123 N. Blount St., Madison, 4/11/89, A, C, 89000232

Bascom Hill Historic District, Bounded by Observatory Dr., University Ave., and N. Park, Langdon, and State Sts., Madison, 9/12/74, A, C, g, 74000065

Bashford, Robert M., House, 423 N. Pinckney St., Madison.3/14/73, B, C, 73000075

Baskerville Apartment Building, 121-129 S. Hamilton St., Madison, 10/13/88, C, 88002006

Bellevue Apartment Building, 29 E. Wilson St., Madison, 3/13/87, C, 87000433

Belmont Hotel, 101 E. Mifflin St., Madison, 1/18/90, A, C, 89002311

Bernard-Hoover Boathouse, 622 E. Gorham St., Madison, 7/30/81, A, 81000036

Biederstaedt Grocery, 851-853 Williamson St., Madison, 3/25/82, A, 82000647

Blackhawk Country Club Mound Group (47DA131), Address Restricted. Madison vicinity, 8/01/79, D, 79000068

Bowen, James B., House, 302 S. Mills St., Madison, 3/01/82, A, C, 82000648

Bradley, Harold C,, House, 106 N. Prospect Ave., Madison, 3/01/82, C, NHL, 72000047

Braley, Judge Arthur B., House, 422 N. Henry St., Madison, 11/28/80, B, 80000116

Bram Mound Group, Late Woodland Stage in Archeological Region 8 MPS, Address Restricted, Dunn, 3/25/93, D, 93000216

Brittingham Park Boathouse, N. Shore Dr., Madison, 6/30/82, A, C, 82000649

Brown, Charles E., Indian Mounds, Address Restricted, Madison vicinity, 1/05/84, D, 84003630

Burrows Park Effigy Mound and Campsite, Address Restricted, Madison vicinity, 12/31/74, D, 74000066

Camp Randall, Camp Randall Memorial Park, Madison, 0/07/71, A, 71000030

Cardinal Hotel, 416 E. Wilson St., Madison, 9/02/82, A, C, 82000650

City Market, 101 N. Blount St., Madison, 11/28/78, C, 78000085

Clarke, Bascom B., House, 1150 Spaight St., Madison, 11/28/80, B, 80000117

Collins, William, House, 704 E. Gorham St., Madison, 12/03/74, C, 74000067

Commons, John R., House, 1645 Norman Way, Madison, 3/14/85, B, 85000572

Crosse, Dr. Charles O., House, 133 W. Main St., Sun Prairie, 2/24/93, C, 93000029

Curtis-Kittleson House, 1102 Spaight St., Madison, 4/10/80, A, B, C, 80000118

Cutter, Judson C., House, 1030 Jenifer St., Madison, 7/12/78, C, 78000086

Dean, Nathaniel W., House, 4718 Monona Dr., Madison, 11/07/80, B, 80000119

Donald Farm, 1972 WI 92, Mount Horeb vicinity, 6/07/84, B, 84003633

Drohman Cabin, 6701 E. Broadway, Madison vicinity, 9/28/81, C, 81000037

Dunroven House, 7801 Dunroven Rd., Dane vicinity, 11/28/80, B, C, 80000120

East Dayton Street Historic District, 649-53 F. Dayton St. and 114 N. Blount St., Madison, 12/27/88, A, 88000217

East Wilson Street Historic District, 402-524 E. Wilson and 1335 Blair Sts., Madison, 4/03/86, A, C, 86000618

Edgewood College Mound Group Archeological District, Late Woodland Stage in Archeological Region 8 MPS, Address Restricted, Madison, 6/07/91, D, 91000669

Elliott, Edward C., House, 137 N. Prospect Ave., Madison, 8/11/78, C, 78000087

Elmside Park Mounds, Late Woodland Stage in Archeological Region 8 (AD 650-1300) MPS, Address Restricted, Madison, 4/10/91, D, 91000358

Ely, Richard T., House, 205 N. Prospect Ave., Madison, 12/16/74, B, C, 74000068

Farwell's Point Mound Group, Address Restricted, Madison vicinity, 12/27/74, D, 74000069

Fess Hotel, 123 E. Doty Street, Madison, 9/21/78, A, C, 78003204

Fire Station No. 4, 1329 W. Dayton St., Madison, 3/01/81, A, 84003037

First Church of Christ Scientist, 315 Wisconsin Ave., Madison, 11/24/82, C, a, 82001841

First Lutheran Church, Pleasant View Rd. at Old Sauk Rd., Middleton, 6/16/88, A, C, a, d, 88000728

First Unitarian Society Meetinghouse, 900 University Bay Dr., Shorewood Hills, 4/11/73, C, a, g, 73000076

Forest Hill Cemetery Mound Group, Address Restricted, Madison vicinity, 12/27/74, D, d, 74000070

Fox Hall, 5183 County Hwy. M, Fitchburg vicinity, 12/01/83, C, 853004273

Gilmore, Eugene A., House, 120 Ely Pl., Madison, 3/14/73, C, 73000077

Grace Episcopal Church, 6 N. Carroll St., Madison, 1/01/76, A, C, a, 76000055

Graves, Sereno W., House, Graves Stone Buildings TR, 4006 Old Stage Rd., Rutland, 9/29/82, B, C, 82000651

Grimm Book Bindery, 454 W. Gilman St., Madison, 4/03/86, C, 86000625

Haiglit, Nicholas, Farmstead, 4926 Lacy Rd., Fitchburg, 10/29/93, C, 93001162

Hall, Samuel, House, 924 Hillside Rd., Athion, 12/23/93, A, C, 93001445

Halvorsun Mound Group, Late Woodland Stage in Archeological Region 8 MPS, Address Restricted, Madison, 3/25/93, D, 93000215

Hauge Log Church, 1 mi. N of Daleyville on CR Z, Daleyville vicinity, 12/31/74, A, C, a, 74000071

Heiney's Meat Market, 1221 Mills St., Black Earth, 9/27/84, C, 84003642

Hiram Smith Hall and Annex, 1545 Observatory Dr., Univ. of WI, Madison, 3/14/85, A, C, 85000573

Hirsig, Louis, House, 1010 Sherman Ave., Madison, 12/02/74, C, 74000072

Hoff Department Store, 101-103 Main St., Mount Horeb, 2/14/89, A, C, 89000005

Horticulture and Agricultural Physics and Soil Science Building, 1525 Observatory Dr., Univ. of WI, Madison, 3/14/85, A, B, C, 85000574

Hunt, Samuel, House, Graves Stone Buildings TR, 632 Center Rd., Rutland, 9/30/82, C, 82000652

Hyer's Hotel, 854 Jenifer St., Madison, 9/22/83, A, C, 83003370

Ingebretson, Gaute, Loft House, 1212 Pleasant Hill Rd., Stoughton vicinity, 3/13/87, A, C, 87000437

Iverson-Johnson House, 327 E. Washington St., Stoughton, 1/21/88, B, C, 87002501

Jackman Building, 111 S. Hamilton St., Madison, 3/27/80, C, 80000121

Jacobs, Herbert A., House, 441 Toepfer Ave., Madison, 7/24/74, C, g, 74000073

Jacobs, Herbert, Second House, 7033 Old Lack Rd., Middleton, 12/31/74, C, g, 74000074

Kayser, Adolph H., House, 802 E. Gorham St., Madison, 11/28/80, C, 80000122

Kehl Winery, E. of Prairie du Sac on WI 188, Prairie du Sac vicinity, 1/02/76, A, C, 76000056

Kohlmann, Friederich, House, W of Springfield Corners off WI 19, Springfield Corners vicinity, 12/27/74, A, C, 74900075

LaFollette, Robert M., House, 733 Lakewood Blvd., Maple Bluff, 10/15166, B, NHL, 66000020

Lake Farms Archeological District, Address Restricted, Madison vicinity, 12/22/78, D, 78000088

Lake View Sanatorium, 1204 Northport Dr., Madison, 4/15/93, A, C, 93000258

Lamb Building, 114 State St., Madison, 8/02/84, C, 84003645

Lamp, Robert M., House, 22 N. Butler St., Madison, 1/03/78, C, 78000089

Langdon Street Historic District, Roughly bounded by Lake Mendota, Wisconsin Ave., Langdon, and N. Lake Sts., Madison, 6/26/86, A, B, C, 86001394

Lathrop Hall, 1050 University Ave., University of Wisconsin Campus, Madison, 7/11/85, A, C, 85001503

Leitch, William T., House, 752 E. Gorham St., Madison, 7/18/75, B, C, 75000061

Lewis Mound Group (47Da74), Address Restricted, McFarland vicinity, 12/15/84, D, 84000819

Library Park, Bounded by Vine, Main, Park and Pearl Sts., Belleville, 1/26/81, A, C, 81000038

Lie, Aslak, Cabin, 3022 County Trunk P, Mount Horeb, 4/03/86, B, C, 86000622

Lincoln School, 728 F. Gorham St., Madison, 8/28/80, C, 80000123

Lockwood Barn, Graves Stone Buildings TR, Old Stage Rd, Rutland, 9/29/82, C, 82000653

Lougee, George A,, House, 620 S. Ingersoll St., Madison, 6/07/78, C, 78000090

Machinery Row, 601-627 Williamson St., Madison, 4/12/82, A, C, 82000654

Madison Masonic Temple, 301 Wisconsin Ave., Madison, 9/13/90, A, C, 90001456

Madison Waterworks, N. Hancock St., Madison, 8/18/80, A, C, 80000125

Mann, John, House, 6261 Nesbitt Rd., Fitchburg vicinity, 7/08/82, C, 82000655

Mazomanie Town Hall, 51 Crescent St., Mazomanie, 10/22/80, A, 80000126

McCoy Farmhouse, S. of Madison at 2925 Syene Rd., Fitchburg, 5/29/80, A, B, 80000124

McFarland House, 5923 Exchange St., McFarland, 11/03/88, A, B, C, 88002228

Mendota State Hospital Mound Group, Madison vicinity, 12/27/74, D, 74000076

Merrill Springs Mound Group II Archeological District, Late Woodland Stage in Archeological Region 8 MPS, Address Restricted, Madison, 6/07/91, D, 91011670

Miller House, 647 E. Dayton St., Madison, 11/08/79, B, b, 79000339

Mills Woods Mound, Late Woodland Stage in Archeological Region 8 MPS, Address Restricted, Madison, 6/07/91, D, 91000667

Mills, Simeon, House, 2709 Sommers Ave., Madison, 8/13/87, B, C, 87001386

Monona Mound (47DA275), Address Restricted, Monona vicinity, 12/01/89, C, 89002064

Moore Mound Group, Late Woodland Stage in Archeological Region 8 MPS, Address Restricted, Dunn, 8/05/93,11, 93000809

Mt. Horeb Opera Block, 109-117 E. Main St., Mt. Horeb, 2/23/89, A, C, 89000068

Naeset, Jens, House, 126 E. Washington, Stoughton, 3/14/85, B, C, 85000577

North Hall, University of Wisconsin, University of Wisconsin campus, Madison, 10/15/66, A, B, NHL, 66900021

Old Executive Mansion, 130 E. Gilman St., Madison, 4/11/73, A, C, 73000078

Old Spring Tavern, 3706 Nakoma Rd, Madison, 1/21/74, A, C, 74000077

Old Synagogue, E. Gorham St. at N. Butler St., Madison, 12/29/70, A, a, 70000030

Old U.S. Forest Products Laboratory, 1509 University Ave., University of Wisconsin campus, Madison, 9/12/85, A, C, 85002332

Orton Park, 1100 Spaight St., Madison, 12/18/78, A, d, 7800009

Orton Park Historic District, Roughly bounded by Spaight St., S. Few St., Lake Monona, and S. Ingersoll St., Madison, 10/31/88, B, C, 88000221

Ott, John George, House, 754 Jenifer St., Madison, 9/23/82, B, C, 82000656

Paoli Mills, 6890 Sun Valley Pkwy., Paoli, 3/30/79, A, 79000337

Phlaum-McWilliams Mound Group, Late Woodland Stage in Archeological Regions MPS, Address restricted, Madison, 6/07/91, D, 91000666

Pierce, Carrie, House, 424 N. Pinckney St., Madison, 10/18/72, C, 72000048

Plough Inn, 3402 Monroe St., Madison, 5/29/80, A, 80000127

Pond, Daniel, Farmhouse, E of Brooklyn on U.S. 14, Brooklyn vicinity, 6/30/80, A, C, 80000128

Quisling Towers Apartments, 1 E. Gilman St., Madison, 1/09/84, C, 84003648

Roe, Ole K., House, 404 S. 5th St., Stoughton, 9/07/84, B, C, 84003652

Savage House, Cooksville MRA, SR 1, Stoughton vicinity, 9/17/80, B, 80000392

Sherman Avenue Historic District, Sherman Ave. roughly between Marston Ave. and N. Brearly St., Madison, 3/22/88, C, g, 88000216

Siggelkow Park Mound Group (47DA504), Address Restricted, McFarland vicinity, 3/14/85, D, 85000576

Simeon Mills Historic District, 102-118 King and 115-123 E. Main Sts., Madison, 6/25/87, A, C, 87001063

South School, 1009 Summit Ave., Stoughton, 9/12/85, C, 85002319

Spring Harbor Mound Group, Late Woodland Stage in Archeological Region 8 MPS, Address Restricted, Madison, 6/07/91, D, 91000668

St. Patrick's Roman Catholic Church, 404 E. Main St., Madison, 9/16/82, C, a, 82000657

St. Peter's Roman Catholic Church, WI K, Ashton, 9/23/80, A, C, a, 89000130

State Historical Society of Wisconsin, 816 State St., Madison, 2/23/72, A, C, 72000040

State Office Building, 1 W. Wilson St., Madison, 1/28/82, C, g, 82000658

Steensland, Halle, House, 315 N. Carroll St., Madison, 11/30/82, A, B. C, 82001843

Stock Pavilion, 1675 Linden Dr., University of Wisconsin Campus, Madison, 7/11/85, C, 85001504

Stoner, Joseph J., House, 321 S, Hamilton St., Madison, 1/17/80, A, B, C, 80000129

Stoughton Main Street Commercial Historic District, Main St. from the Yahara River to Forest St., Stoughton, 10/21/82, C, 82001842

Stoughton Universalist Church, 324 S. Page St., Stoughton, 9/30/82, A, C, a, 82900659

Stricker Pond I Site (47DA424), Address Restricted, Middleton, 7/16/79, D, 79000069

Suhr, John J., House, 121 Langdon St., Madison, 6/17/82, B, C, 82000660

Thompson's Block, 119 E. Main St., Madison, 6/07/84, C, 84003654

Thorstrand, 1-2 Thorstrand Rd,, Madison, 8/11/80, B, 80000131

University Heights Historic District, Roughly bounded by Regent, Allen, Lathrop Sts., and Kendall Ave. (both sides), Madison, 12/17/82, B, C, 82001844

University of Wisconsin Science Hall, 550 N. Park St., Madison, 11/04/93, A, B, NHL, 93001616

Vilas Circle Bear Effigy Mound and the Curtis Mounds, Address Restricted, Madison vicinity, 12/30/74, D, 74000078

Vilas Park Mound Group, Late Woodland Stage in Archeological Region 8 (AD 650-1300) MPS, Address Restricted, Madison, 4/10/91, D, 91000357

Wakeley-Giles Commercial Building, 117-119 E. Mifflin St., Madison, 2/23/88, A, B, 88000081

Washburn Observatory and Observatory Director's Residence, 1401 and 1225 Observatory Dr., Univ. of WI, Madison, 3/14/85, A, B, C, 85000575

Waunakee Railroad Depot, South and Main Sts., Waunakee, 2/14/78, A, 78000092

West Madison Depot, Chicago, Milwaukee, and St. Paul Railway, 640 W. Washington Ave., Madison, 5/09/85, A, C, 85000990

West School, 404 Garfield St., Stoughton, 1/22/92, A, 91002992

Wiedenbeck-Dobelin Warehouse, 619 W. Mifflin St., Madison, 12/23/86, A, C, 86003473

Wisconsin Memorial Hospital Historic District, 816 Troy Dr., Madison, 11/03/88, A, 88002183

Wisconsin State Capitol, Capitol Sq., Madison, 10/15/70, A, C, 70000031

DODGE COUNTY

Beaumont Hotel, 45 Main St., Mayville, 1/13/88, C, 87002238

Historic Places

Central State Hospital Historic District, Lincoln St. between Beaver Dam and Mason Sts., Waupun, 9/13/91, A, 91001395

Dahl, Martin K., House, 314 Beaver Dam St., Waupun, 9/11/75, B, C, 75000062

Dodge County Courthouse, County Courthouses of Wisconsin TR, 220 E. State St., Juneau, 3/09/82, C, g, 82000661

Dodge County Historical Museum, 127 S. Spring St., Beaver Dam, 7/07/81, C, 81000039

Fox Lake Railroad Depot, Cordelia St. and S. College Avenue, Fox Lake, 5/22/78, A, 78000093

Greenfield, Willard, Farmstead, N. 7436 WI Trunk Hwy. 26, Burnett Township, Horicon vicinity, 11/05/92, C, 92001557

Hartwig, Ferdinand C., House, 908 Country Lane, Watertown, 6/17/82, A, 82000662

Hollenstein Wagon and Carriage Factory, Bridge and German Sts., Mayville, 7/27/79, A, 79000070

Horicon Site, E. of Waupun, Waupun vicinity, 1/31/79, D, 79003492

Hotel Rogers, 103 E. Maple Ave., Beaver Dam, 3/02/89, A, C, 89000120

Hustis, John, House, N. Ridge St., Hustisford, 3/10/83, B, b, 83003371

Hutchinson Memorial Library, Public Library Facilities of Wisconsin MPS, 228 N. High St., Randolph, 11/15/90, A, C, 09001705

Indian Point Site, Address Restricted, Fox Lake vicinity, 9/13/90, D, 90001459

Schoenicke Barn, NE of Watertown on Venus Rd., Watertown vicinity, 9/19179, C, 79000071

St. Joseph's Roman Catholic Church, WI Q and Rich Rd., Shields, 7/02/80, A, C, a, 80004480

St. Mark's Episcopal Church, 130 E. Maple St., Beaver Dam, 11/28/80, C, a, b, 80000132

Swan House and Vita Spring Pavilion, 230 Park Ave., Beaver Dam, 4/09/80, B, C, 80000133

Van Brunt, Daniel C, House, 139 W. Lake St., Horicon, 9/14/81, B, C, 81000040

Waupun Public Library, 22 S. Madison St., Waupun, 9/04/79, A, C, 79000072

White Limestone School, N. Main St. between Dayton and Buchanan Sts., Mayville, 10/22/76, A, C, 70000057

Williams Free Library, 105 Park Ave., Beaver Dam, 8/07/74, C, 74000079

Wisconsin State Prison Historic District, 200 S. Madison St., Waupun, 1/22/92, A, C, 91001994

DOOR COUNTY

Anderson Dock Historic District, Ephraim MRA, Roughly bounded by Anderson Lane and North Water St., Ephraim, 6/11/85, A, 85001249

Baileys Harbor Range Light, Roughly Co. Rd. Q, Ridges Rd., and WI 57, Baileys Harbor, 9/21/89, A, C, 89001466

Bohianen's Door Bluff Pictographs, Indian Rock Art Sites MPS, Address Restricted, Liberty Grove vicinity, 9/02/93, D, 93000881

Cana Island Lighthouse, NE of Baileys Harbor on E. side of Cana Island, Baileys Harbor vicinity, 1/21/76, A, 76000201

Carnegie Free Library, 354 Michigan St., Sturgeon Bay, 12/29/88, A, C, 88003069

Chambers Island Lighthouse, 7 mi. NW of Fish Creek at NW tip of Chambers Island, Fish Creek vicinity, 8/19/75, A, 75000063

Church of the Atonement, Fire No. 9410, Fish Creek, 1/07/85, A, C, a, 85000487

Clearing, The, Off WI 42, Ellison Bay, 12/31/74, B, C, 74000080

Cupola House, 7836 Egg Harbor Rd., Egg Harbor, 7/16179, B, C, 79000073

Eagle Bluff Lighthouse, 3.5 mi. N of Fish Creek on Shore Rd., in Peninsula State Park, Fish Creek vicinity, 10/15/70, A, C, 70000032

Ephraim Moravian Church, Ephraim MRA, 9970 Moravia St., Ephraim, 3/27/85, A, a, b, 85000662

Ephraim Village Hall, Ephraim MRA, 9996 S. Water St., Ephraim, 3/27/85, A, C, 85000663

Free Evangelical Lutheran Church-Bethania Scandinavian Evangelical Lutheran Congregation, Ephraim MRA, 3028 Church St., Ephraim, 3/27/85, A, a, 85000664

Gibraltar District School No. 2, Ephraim MRA, 9988 Moravia St., Ephraim, 6/11/85, A, 85001250

Historic Places

Globe Hotel, 8090 Main St., Baileys Harbor, 1/28/82, B, C, 82000663

Globe Hotel, 8090 Main St., Baileys Harbor, 1/28/82, B, C, 82004661

Hillside Hotel, Ephraim MRA, 9980 S. Water St., Ephraim, 3/27/85, A, 85000665

Jischke's Meat Market, 414 Maple Dr., Sister Bay, 9/11/86, A, C, 86002306

LOUISIANA (Shipwreck), Great Lakes Shipwrecks of Wisconsin MP, Address Restricted, Washington vicinity, 3/19/92, C, D, 92000104

Larson, L. A., & Co. Store, 306 S. 3rd Ave., Sturgeon Bay, 6/19/85, A, C, 85001357

Louisiana Street/Seventh Avenue Historic District, Roughly bounded by Louisiana and Kentucky Sts., N. 5th, N. 7th, and N. 8th Aves., Sturgeon Bay, 9/22/83, C, 83003372

Namur Belgian-American District, Roughly bounded by CR K, Brussels Rd., WI 57, Belgian Dr., and the Green Bay, Namur vicinity, 11/06/89, A, C, a, d, NHL, 87002553

Peterson, Peter, House, Ephraim MRA, 10020 N. Water St., Ephraim, 3/27/85, A, B, a, 85000666

Pilot Island Light, Portes des Norts Passage, Gills Rock vicinity, 11/21/83, A, 83004279

Pilot Island NW Site, Great Lakes Shipwrecks of Wisconsin MRS, Address Restricted, Washington vicinity, 3/19/92, D, 92000103

Plum Island Range Rear Light, U.S. Coast Guard Lighthouses and Light Stations on the Great Lakes TR, Plum Island, Gills Rock vicinity, 7/19/54, A, C, 84003659

Porte des Morts Site, Address Restricted, Northport vicinity, 3/16/76, D, 76000058

Pottawatomie Lighthouse, NW Rock Island, Washington Island vicinity, 4/20179, A, 79000074

Rock Island Historic District, Rock Island, off NE tip of Washington Island, Washington vicinity, 5/19/72, D, 72000050

Sherwood Point light Station, U.S. Coast Guard Lighthouses and Light Stations on the Great Lakes TR, Sherwood Point Road on Green Bay, Sturgeon Bay vicinity, 7/19/84, A, C, 84003663

Sturgeon Bay Canal Lighthouse, U.S. Coast Guard Lighthouses and Light Stations on the Great Lakes TR, Sturgeon Bay Canal, Sturgeon Bay vicinity, 7/19/84, A, C, 84003666

The Encyclopedia of Wisconsin

Third Avenue Historic District, Roughly hounded by Kentucky St., N. 2nd, N. 3rd, and S. 3rd Aves., Sturgeon Bay, 0/06/83, A, C, 83004282
Thordarson Estate Historic District, Chester H. Thordarson Estate TR, Rock Island State Park, Washington Island vicinity, 3/21/85, C, 85000641
Water Tower, Chester H. Thordarson Estate TR, Rock Island State Park, Washington Island vicinity, 3/21/85, C, 85000640
Whitefish Dunes-Bay View Site, Address Restricted, Sevastopol vicinity, 12/28/90, D, 90001960

DOUGLAS COUNTY

Berkshire Block, Speculative Commercial Blocks of Superior's Boom Period 1888-1892 TR, 917-927 Tower Ave., Superior, 6/27/85, A, C, 85001466
Brule-St. Croix Portage, Brule River State Park, Solon Springs vicinity, 10/15/70, A, 70000033
Davidson Windmill, SE of Superior on WI 13, Superior vicinity, 8/03/79, A, C, 79000075
Douglas County Courthouse, County Courthouses of Wisconsin TR, 1313 Belknap St., Superior, 3/09/82, C, 82000664
Empire Block, Speculative Commercial Blocks of Superior's Boom Period 1888-1892 TR, 1202-1208 Tower Ave., Superior, 6/27/85, A, C, 85001467
Lake Nebagamon Auditorium, 1st St., Lake Nebagamon, 9/14/81, A, C, g, 81000041
METEOR (Whaleback carrier), NW tip of Barkers Island, Superior, 9/09/74, A, 74000083
Maryland Block, Speculative Commercial Blocks of Superior's Boom Period 1888-1892 TR, 1221-1227 Tower Ave., Superior, 6/27/85, A, C, 85001468
Massachusetts Block, Speculative Commercial Blocks of Superior's Boom Period 1888-1892 TR, 1525-1531 Tower Ave., Superior, 6/27/85, A, C, 85001469
Minnesota Block—Board of Trade Bldg., Speculative Commercial Blocks of Superior's Boom Period 1888-1892 TR, 1501-1511 Tower Ave., Superior, 6/27/85, A, C, 85001470
New Jersey Building, 1422-1432 Tower Ave. and 17051723 Belknap Ave., Superior, 9/22/83, A, C, 83003373

New York Block, Speculative Commercial Blocks Superior's Boom Period 1888-1892 TR, 1402-1412 Tower Ave., Superior, 6/27/85, A, 85001472

Northern Block, Speculative Commercial Blocks of Superior's Boom Period 1888-1892 TR, 2229 East 5th St., Superior, 6/27/85, A, C, 85001471

Pattison, Martin, House, 906 E. 2nd St., Superior, 2/12/81, B, 81000042

Trade and Commerce Building, 916 Hammond Ave., Superior, 5/08/79, A, C, 79000076

Washington Block, Speculative Commercial Blocks of Superior's Boom Period 1888-1892 TR, 1517-1523 Tower Ave., Superior, 6/27/85, A, C, 85001473

Wemyss Building, Speculative Commercial Blocks of Superior's Boom Period 1888-1892 TR, 1301-1305 Tower Ave., Superior, 6/27/85, A, C, 85001474

DUNN COUNTY

Menomonie Downtown Historic District, Roughly bounded by Main and Crescent Sts., Fifth St., Wilson, and Second St. and Broadway, Menomonie, 7/14/86, A, B, C, 86001667

Tainter, Louis Smith, House, Broadway at Crescent, Menomonie, 7/18/74, B, C, 74000082

Tainter, Mabel, Memorial Building, 205 Main St., Menomonie, 7/18/74, B, C, 74000083

EAU CLAIRE COUNTY

Barber, James, House, Eau Claire MRA, 132 Marston Ave., Eau Claire, 1/28/83, B, C, 83003374

Barnes Block, 15-21 S. Barstow St., Eau Claire, 1/22/82, C, 82000665

Barron, Martin Van Buren, House, Eau Claire MRA, 221 Washington St., Eau Claire, 1/28/83, C, 83003375

Brice, Orlando, House, Eau Claire MRA, 120 Marston Ave., Eau Claire, 1/28/83, C, 83003376

California Wine and Liquor Store, 201 Farmers St., Fairchild, 3/01/82, C, 82000666

Chicago, St. Paul, Minneapolis & Omaha Railroad Depot, Eau Claire MRA, 324 Putnam Ave., Eau Claire, 10/24/85, C, 85003383

Christ Church Cathedral and Parish House, Eau Claire MRA, 510 S. Farwell St., Eau Claire, 1/28/83, C, a, 83003377

City Hall, Eau Claire MRA, 203 S. Farwell St., Eau Claire, 1/28/83, C, 83003378

Cobblestone House, 1011 State St., Eau Claire, 11/19/74, C, 74000094

Community House, First Congregational Church, 310 Broadway, Eau Claire, 7/18/74, C, a, 74000085

Dells Mill, About 3 mi. NNW of Augusta off WI 27, Augusta vicinity, 12/24/74, A, 74000086

Drummond, David, House, 1310 State St., Eau Claire, 7/30/74, B, C, 74000087

Eau Claire High School, Eau Claire MRA, 314 Doty St., Eau Claire, 1/28/83, C, 83003379

Eau Claire Public Library, Eau Claire MRA, 217 S. Farwell St., Eau Claire, 1/28/83, C, 83003380

Eichert, Christine, House, Eau Claire MRA, 527 N. Barstow St., Eau Claire, 1/28/83 C, 83003381

Emery Street Bungalow District, Eau Claire MRA, Emery St. between Chauncey and Agnes Sts., Eau Claire, 5/20/83, C, 83003382

Johnson, John, Saloon, Eau Claire MRA, 216 Fifth Ave., Eau Claire, 1/28/83, C, 83003383

Kaiser Lumber Company Office, Eau Claire MRA, 1004 Menomonie St., Eau Claire, 1/28/83, A, C, 83003384

Kenyon, A. L., House, Eau Claire MRA, 333 Garfield Ave., Eau Claire, 1/28/83, C, 83003385

Kline's Department Store, Eau Claire MRA, 610 S. Barstow St., Eau Claire, 6/14/84, C, 84003669

Merrill, Levi, House, Eau Claire MRA, 120 Ferry St., Eau Claire, 6/20/85, C, 85001358

Ottawa House, Eau Claire MRA, 602 Water St., Eau Claire, 1/28/83, C, 83003386

Owen, John S., House, Eau Claire MRA, 907 Porter Ave., Eau Claire, 1/28/83, B, 83003387

Pioneer Block, 401409 Water St., Eau Claire, 8/27/80, C, 80000134

Randall, Adin, House, Eau Claire MRA, 526 Menomonie St., Eau Claire, 1128/83, B, 83003389

Randall Park Historic District, Eau Claire MRA, Roughly bounded by Lake and Niagara Sts., 3rd and 5th Aves., Eau Claire, 5/20/83, C, 83003390

Sacred Heart Church, Eau Claire MRA, 418 N. Dewey St., Eau Claire, 3/03/83, C, a, 83003391

Schofield Hall, Eau Claire MRA, 105 Garfield Ave., Eau Claire, 1/28/83, A, 83003393

St. Joseph's Chapel, Sacred Heart Cemetery, Omaha St., Eau Claire, 1/14/88, C, a, 87002436

St. Patrick's Church, Eau Claire MRA, 322 Fulton St., Eau Claire, 1/28/83, C, a, 83003392

Steven House, 216 Hudson Ave., Eau Claire, 3/01/82, C, 82000667

Temple of Free Masonry, 616 Graham Ave., Eau Claire, 1/14/88, C, 87002450

Third Ward Historic District, Eau Claire MRA, Roughly bounded by Chippewa River, Park Pl., Gilbert Ave., and Farwell St., Eau Claire, 5/21/83, C, 83003394

Union National Bank, Eau Claire MRA, 131 S. Barstow St., Eau Claire, 1/28/83, C, 83003395

US Post Office and Courthouse, 500 S. Barstow Commons, Eau Claire, 7/25/91, A, C, 91000899

Walter-Heins House, 605 N. Barstow St., Eau Claire, 3/19/82, C, 82000668

Wilcox, Roy, House, Eau Claire MRA, 104 Wilcox St., Eau Claire, 1/28/83, B, 83003396

Winslow, George F., House, 210 Oakwood Pl., Fan Claire 12/08/78, C, 78000094

FLORENCE COUNTY

Fay Outlet Site (47FL13), Address Restricted, Long Lake vicinity, 1/17/89, D, 88000647

Fern School, SW of Florence on WI 101, Florence vicinity, 3/20/81, A, 81000043

Florence County Courthouse and Jail, County Courthouses of Wisconsin TR, 501 Lake St., Florence, 12/02/85, C, 85003029

FOND DU LAC COUNTY

Aetna Station No. 5, 193 N. Main St., Fond du Lac, 12/12/76, A, C, 76000059

Ceresco Site, Bounded by North, Church, Union, and both sides of Warren Sts., Ripon, 9/05/75, A, 75000064

Chicago and Northwestern Railroad Depot, 182 Forest Ave., Fond du Lac, 8/10/90, A, C, b, 90001232

Club Harbor, Jct. of WI 151 and WI W, Pipe, 1/22/80, A, 80000135

End of the Trail, Madison St. (Shaler Park), Waupun, 8/29/80, A, 80000136

First Baptist Church of Fond du Lac, 90 S. Many St., Fond du Lac, 12/29/86, C, a, 86003522

First Congregational Church, 220 Ransom St., Ripon, 9/04/79, C, a, 79000077

Galloway, Edwin H., House, 336 E. Pioneer Rd., Fond du Lac, 5/28/76, B, C, 76000060

Horner, John Scott, House, 336 Scott St., Ripon, 9/27/84, B, C, 84003672

Hotel Calumet, 170 Forest Ave., Fond du Lac, 3/20/92, C, 92000111

Hotel Retlaw, 15 E. Division St., Fond du Lac, 9/07/84, A, C, 84003673

Little White Schoolhouse, SE corner of Blackburn and Blossom Sts., Ripon, 8/14/73, A, b, NHL, 73000079

Moose Temple, 17-23 Forest Ave., Fond du Lac, 4/22/93, A, C, 93000340

Octagon House, 276 Linden St., Fond du Lac, 11/03/72, C, 72000051

Pedrick, Marcellus, House, 515 Ransom Ave., Ripon, 9/29/76, C, 76000061

Pipe Site, NE of Fond du Lac, Fond du Lac vicinity, 12/22/78, D, 78000095

Raube Road Site, Address Restricted, Springvale, 6/04/92, A, C, D, 92000589

Recording Angel, The, Forest Mound Cemetery, N. Madison St., Waupun, 7/15/74, C, f. 74000088

Saint John Evangelical Lutheran Church, 670 County Trunk Hwy. S, New Fane, 4/15/86, C, a, 86000794

St. John the Baptist Catholic Church, Off WI Q, Johnsburg, 10/29/80, A, C, a, 80000137

St. Matthias Mission, 1081 County Trunk S, New Fane vicinity, 10/13/88, A, a, 88001838

St. Peter's Episcopal Church, 217 Houston St., Ripon, 12/31/74, C, a, 74000089

Watson Street Commercial Historic District, Roughly, Watson St. from Seward to Jackson Sts. and Jackson and Scott Sts, from Watson to Blackburn Sts., Ripon, 9/27/91, A, C, 91001396

Woodruff, Jacob, House, 610 Liberty St., Ripon, 12/30/74, C, 74000090

FOREST COUNTY

Chicago and North-Western Land Office, Public Library Facilities of Wisconsin MPS, 4556 N. Branch St., Waupun, 12/23/93, A, 93001446

Franklin Lake Campground, National Forest Rd. 2181, Alvin vicinity, 9/28/88, A, C, 88001573

GRANT COUNTY

Agriculture and Manual Arts Building/Platteville State Normal School, Univ. of WI, Platteville, Platteville, 3/14185, A, C, 85000578

Arthur, L. J., House, 210 N. Jefferson St., Lancaster, 9/05/85, C, 85001951

Ballantine, James, House, 720 North 4th Street, Bloomington, 6/07/76, C, 76000062

Bass Site (47GT25), Address Restricted, Lancaster vicinity, 9/09/82, D, 82000669

Beebe House, 390 W. Adams St., Platteville, 8/07/79, B, C, 79000078

Boscobel High School, 207 Buchanan St., Boscobel, 12/30/86, A, C, 86003518

Denniston House, 117 E. Front St., Cassville, 2/20/75, A, B, 75000213

Evans, Jonathan H., House, 440 W. Adams St., Platteville, 6/01/82, A, 8,82000670

First Congregational Church, 80 Market, Platteville, 6/19/85, C, a, 85001359

Grant County Courthouse, 126 W. Main St., Lancaster, 10/19/78, A, C, 78000096

Hazel Green Town Hall, 2130 N. Main St., Hazel Green, 1/26/89, A, C, 88003231

Lancaster Municipal Building, 206 S. Madison St., Lancaster, 3/10/83, C, 83003397

Main Street Commercial Historic District, Roughly bounded by Chestnut, Furnace, Bonson, Mineral, Oak, and Pine, Platteville, 3/09/90, A, C, 90000377

Mitchell-Rountree House, Jewett and Lancaster Sts., Platteville, 2/23/72, C, 72000052

Parker, Dwight T., Public Library, 925 Lincoln Ave., Fennimore, 3/10/83, C, 83003398

Potosi Brewery, Main St., Potosi, 11/19/80, A, 80000138

Rountree Hall, 30 North Elm St., Platteville, 12/17/74, A, C, 74000091

Rountree, J. H., Mansion, 150 Rountree Ave., Platteville, 6/13/86, B, C, 86001307

St. John Mine, WI 133, Potosi, 6/04/79, A, 79000079

Stonefield, 2.5 mi. W of Cassville, on CR VV, Cassville vicinity, 5/19/70, B, C, 70000034

GREEN COUNTY

Bingham, Judge John A., House, 621 14th Ave., Monroe, 1/02/76, B, 76000063

Bintliff, Gen. James, House, 723 18th Ave., Monroe, 5/14/79, B, C, 79000080

Caradine Building, 1007 16th Ave., Monroe, 5/08/79, A, C, 79000081

Chenoweth, Frank L., House, 2004 10th St., Monroe, 10/08/76, C, 70000064

Exchange Square Historic District, Roughly bounded by 10th, RR tracks, E. 2nd and W. 3rd Aves., Brodhead, 11/15/84, A, C, 84000724

First Methodist Church, 11th St. and 14th Ave., Monroe, 2/25/75, A, C, a, 75000065

Freitag's Pure Oil Service Station, 1323 9th St., Monroe, 1/15/80, A, C, 80000139

Green County Courthouse, Courthouse Sq., Monroe, 3/23/78, A, B, C, 78000097

Hulburt, C. D., House, 1205 13th Ave., Monroe, 5/08/79, C, 79000082

Jennings, Janet, House, 612 22nd Ave., Monroe, 1/02/76, B, b, 76000065

Monroe Commercial District, Roughly bounded by 15th and 8th Aves., 9th and 13th Sts., Monroe, 5/06/82, A, C, g, 82000671

Regez, Jacob, Sr., House, 2121 7th St., Monroe, 1/17/80, A, B, C, 80000140

Smith, Francis West, House, 1002 W. 2nd Ave., Brodhead, 4/37/79, C, 79000083

West, Gen. Francis H., House, 1410 17th Ave., Monroe, 1/01/75, C, 75000066

White, F. F., Block, 1514-1524 11th St., Monroe, 1/31/79, A, B, C, 79000084

GREEN LAKE COUNTY

Beckwith House Hotel, 101 W. Huron St., Berlin, 9/13/91, A, 91001389

Beckwith, Nelson F., House, 179 E. Huron St., Berlin, 4/06/90, C, 90000575

Green Lake County Courthouse, County Courthouses of Wisconsin TR, 492 Hill St., Green Lake, 3/09/82, C, 82000672

Hamilton-Brooks Site, S. of Berlin, Berlin vicinity, 12/19/78, D, 78000098

Huron Street Historic District, Roughly, Huron St. from Fox R. to 124 E. Huron, including adjacent side streets, Berlin, 8/31/92, A, C, 92003140

Wisconsin Power and Light Berlin Power Plant, 142 Water St., Berlin, 3/19/92, A, C, 92000157

IOWA COUNTY

Archeological Site No. 47IA168, Wisconsin Indian Rock Art Sites MPS, Address Restricted, Brigham, 8/21/92, D, 92001025

Archeological Site No. 47IA167, Wisconsin Indian Rock Art Sites MPS, Address Restricted, Brigham, 8/21/92, D, 92001026

Brisbane, William Henry, House, Reimann Rd., .6 mi. S of US 14, Arena, 9/13/90, C, 90001458

Carden Rockshelter, Wisconsin Indian Rock Art Sites MPS, Address Restricted, Brigham, 8/05/93, D, 93000808

Cassidy Farmhouse, Barneveld MRA, WI   K N. of US 18/151, Barneveld, 9/29/86, C, 86002297

DNR No. 4 Rockshelter, Wisconsin Indian Rock Art Sites MPS, Address Restricted, Brigham vicinity, 1/30/91, D, 00002156

DNR No. 5 Archeological Site, Wisconsin Indian Rock Art Sites MPS, Address Restricted, Brigham, 5/21/92, D, 92000592

Gottschall Site (47IA80), Address Restricted, Highland vicinity, 6/30/83, D, 83003399

Grove Street Historic District, Barneveld MRA, 304-316 Grove St., Barneveld, 9/29/86, A, C, 86002313

Harris House, Barneveld MRA, 202 W. Wood St., Barneveld, 9/29/86, C, 86002299

Hole-in-the-Wall #1 Cave, Wisconsin Indian Rock Art Sites MPS, Address Restricted, Brigham vicinity, 1/30/91, D, 90002357

Hyde Chapel, 1 mi. S of CTH H on CTH T, Ridge way, 10/13/88, C, a, d, 88002002

Ihm House, Barneveld MRA, 203 N. Garfield St., Barneveld, 9/29/86, C, 86002301

Iowa County Courthouse, NW corner of Iowa and Chapel Sts., Dodgeville, 2/01/72, C, 72000053

Kittleson House, Barneveld MRA, 104 W. Wood St., Barneveld, 9/29/86, C, 86002304

Linden High School, 344 E. Main St., Linden, 11/04/93, A, C, 93001168

Linden Methodist Church, Main and Church Sts., Linden, 10/19/78, A, C, a, 78000099

Mayland Cave, Address Restricted, Dodgeville vicinity, 12/22/78, D, 78000100

McCoy Rock Art Site, Wisconsin Indian Rock Art Sites MPS, Address Restricted, Moscow, 4/19/91, D, 91000467

Mineral Point Hill, Roughly bounded by WI 23, Copper, Dodge, and Shake Rag Sts., Mineral Point, 10/26/72, A, C, 72000054

Mineral Point Historic District, Roughly bounded by Ross, Shake Rag, 9th, and Bend Sts., Mineral Point, 7/30/71, A, C, 71000037

Old Rock School, 914 Bequette St., Dodgeville, 12/18/78, A, C, e, 78000101

Pendarvis, 114 Shake Rag St., Mineral Point, 1/25/71, A, C, 71000038

Roberts House, Barneveld MRA, 302 Front St., Barneveld, 9/01/88, C, 86002311

Roethlisberger House, Barneveld MRA, 205 N. Grove St., Barneveld, 9/29/86, C, 86002312

Sawle Mound Group Archeological District, Late Woodland Stage in Archeological Region 8 MPS, Address Restricted, Arena, 6/07/91, D, 91000672

Shot Tower, SE of Spring Green in Tower Hill State Park, Spring Green vicinity, 4/03/73, A, C, 73000080

Taliesin, 2 mi. S. of Spring Green on WI 23, Spring Green vicinity, 4/14/73, A, C, g, NHL, 73000081

Unity Chapel, So Spring Green off WI 23, Spring Green vicinity, 7/18/74, C, a, 74000092

IRON COUNTY

Annala Round Barn, S of Hurley, Hurley vicinity, 8/27/79, A, C, 79000085

Montreal Company Location Historic District, WI 77, Montreal, 5/23/80, A, 80000141

Old Iron County Courthouse, 303 Iron St., Hurley, 7/26/77, A, C, 77000031

JACKSON COUNTY

Gullickson's Glen, Address Restricted, Black River Falls vicinity, 12/21/78, D, 78000102

Silver Mound Archeological District, Address Restricted, Alma Center vicinity, 1 /17/75, D, 75000067

Union High School, N. 3rd St., Black River Falls, 1120/78, C, 78000103

JEFFERSON COUNTY

Aztalan, Near Lake Mills on WI 89, Aztalan State Park, Lake Mills vicinity, 10/15/66, D, e, NHL, 66000022

Beals and Torrey Shoe Co. Building, 100 W. Milwaukee St., Watertown, 12/06/84, A, 84000699

Bean Lake Islands Archeological District, Address Restricted, Lake Mills, 8/12/82, D, 82000673

Carcajou Point (47JE2), Address Restricted, Busseyville vicinity, 9/18/79, D, 79000088

Carcajou Point Site (Boundary Increase), Address Restricted, Sumner, 9/05/91, D, 91001370

Chicago and Northwest Railroad Passenger Station, 725 W. Main St., Watertown, 3/28/79, A, C, 79000086

Copeland-Ryder Company, 411 Wisconsin Dr., Jefferson, 4/13/89, A, 89000233

Crab Apple Point Site, Address Restricted, Edgerton vicinity, 12/22/78, D, 78000104

Enterprise Building, 125 W. Main St., Palmyra, 6/05/75, A, C, 75000068

Fargo, Enoch J., House, 406 Mulberry St., Lake Mills, 7/08182, B, C, 82000674

Fargo, L. D., Public Library, 120 E. Madison St., Lake Mills, 1/18/82, A, C, 82000675

First Kindergarten, 919 Charles St., Watertown, 2/23/72, A, B, b, 72000055

Fuermann, August, Jr., and Eliza, House, 500 S. Third St., Watertown, 7/27/89, C, 89001002

Haight Creek Mound Group (47JE38), Address Restricted, Fort Atkinson vicinity, 8/05/85, D, 85001751

Highsmith Site, NE of Fort Atkinson, Fort Atkinson vicinity, 12/01/78, D, 78000106

Hoard Mound Group (47JE33), Address Restricted, Fort Atkinson vicinity, 5/10/84, D, 84003678

Hoard's Dairyman Farm, N of Fort Atkinson, Fort Atkinson vicinity, 8/29/78, A, B, 78000105

Hoard, Arthur R., House, 323 Merchants Ave., Fort Atkinson, 11/30/82, B, C, 82001845

Jefferson Fire Station, 146 E. Milwaukee St., Jefferson, 12/06/84, A, C, 84000695

Jefferson Public Library, 305 S. Main St., Jefferson, 1/17/80, C, 80000142

Jones Dairy Farm, Jones Ave., Fort Atkinson, 12/27/78, A, B, g, 78000107

Main Street Commercial Historic District, Roughly Main St. from N. Washington St. to S. Seventh St., Watertown, 6/02/89, A, C, 89000483

Main Street Historic District, Roughly Main St. from Sherman Ave, to S. 3rd St., Fort Atkinson, 6/07/84, A, C, 84003683

May, Eli, House, 407 E. Milwaukee Ave., Fort Atkinson, 9/14/72, A, D, 72000056

McKenzie, Monroe, House, 226 Main St., Palmyra, 6/19/85, C, 85001360

Merchants Avenue Historic District, Roughly bounded by S. Third St. E and S. Milwaukee Ave. E, Foster St., Whitewater, and Merchant Aves., Fort Atkinson, 6/13/86, B, C, 86001303

Octagon House, 919 Charles St., Watertown, 11/23/71, C, 71000039

Panther Intaglio Effigy Mound, Address Restricted, Fort Atkinson vicinity, 10/15/70, D, 70000035

Pioneer Aztalan Site, SE corner at jct. of SR B and SR Q, Aztalan, 2/25/75, A, C, b, 75000069

Pitzner Site (47JE676), Jefferson vicinity 7/06/82, D, 82000676

Puerner Block-Breunig's Brewery, 101-115 E. Racine, 110-112 N. Main St., Jefferson, 6/14/84, A, C, 84003687

Smith, Richard C., House, 332 E. Linden St., Jefferson, 4/19/79, C, g, 79000338

St. Paul's Episcopal Church, 413 S. 2nd St., Watertown, 11/07/79, C, a, 79000087

St. Wenceslaus Roman Catholic Church, SE of Waterloo at jct. of Blue Point and Island Rds., Waterloo vicinity, 5/12/75, A, C, a, 75000070

JUNEAU COUNTY

Boorman, Benjamin, House, 211 N. Union St., Mauston, 5/04/76, B, C, 76000066

Cranberry Creek Archeological District, Address Restricted, Necedah National Wildlife Refuge vicinity, 7/10/84, D, 84003689

Gee's Slough Mound Group, Address Restricted, New Lisbon vicinity, 3/08/78, D, 78000108

Juneau County Courthouse, County Courthouses of Wisconsin TR, 220 E. State St., Mauston, 11/04/82. A, g, 82001846

Weston-Babcock House, Main St., Necedah, 1/29/79, A, C, 79000089

KENOSHA COUNTY

Barnes Creek Site Address Restricted, Kenosha vicinity, 7/20/77, D, NHL, 77000032
Boys and Girls Library, 5810 8th Ave., Kenosha, 10/24/80, A, B, C, 80000144
Chesrow Site, S. of Kenosha on WI 32, Kenosha vicinity, 11/30/78, D, 78000100
Civic Center Historic District, Roughly bounded by 55th St., 8th Ave., 58th St., and 10th Ave., Kenosha, 7/26/80, A, C, b, 89000069
Kemper Hall, 6501 3rd Ave., Kenosha, 6/07/76, B, C, a, 76000067
Kenosha County Courthouse and Jail, County Courthouses of Wisconsin TR, 912 56th St., Kenosha, 3/09/82, A, 0,82000677
Kenosha Light Station, 5117 Fourth Ave., Kenosha, 6/28/90, A, 90000005
Library Park Historic District, Roughly bounded by 59th St., 7th Ave., 61st St., and 8th Ave., Kenosha, 11/29/88, A, B, C, a, 88002657
Manor House, 6536 3rd Ave., Kenosha, 10/29/80, C, 80000145
McCaffary, John, House, 5732 13th Court, Kenosha, 1/31/78, A, B, 78000110
Simmons, Gilbert M., Memorial Library, 711 59th Pl., Kenosha, 12/17/74, C, f, 74000093
St. Matthew's Episcopal Church, 5900 7th Ave., Kenosha, 6/0679, A, C, a, 79000090
Third Avenue Historic District, Along Third Ave. between 61st and 66th Sts., Kenosha, 11/01/88, A, B, C, 5,88002022
Weed, Justin, House, 3509 Washington Rd., Kenosha, 12/03/74, C, 74000094
Wehmhoff Mound (47KN15), Address Restricted, Wheatland vicinity, 11/21/85, A, D, 85002971

KEWAUNEE COUNTY

Deuman, Art, Fishing Shanty, Church St. at the Alinapee P., Algoma, 12/10/93, A, 93001428
Pilgrim Family Farmstead, SW of Kewanee on Church Rd., Kewaunee, 5/08/79, A, B, C, 79000091

St. Lawrence Catholic Church, Jct. Of WI 163 and County Hwy., J, Stangelville, 2/21/89, A, C, a, b, d, 89000056

LA CROSSE COUNTY

Agger Rockshelter, Address Restricted, Stevenstown vicinity, 3/25/88, D, 87002239

Anderson, Mons, House, 410 Cass St., La Crosse, 5/06/75, B, C, 75000071

Barron, E. R., Building, 426-430 Main St., La Crosse, 6/19/85, A, C, 85001302

Bridge No. 1, Van Loon Wildlife Area Truss Bridge TR, NW of La Crosse, La Crosse vicinity, 2/27/80, A, C, 80000146

Bridge No. 2, Van Loon Wildlife Area Truss Bridge TR, NW of La Crosse, La Crosse vicinity, 2/27/80, A, C, 80000147

Bridge No. 3, Van Loon Wildlife Area Truss Bridge TR, NW of La Crosse, La Crosse vicinity, 2/27/80, A, C, 80000148

Bridge No. 4, Van Loon Wildlife Area Truss Bridge TR, NW of La Crosse, La Crosse vicinity, 2/27/80, A, C, 50000149

Bridge No. 5, Van Loon Wildlife Area Truss Bridge TR, NW of La Crosse, La Crosse vicinity, 2/27/80, A, C, 80900150

Bridge No. 6, Van Loon Wildlife Area Truss Bridge TR, NW of La Crosse, La Crosse vicinity, 2/27/80, A, C, 80000151

Chambers-Markle Farmstead, 6104 WI 35, La Crosse, 3/22/91, C, 91000341

Chase, Dr. H. H., and Henry G. Wohlhuter Bungalows, 221 and 223 S. 11th St., La Crosse, 6/30/83, C, 83003400

Christ Church of La Crosse, 831 Main St., La Crosse, 6/19/85, C, a, 85001361

Freight House, 107-109 Vine St., La Crosse, 3/02/82, A, C, 82000678

Garland, Hamlin, House, 357 W. Garland St., West Salem, 11/11/71, B, NHL, 71000010

Hixon, Gideon C., House, 429 N. 7th St., La Crosse, 12/30/74, B, C, 74000095

La Crosse County School of Agriculture and Domestic Economy, 700 Wilson Ave., Onalaska, 3/13/87, A, C, 87000438

Laverty-Martindale House, 237 S. 10th St., La Crosse, 11/23/77, C, 77000033

Main Hall/La Crosse State Normal School, 1724 State St., Univ. of WI, La Crosse, La Crosse, 3/14/85, A, C, 85000579

Midway Village Site, W of Holmen, Holmen vicinity, 12/18/78, D, 75000111

Nichols, Frank Eugene, House, 421 N. Second St., Onalaska, 2/11/93, B, 93000027

Ott, Will, House, 1532 Madison St., La Crosse, 1/15/80, B, C, 80000152

Our Lady of Sorrows Chapel, 519 Losey Blvd., S, La Crosse, 9/11/86, C, a, 86002302

Overhead Site, S. of La Crosse, La Crosse vicinity 12/18/78, D, 78000112

Palmer Brother's Octagons, 358 N. Leonard St. and WI 16, West Salem and Vicinity, 8/07/79, C, b, 79000092

Physical Education Building/La Crosse State Normal School, UW La Crosse Campus off US 16, La Crosse, 4/11/85, A, C, 85000791

Powell Place, 200-212 Main St., La Crosse, 12/22/83, B, C, 83004299

Roosevelt, W. A., Company, 230 N. Front St., La Crosse, 2/16/84, A, C, 84003690

Samuels' Cave, Address Restricted, Barre Mills vicinity, 6/11/91, A, D, 86003275

Sand Lake Archeological District, Address Restricted, Onalaska vicinity, 4/20/84, D, 84003694

Sand Lake Site (47LC44), Address Restricted, Onalaska vicinity, 6/30/83, D, 53003401

Smith Valley School, 4130 Smith Valley Rd., La Crosse vicinity, 7/30/81, A, 51000044

Swennes Archeological District, Address Restricted, Onalaska vicinity, 7/18/85, D, 85001573

U.S. Fish Control Laboratory, Riverside Park, La Crosse, 9/17/81, A, 81000045

Valley View Site, N of Medary, Medary vicinity, 12/15/78, D, 78000113

Vincent, James, House, 1024 Cass St., La Crosse, 10/20/88, C, 88002024

Waterworks Building, 119 King St., La Crosse, 7/27/79, C, 79000093

Wisconsin Telephone Company Building, 125 N. 4th St., La Crosse, 3/07/85, C, 85000491

Zeisler George, Building, 201 Pearl St., La Crosse, 2/25/93, C, 93000069

LAFAYETTE COUNTY

First Capitol, N of Belmont off U.S. 151, Belmont vicinity, 4/28/70, A, 70000036

Gratiot House, S. of Shullsburg on Rennick Rd., Shullsburg vicinity, 1/08/80, A, C, 80000153

Lafayette County Courthouse, 626 Main St., Darlington, 12/22/78, A, C, 78000114

St. Augustine Church, Off CR W, New Diggings, 2/23/72, C, a, 72000057

Star Theatre, 200 S. North St., Argyle, 11/07/80, A, C, 80000154

Water Street Commercial Historic District, Roughly Water St., from Judgement to Kennedy Sts., and Gratiot St. from Water to Church Sts., Shullsburg, 6/28/90, A, C, a, 90000998

LANGLADE COUNTY

Antigo Depot, 522 Morse St., Antigo, 2/10/92, A, C, 92000029

Antigo Opera House, 1016 5th Ave., Antigo, 1/12/84, A, 84003699

Antigo Public Library and Deleglise Cabin, 404 Superior St., Antigo, 12/18/78, A, B, C, b, 78000115

Langlade County Courthouse, 800 Clermont St., Antigo, 7/25/77, C, 77000034

LINCOLN COUNTY

Lincoln County Courthouse, 1110 E. Main St., Merrill, 4/19/78, A, C, 78000116

Merrill City Hall, 717 E. 2nd St., Merrill, 7/12/78, A, 78000117

Scott, T. B., Free Library, E. 1st St., Merrill, 1/21/74, A, B, C, 74000096

MANITOWOC COUNTY

Eighth Street Historic District, Roughly bounded by Buffalo St., Eighth and Seventh Sts., Hancock St., and Tenth, Ninth and Quay Sts,, Manitowoc, 3/17/88, A, C, 88000215

Frenchside Fishing Village, Twenty-first, Jackson, East, Sixteenth, Harbor, and Rogers Sts., Two Rivers, 1/06/87, A, 86003580

Loreto Shrine Chapel, Colony of St. Gregory of Nazianzen TR, Off WI A, St. Nazianz, 6/07/82, A, a, 82000679

Lutze Housebarn, 13634 S. Union Rd., Newton vicinity, 6/07/84, A, C, 84003702

Manitowoc County Courthouse, 8th and Washington Sts., Manitowoc, 4/16/81. A, C, 81000047

Rawley Point Light Station, U.S. Coast Guard Lighthouses and Light Stations on the Great Lakes TR, Point Beach State Forest, Two Rivers vicinity, 7/19/84, A, C, 84003706

Rock Mill, Off U.S. 141, Maribel, 6/21/82, C, 82000680

St. Gregory's Church, Colony of St. Gregory of Nazianzen TR, 212 Church St., St. Nazianz, 6/07/82, A, a, 82000681

USS COBIA (submarine), 809 S. Eighth St., Manitowoc, 1/14/86, A, g, NHL, 86000087

Vilas, Joseph, Jr., House, 610-616 N. 8th St., Manitowoc, 4/29/77, B, C, 77000035

MARATHON COUNTY

Andrew Warren Historic District, Roughly bounded by Fulton, Grant, 4th, and 7th Sts., Wausau, 1/05/84, A, C, 84003708

Bird, C. B., House, Eschweiler TR of Marathon County, 522 McIndoe St., Wausau, 5/01/80, B, C, 80000155

Dessert, Joseph, Library, Eschweiler TR of Marathon County, 123 Main St., Mosinee, 5/01/80, B, C, 80000156

Dunbar, C. F., House, Eschweiler TR of Marathon County, 929 McIndoe St., Wausau, 5/01/80, C, 80000157

Everest, D.C., House, Eschweiler TR of Marathon County, 1206 Highland Park Blvd., Wausau, 5/01/80, B, C, 80000158

First Universalist Church, Eschweiler TR of Marathon County, 504 Grant St., Wausau, 5/01/80, C, a, 80000159

Fricke-Menzner House, 105 Main St., Marathon, 7/16/92, B, C, 92000856

Fromm, Walter and Mabel, House, Off WI 107, Hamburg, 6/17/82, C, 82000682

Jones, Granville D., House, 915 Grant St., Wausau, 12/07/77, B, C, 77000036

Maine Site (47MR22), Address Restricted, Brokaw vicinity, 7/19/84, D, 84003711

Marathon County Fairgrounds, Eschweiler TR of Marathon County, Stewart Ave., Wausau, 5/01/80, A, C, 80000160

Mathie, Karl, House, Eschweiler TR of Marathon County, 202 Water St., Mosinee, 5/01/80, B, C, 80000161

Miller, Henry, House, 1314 Grand Ave., Wausau, 6/14/82, B, C, b, 82000683

Schuetz, E. K., House, Eschweiler TR of Marathon County, 930 Franklin St., Wausau, 5/01/80, B, C, 80000162

Single, Benjamin, House, W. of Wausau at 4708 Stettin Dr., Wausau vicinity, 11/24/80, B, C, 80000163

Stewart, Hiram C., House, 521 Grant St., Wausau, 8/30/74, C, 74000097

Wausau Club, 309 McClellan St., Wausau, 9/14/89, A, C, 89001420

Wegner, C. H., House, Eschweiler TR of Marathon County, 906 Grant St., Wausau, 5/01/80, B, C, 80000164

Wright, Ely, House, 901 6th St., Wausau, 3/01/82, C, 82000684

Yawkey, Cyrus C., House, 403 McIndoe St., Wausau, 12/31/74, B, C, 74000098

MARINETTE COUNTY

Amberg Town Hall, Grant St., Amberg, 3/20/81, A, C, 81000048

Dunlap Square Building, 1821 Hall St., Marinette, 2/24/92, C, 92000026

Lauerman Brothers Department Store, 1701-1721 Dunlap Sq., Marinette, 2/24/92, A, C, b, 92000027

Lauerman, F. J., House, 383 State St., Marinette, 8/14/79, A, B, C, 79900094

Peshtigo Fire Cemetery, Oconto Ave. between Peck and Ellis Aves., Peshtigo, 10/15/70, A, f, 70000037

MARQUETTE COUNTY

Bonnie Oaks Historic District, Grouse Dr., Briggsville vicinity, 4/03/86, B, D, 86000626

Fountain Lake Farm, Co. Hwy. F. and Gillette Rd., Montello vicinity, 6/21/90, B. NHL, 90000471

Marquette County Courthouse and Marquette County Sheriff's Office and Jail, County Courthouses of Wisconsin TR, 77 W. Park St., Montello, 3/09/82, C, 82000685

MILWAUKEE COUNTY

Abbot Row, 1019-1013 E. Ogden Ave., Milwaukee, 3/03/83, C, 83003402

Abresch, Charles, House, West Side Area MRA, 2126 W. Juneau Ave., Milwaukee, 1/16/86, B, C, 86000095

Adler, Emanuel P., House, 1681 N. Prospect Ave., Milwaukee, 9/13/91, C, 91001397

All Saints' Episcopal Cathedral Complex, 804-828 E. Juneau Ave., Milwaukee, 12/27/74, A, C, a, 74000099

Allis, Charles, House, 1630 E. Royall Pl., Milwaukee, 1/17/75, B, C, 75000072

American System Built Homes–Burnham Street District, W. Burnham St., Milwaukee, 9/12/85, C, 85002166

Annunciation Greek Orthodox Church, 9400 W. Congress St., Wauwatosa, 12/19/74, C, a, g, 74000100

Arndt, Rufus, House, Ernest Flagg Stone Masonry Houses of Milwaukee County TR, 4524 N. Cramer St., Whitefish Bay, 9/12/85, C, 85002016

Astor on the Lake, 924 E. Juneau Ave., Milwaukee, 9/06/84, C, 84003715

Baasen House–German YMCA, Brewers' Hill MRA, 1702 N. 4th St., Milwaukee, 8/02/84, A, 84003718

Barfield-Staples House, Ernest Flagg Stone Masonry Houses of Milwaukee County TR, 5461-5463 Danbury Rd., Whitefish Bay, 9/12/85, C, 85002017

Baumbach Building, 302 N. Broadway St., Milwaukee, 3/03/83, C, 83003403

Bay View Historic District, Roughly bounded by Lake Michigan, Meredith, Superior, Neck, Wentworth, Pryor, Clair, RR tracks and Conway St., Milwaukee, 8/23/82, A, C, 82000686

Blatz Brewery Complex, 1101-1147 N. Broadway, Milwaukee, 4/15/86, A, C, 86000793

Blatz, Valentin, Brewing Company Office Building, 1120 N. Broadway, Milwaukee, 3/31/83, A, C, 83003404

Bogk, Frederick C., House, 2420 N. Terrace Ave., Milwaukee, 10/18/72, C, 72000058

Bossert, Thomas, House, Ernest Flagg Stone Masonry Houses of Milwaukee County TR, 2614 E. Menlo Blvd., Shorewood, 9/12/85, C, 85002018

Brown Deer School, 4800 W. Green Brook Dr., Brown Deer, 12/10/93, A, C, b, 93001427

Buemming, Herman W., House, 1012 E. Pleasant St., Milwaukee, 1/18/90, C, 89002315

Burnham, J. L., Block, 907-911 W. National Ave., Milwaukee, 2/11/88, A, C, 88000086

Calkins, Elias A., Doublehouse, 1612-1614 E. Kane Pl., Milwaukee, 1/18/90, C, 89002313

Calvary Presbyterian Church, West Side Area MRA, 935 W. Wisconsin Ave., Milwaukee, 3/10/86, C, a, 86000098

Carpenter, Michael, House, West Side Area MRA, 1115 Thirty-fifth St., Milwaukee, 1/16/86, C, a, 86000096

Cass-Juneau Street Historic District, Roughly bounded by E. Knapp and Marshall Sts., Juneau Ave., and Van Buren St., Milwaukee, 11/03/88, C, a, 88002389

Cass-Wells Street Historic District, 712, 718, and 724 E. Wells St. and 801, 809, 815, 819, and 823 N. Cass St., Milwaukee, 6/13/86, C, 86001325

Central Library, 814 W. Wisconsin Ave., Milwaukee, 12/30/74, C, 74000101

Chief Lippert Fire Station, 642 W. North Ave., Milwaukee, 10/28/88, C, 88002007

Christ Evangelical Lutheran Church, 2235 W. Greenfield Ave., Milwaukee, 9/25/87, C, a, 87001735

Church Street Historic District, 1448-1630 Church St. and 7758 W. Menomonee River Pkwy., Wauwatosa, 8/10/89, C, 89001099

Church, Benjamin, House, Parkway Dr., Eastabrook Park, Shorewood, 2/23/72, C, b, 72000059

Coast Guard Station, Old, 1600 N. Lincoln Memorial Dr., Milwaukee, 8/07/89, A, C, 89001047

Concordia Historic District, West Side Area MRA, Roughly bounded by West State, N. 27th, W. Killbourn Ave. and N. 35th St., Milwaukee, 7/30/85, A, B, C, g, 85001688

Cook, Thomas, House, West Side Area MRA, 853 N. Seventeenth St., Milwaukee, 1/16/86, C, 86000104

The Encyclopedia of Wisconsin

Cords, Erwin, House, Ernest Flagg Stone Masonry Houses of Milwaukee County TR, 1913 E. Olive St., Shorewood, 9/12/85, C, 85002019

Curtin, Jeremiah, House, 8685 W. Grange Ave., Greendale, 11/07/72, B, C, 72000060

Dahinden, Edward J., House, West Side Area MRA, 3316 W. Wisconsin Ave., Milwaukee, 2/25/86, C, 86000313

Damon, Lowell, House, 2107 N. Wauwatosa Ave., Wauwatosa, 2/23/72, C, 72000061

Davis, H. R., House, Ernest Flagg Stone Masonry Houses of Milwaukee County TR, 6839 Cedar St., Wauwatosa, 9/12/85, C, 85002020

Desmond-Farnham-Hustis House, 1535 N. Marshall St., Milwaukee, 1/18/90, C, 89002314

Eagles Club, West Side Area MRA, 2401 W. Wisconsin Ave., Milwaukee, 7/29/86, C, g. 86002096

East Brady Street Historic District, E. Brady St. from N. Farwell Ave. to N. Van Buren St., Milwaukee, 3/09/90, A, C, a, b, 90000363

East Side Commercial Historic District, Roughly bonded by E. Wells St., N. Jefferson St. and N. Broadway, Michigan and E. Clybourn, and N. Water Sts., Milwaukee, 9/23/86, A, C, g, 86002325

Elderwood, 6789 N. Elm Tree Rd., Glendale, 12/04/80, C, 80000165

Esbenshade, Abraham H., House, West Side Area MRA, 3119 W. Wells St., Milwaukee, 1/16/86, C, 86000106

Federal Building, 515-519 E. Wisconsin Ave., Milwaukee, 3/14/73, C, 73000082

Fiebing, J. H., House, Ernest Flagg Stone Masonry Houses of Milwaukee County TR, 7707 Stickney, Wauwatosa, 9/12/85, C, 85002021

Fiebing, Otto F., House, Ernest Flagg Stone Masonry Houses of Milwaukee County TR, 302 N. Hawley Rd., Milwaukee, 9/12/85, C, 85002022

First Church of Christ, Scientist, 1443-1451 N. Prospect Ave., Milwaukee, 3/08/59, C, a, 89000070

First Unitarian Church, 1009 E. Ogden Ave., Milwaukee, 12/30/74, C, a, 74000102

First Ward Triangle Historic District, Roughly Franklin Pl., N. Prospect and E. Juneau Aves., and E. Knapp St., Milwaukee, 3/19/87, B, C, 87000489

Forest Home Cemetery and Chapel, 2405 Forest Home Ave., Milwaukee, 11/03/80, A, B, C, d, 80000166
Foth, Christian, House, 1209-1211 S. Seventh St., Milwaukee, 3/22/88, C, 88000218
Fourth Street School, Brewers' Hill MRA, 333 W. Galena St., Milwaukee, 8/02/84, B, C, NHL, 84013720
Gabel, George, House, Ernest Flagg Stone Masonry Houses of Milwaukee County TR, 1600 N. Cramer St., Whitefish Bay, 9/12/85, C, 85002023
Gallun Tannery Historic District, Brewers' Hill MRA, Holton and Water Sts., Milwaukee, 8/02/84, A, C, 84003721
Garden Homes Historic District, Roughly bounded by W. Ruby and N. Teutonia Aves., N. 24th Pl., W. Atkinson Ave. and N. 27th St., Milwaukee, 5/04/90, A, 90000669
George, Warren B., House, Ernest Flagg Stone Masonry Houses of Milwaukee County TR, 7105 Grand Pkwy., Wauwatosa, 9/12/85, C, 85002024
German-English Academy, 1020 N. Broadway, Milwaukee, 4/11/77, A, C, 77000037
Germania Building, 135 W. Wells St., Milwaukee, 7107/83, A, B, C, g, 83003405
Gesu Church, West Side Area MRA, 1145 W. Wisconsin Ave., Milwaukee, 1/16/86, C, a, 86000108
Graham Row, 1501,1503, and 1507 N. Marshall St., Milwaukee, 7127/79, C, 70000095
Grand Avenue Congregational Church, West Side Area MRA, 2133 W. Wisconsin Ave., Milwaukee, 1/16/86, C, a, 86000110
Grant, Paul S., House, Ernest Flagg Stone Masonry Houses of Milwaukee County TR, 984 Circle Dr., Whitefish Bay, 9/12/85, C, 85002025
Greene, Thomas A., Memorial Museum, 3367 N. Downer Ave., Milwaukee, 11/04/93, A, B, NHL, 93001615
Hardie, Harrison, House, Ernest Flagg Stone Masonry Houses of Milwaukee County TR, 4540 N. Cramer St., Whitefish Bay, 9/12/85, C, 85002026
Hart, Thomas B., House, 1609 Church St., Wauwatosa, 0/10/85, B, C, 85003135
Hatch, Horace W., House, Ernest Flagg Stone Masonry Houses of Milwaukee County TR, 739 E. Beaumont, Whitefish Bay, 9/12/85, C, 85002027
Henni Hall, 3257 S. Lake Dr., St. Francis, 7/24/74, A, C, a, 74000103

Highland Avenue Methodist Church, West Side Area MRA, 2024 W. Highland Ave., Milwaukee, 1/16/85, A, C, a, 86000114

Highland Boulevard Historic District, West Side Area MRA, W. Highland Blvd. roughly bounded by N. 33rd and N. 29th Sts., Milwaukee, 7/30/85, A, B, C, 85001686

Historic Third Ward District, Bounded by the Milwaukee River, C and NW BR, and E. St. Paul and N. Jackson Sts., Milwaukee, 3/08184, A, C, 84003724

Hoelz, Alfred M., House, Ernest Flagg Stone Masonry Houses of Milwaukee County TR, 3449-3451 Frederick Ave., Milwaukee, 9/12185, C, 85002029

Holy Trinity Roman Catholic Church, 605 S. 4th St., Milwaukee, 11/07/72, A, C, a, 72000062

Home Office, Northwestern Mutual Life Insurance Company, 605-623 N. Broadway, Milwaukee, 3/20/73, A, C, 73000083

Hopkins, Willis, House, Ernest Flagg Stone Masonry Houses of Milwaukee County TR, 325 Glenview, Wauwatosa, 9/12/85, C, 85002030

Howie, David W., House, West Side Area MRA, 3026 W. Wells St., Milwaukee, 1/16/86, C, 86000116

Immanuel Presbyterian Church, 1100 N. Astor St., Milwaukee, 12127/74, C, a, 74000101

Iron Block, 205 E. Wisconsin Ave., Milwaukee, 12/27/74, C, 74000105

Jenkins, Halbert D., House, Ernest Flagg Stone Masonry Houses of Milwaukee County TR, 1028 E. Lexington Blvd., Whitefish Bay, 9/12/85, C, 85002031

Johnston Hall, West Side Area MRA, 1121 W. Wisconsin Ave., Milwaukee, 1/16/86, A, C, 86000018

Kalvelage, Joseph B., House, 2432 W. Kilbourn Ave., Milwaukee, 5/23/78, C, 78000118

Ketter, Frederick, Warehouse, Brewers' Hill MRA, 325 W. Vine St., Milwaukee, 8/02/84, C, 84003725

Kilbourn Avenue Row House Historic District, West Side Area MRA, Roughly bounded by N. Fourteenth St., W. Kilbourn Ave., and N. Fifteenth St., Milwaukee, 2125/86, C, 86000311

Kilbourn Masonic Temple, West Side Area MRA, 527 N. Eleventh St., Milwaukee 1/16/86, C, 86000121

Knapp-Astor House, 930 E. Knapp St. and 1301 N. Astor St., Milwaukee, 3127180, C, 80000167

Kneeland-Walker House, 7406 Hillcrest Dr., Wauwatosa, 1/19/89, C, 88003212

Knickerbocker Hotel, 1028 E. Juneau Ave., Milwaukee, 6/02/88, C, 88000680

Lohman Funeral Home and Livery Stable, 804 W. Greenfield and 1325 S. Eighth, Milwaukee, 3/17/88, A, C, 85000220

Machek, Robert, House, 1305 N. 19th St., Milwaukee, 10/28/77, C, 77000038

Mackie Building, 225 E. Michigan St., Milwaukee, 4/03/73, A, C, 73000084

Mayer Boot and Shoe Company Building, Brewers' Hill MRA, 116 E. Walnut St., Milwaukee, 8/02/84, A, C, 84003725

McEwens, John F., House, Ernest Flagg Stone Masonry Houses of Milwaukee County TR, 829 E. Lake Forest, Whitefish Bay, 9/12/85, C, 85002032

McKinley Boulevard Historic District, West Side Area MRA, W. McKinley Blvd. between N. 34th & N. 27th Sts., Milwaukee, 7/30/85, A, C, 85001687

Meyer, Henry A., House, Ernest Flagg Stone Masonry Houses of Milwaukee County TR, 3559 N. Summit Ave., Shorewood, 9/12/85, C, 85002033

Meyer, Starke, House, Ernest Flagg Stone Masonry Houses of Milwaukee County TR, 7896 N. Club Circle, Fox Point, 9/12/85, C, 85002034

Milwaukee City Hall, 200 E. Wells St., Milwaukee, 3/14/73, C, 85002034

Milwaukee County Courthouse, County Courthouses of Wisconsin TR, 901 N. 9th St., Milwaukee, 3/09/82, A, C, 82000687

Milwaukee County Dispensary and Emergency Hospital, 2430 W. Wisconsin Ave., Milwaukee, 3/21/55, A, B, C, 85000039

Milwaukee County Historical Center, 910 N. 3rd St., Milwaukee, 3/14/73, A, C, 73000086

Milwaukee Fire Department High Pressure Pumping Station, 2011 S. 1st St., Milwaukee 7/07/81, A, C, 81000049

Milwaukee News Building and Milwaukee Abstract Association Building, 222 E. Mason St., Milwaukee, 3/01/82, A, C, 82000688

Milwaukee Normal School-Milwaukee Girls' Trade and Technical High School, West Side Area MRA, 820 W. Wells St., Milwaukee, 1/16/86, A, B, C, 86000123

Milwaukee-Downer 'Quad', NW corner of Hartford and Downer Aves., Milwaukee 1/17/74, A, C, 74000106

Mitchell Building, 207 E. Michigan St., Milwaukee, 4/03/73, A, C, 7300008

Morgan, George E., House, Ernest Flagg Stone Masonry Houses of Milwaukee Country TR, 4448 N. Maryland Ave., Shorewood, 9/12/85, C, 85002035

New Coeln House, 5905 S. Howell Ave., Milwaukee, 2/11/88, A, C, 88000083

North First Street Historic District, Brewers' Hill MRA, Roughly 1st and 2nd Sts. between North and Center Sts., Milwaukee, 8/02/84, A, C, 84003731

North Point Lighthouse, U.S. Coast Guard Lighthouses and Light Stations on the Great Lakes TR, Wahl St. at Terrace, Milwaukee, 7/19184, A, C, 84003732

North Point South Historic District, Roughly bounded by North Ave., Summit, Terrace, and Lafayette Sts., Milwaukee, 9/04/79, C, 79000322

North Point Water Tower, E. North Ave. between N. Lake Dr., and N, Terrace Ave., Milwaukee, 2/23/73, C, 73000088

North Third Street Historic District, Brewers' Hill MRA, Roughly N. 3rd St. between N. 3rd Ave. and Vine St., Milwaukee, 8/02/84, A, C, 84003733

Norton, Pearl C., House, Ernest Flagg Stone Masonry Houses of Milwaukee County TR, 2021 Church St., Wauwatosa, 9/12/55, C, 85002036

Old St. Mary's Church, 844 N. Broadway, Milwaukee, 3107173, A, C, a, 73090953

Old World Third Street Historic District, N. Old World Third St., W. Highland Ave., and W. State St., Milwaukee, 3/19/87, A, C, 87000494

Oliver, Joseph B., House, 1516 E. Brady St., Milwaukee, 1/18/90, C, b, 80002312

Oneida Street Station, 108 E. Wells and 816 N. Edison Sts., Milwaukee, 12/06/84, A, C, 84000701

Pabst Brewery Saloon, West Side Area MRA, 1338-1340 W. Juneau Ave., Milwaukee, 1/16/86, C, a, 86000125

Pabst Theater, 144 E. Wells St., Milwaukee, 4/11/72, A, C, NHL, 72000063

Pabst, Frederick, House, 2000 W. Wisconsin Ave., Milwaukee 4/21/75, B, C, 75000073

Painesville Chapel, 2741 W. Ryan Rd., Franklin, 11/07/77, A C a, 77900039

Plankinton-Wells-Water Street Historic District, Roughly bounded by Wells, Bridge, N. Water, E. Mason, W. Wells, and N. Second Sts., Milwaukee 6/13/86, A, C, 86001328

Prospect Avenue Apartment Buildings Historic District, N. Prospect Ave. area roughly between E. Kane Pl. and E. Windsor St., Milwaukee, 4/19/90, C, 90000640

Prospect Avenue Mansions Historic District, 1363-1551 N. Prospect Ave., Milwaukee, 4/07/90, C, 90000478

Public School No. 27, Brewers' Hill MRA, 2215 N. 4th St., Milwaukee, 8/02/84, C, 84003735

Pythian Castle Lodge, 1925 W. National Ave., Milwaukee, 2/25/88, A, C, 88000089

Quarles, Charles, House, 2531 N. Farwell Ave., Milwaukee, 7/27/79, B, C, 79000096

Saint George Melkite Catholic Church, West Side Area MRA, 1017 W. State St., Milwaukee, 1/16/86, A, C, a, 86000128

Saint Peter's Evangelical Lutheran Church, 1204, 1213, 1214 and 12 15 S. Eighth St., Milwaukee, 9/25/87, C, a, 87001736

Saint Vincent's Infant Asylum, 809 W. Greenfield Ave., Milwaukee, 9/25/87, A, C, 87001742

Salem Evangelical Church, 1025 & 1037 S. Eleventh St., Milwaukee, 10/01/87, C, a, 87001760

Schlitz, Joseph, Brewing Company Saloon, 2414 S. St. Clair St., Milwaukee, 4/11/77, A, C, 77000040

Schlitz, Victor, House, West Side Area MRA, 2004 W. Highland Ave., Milwaukee, 1/16/86, C, 86000145

Schuster, George, House and Carriage Shed, West Side Area MRA, 3209 W. Wells St., Milwaukee, 1/16/86, C, 86000137

Second Church of Christ Scientist, West Side Area MRA, 2722 W. Highland Blvd., Milwaukee, 1/16/86, C, a, 86000139

Shorecrest Hotel, 1962 N. Prospect Ave., Milwaukee, 9/07/84, C, 84003737

Shorewood Village Hall, 3930 N. Murray Ave., Shorewood, 9/07/84, A, 84003739

Sivyer, Fred, House, West Side Area MRA, 761 N. Twenty-fifth St., Milwaukee, 1/36/86, C, 86000341

Sixth Church of Christ, Scientist, 1036 N. Van Buren St., Milwaukee, 3/27/80, A, C, a, 80000168

Smith, Lloyd R., House, 2220 N. Terrace Ave., Milwaukee, 12/30/74, A, C, 74000107

South Branch Library, 931 W. Madison St., Milwaukee, 2/11/88, A, C, 88000084

South First and Second Street Historic District, Roughly bounded by Menomonee River, Chicago & N. Western RR, Seeboth, S. First, Oregon, & S. Second Sts., Milwaukee, 11/30/57, A, C, 87002092

South Milwaukee Passenger Station, Milwaukee Ave., South Milwaukee, 8/03/78, A, C, 78000119

Sperling, Frederick, House, Ernest Flagg Stone Masonry Houses of Milwaukee County TR, 1016 E. Lexington Blvd., Whitefish Bay, 9/12/85, C, 85002037

Spring Grove Site, Address Restricted, Milwaukee vicinity, 9/10/79, A, D, 79000097

St. James Episcopal Church, 833 W. Wisconsin Ave., Milwaukee, 6/27/79, A, C, a, 79090098

St. John's Roman Catholic Cathedral, 812 N. Jackson St., Milwaukee, 12/31/74, A, C, a, e, 74000108

St. Josaphat Basilica, 691 W. Lincoln Ave., Milwaukee, 3/07/73, A, C, a, 73000089

St. Martini Evangelical Lutheran Church, 1557 W. Orchard St., Milwaukee, 9/25/87, C, a, 87001741

St. Patrick's Roman Catholic Church, 1105 S. 7th St., Milwaukee, 12/16/74, C, A, 74000109

St. Paul's Episcopal Church, 904 E. Knapp St., Milwaukee, 12/27/74, C, a, 74000110

State Bank of Wisconsin, 210 E. Michigan St., Milwaukee, 3/08/84, A, C, 84003742

Steinmeyer, William, House, Brewers' Hill MRA, 1716-1722 N. 5th St., Milwaukee, 10/11/84, C, 84000102

Sunnyhill Home, 8000 W. Milwaukee Ave., Wauwatosa, 5/07/80, B, C, 80000169

Town of Milwaukee Town Hall, 5909 N. Milwaukee River Pkwy., Glendale, 10/09/86, A, C, 86002852

Trimborn Farm, 8801 W. Grange Ave., Greendale, 7/31/80, A, C, 80000170

Trinity Evangelical Lutheran Church, 1046 N. 9th St., Milwaukee, 5/08/79, A, C, a, 79000099

Tripoli Temple, West Side Area MRA, 3000 W. Wisconsin Ave., Milwaukee, 1/16/86, A, C, 86000142

Historic Places

Turner Hall, 1034 N. 4th St., Milwaukee, 11/07/77, A, C, 77900041

Uihlein, Herman, House, 5270 N. Lake Dr., Whitefish Bay, 12/22/83, C, 83004313

Ullius, Fred W., Jr., House, Ernest Flagg Stone Masonry Houses of Milwaukee County TR, 5775 N. Santa Monica Blvd., Whitefish Bay, 1/07/87, C, 86003658

Van Altena, William, House, Ernest Flagg Stone Masonry Houses if Milwaukee County TR, 1916 E. Glendale, Whitefish Bay, 9/12/85, C, 85002038

Van Devan G. B., House, Ernest Flagg Stone Masonry Houses of Milwaukee County TR, 4601 N. Murray Ave., Whitefish Bay, 9/12/55, C, 85002039

Vine-Reservoir Historic District, Brewers' Hill MRA, Vine, Reservoir, Palmer, 1st, 2nd, and Brown Sts., Milwaukee, 8/02/84, C, 84003745

Walker's Point Historic District, Roughly bounded by the Freeway, Menomonee Canal, Scott, 2nd, and W. VA Sts., Milwaukee, 12/19/78, A, C, 78000120

Walker, Harry B., House, West Side Area MRA, 3130 W. Wells St., Milwaukee, 1/16/86, C, 86900144

Ward Memorial Hall, 5000 W. National Ave., Wood, 9/06/84, A, C, 84003748

Washington Highlands Historic District, Bounded by N. 68th St., W Lloyd St., N. 60th St., and Milwaukee Ave., Wauwatosa, 12/18/89, A, C, g, 89002121

Williams, Frank J., House, Ernest Flagg Stone Masonry Houses of Milwaukee County TR, 912 E. Lexington Blvd., Whitefish Bay, 9/12/85 C, 85002040

Woman's Club of Wisconsin, 813 E. Kilbourn Ave., Milwaukee, 10/04/82, A, C, 82001847

MONROE COUNTY

Kendalls Depot, N. Railroad St., Kendall, 8/12/81, C, 01000050

Monroe County Courthouse, County Courthouses of Wisconsin TR, 418 W. Main St., Sparta, 3/09/82, C, 82000689

Sparta Free Library, Court and Main Sts., Sparta, 9/03/81, C, 81000051

Sparta Masonic Temple, 200 W. Main St., Sparta, 9/25/87, C, 87001734

St. John's Episcopal Church, 400 N. Water St., Sparta, 3/18/83, C, a, 83003406
Tomah Public Library, 716 Superior Ave., Tomah, 5/28/76, C, 76000068

OCONTO COUNTY

Beyer Home Museum, 917 Park Ave., Oconto, 8/14/79, B, C, 79000100
Campbell, John G., House, 916 Park Ave., Oconto, 1/15/50, C, 80000171
First Church of Christ, Scientist, Chicago and Main Sts., Oconto, 11/19/74, A, C, a, 74000111
Holt and Balcom Logging Camp No. 1, E. of Lakewood, Lakewood vicinity, 12/22/78, A, C, 78000121
Holt-Balcom Lumber Company Office, 106 Superior Ave., Oconto, 11/13/76, A, 76000069
Jones, Huff, House, 3315 Main St., Oconto, 2/22/78, A, 78000122
Oconto County Courthouse, County Courthouses of Wisconsin TR, 300 Washington St., Oconto, 3/09/82, C, 82000690
Oconto Main Post Office, 141 Congress St., Oconto, 8/28/80, B, C, 80004479
Oconto Site, Copper Culture State Park, Oconto, 10/15/60, D, NHL, 66000023
Scofield, Gov. Edward, House, 610 Main St., Oconto, 4/11/73, B, 73000090
St. Mark's Episcopal Church, Guild Hall and Vicarage, 408 Park Ave., Oconto, 8/01/85, C, a, 85001684
St. Peter's and St. Joseph's Catholic Churches, 516 Brazeau Ave. and 705 Park Ave., Oconto, 11/10/80, A, C, a, 80000172
West Main Street Historic District, Main St. from Duncan to Erie Sts., Oconto, 5/14/79, B, C, 79000101

ONEIDA COUNTY

First National Bank, 8 W. Davenport St., Rhinelander, 8/14/73, C, 73000091
Mecikalski General Store, Saloon, and Boardinghouse, 465 Max Rd., Jennings, 3/22/84, C, 84003751

Historic Places

Oneida County Courthouse, S. Oneida Ave., Rhinelander, 3/20/81, C, 81000052

Tomahawk Lake Camp Historic District, 8500 Raven Rd., Lake Tomahawk, 1/30/92, A, 91001987

OUTAGAMIE COUNTY

Black, Merritt, House, Kaukauna MRA, 104 River Rd., Kaukauna, 3/29/84, C, 84003752

Brokaw, Norman, House, Kaukauna MRA, 714 Grignon St.,. Kaukauna, 3/29/84, B, 84003754

College Avenue Historic District, 215 W. to 109 E. and 110 W. to 102 E. College Ave., 106-114 N. Oneida St., Appleton, 12/02/82, A, C, 82001848

Fargo's Furniture Store, Kaukauna MRA, 172-176 W. Wisconsin Ave., Kaukauna, 3/29/84, C, 84003755

Fox River Paper Company Historic District, 405-406, 415 S. Olde Oneida St., Appleton, 4/19/90, A, C, 90000639

Free Public Library of Kaukauna, Kaukauna MRA, 111 Main Ave., Kaukauna, 3/29/84, A, 84003756

Greenville State Bank, 252 Municipal Dr., Greenville, 9/23/82, A, 82000691

Grignon, Charles A., House, Augustine St., Kaukauna, 10/18/72, A B, C, 72000064

Hearthstone, 625 W. Prospect Ave., Appleton, 12/02/74, A, 74000112

Holy Cross Church, Kaukauna MRA, 309 Desnoyer St., Kaukauna, 3/29/84, C, a, 84003758

Hortonville Community Hall, 312 W. Main St., Hortonville, 1/23/81, A, C, 81000053

Klein Dairy Farmhouse, Kaukauna MRA, 1018 Sullivan Ave., Kaukauna, 3/29/84, A, C, 84003760

Kronser, Joseph, Hotel and Saloon, 246 Municipal Dr., Greenville, 7/28/88, A, C, 88001153

Kuehn Blacksmith Shop-Hardware Store, Kaukauna MRA, 148-152 E. 2nd St., Kaukauna, 3/29/84, C, 84003761

Lindauer and Rupert Block, Kaukauna MRA, 137-141 E. 2nd St., Kaukauna, 3/29/84, A, C, 84003763

Main Hall, Lawrence University, 400-500 E. College Ave., Appleton, 1/18/74, A, C, 74000113

Martens, Julius. J., Company Building, Kaukauna MRA, 124-128 E. 3rd St., Kaukauna, 3/29/84, A, 8, C, 84003764

Masonic Temple, 330 E. College Ave., Appleton, 9/12/85, A, C, 85002330

Meade, Capt. Matthew J., House, Kaukauna MRA, 309 Division St., Kaukauna, 3/29/84, B, 84003765

Nicolet Public School, Kaukauna MRA, 109 E. 8th St., Kaukauna, 3/29/84, C, 84003767

Peters, George, House, 305 N., Maple St., Black Creek, 6/18/87, C, 87000989

St. Andrews, Frank, House, Kaukauna MRA, 320 Dixon St., Kaukauna, 3/29/84, C, 84003768

St. Mary's Catholic Church, Kaukauna MRA, 119 W. 7th St., Kaukauna, 3/29/84, A, C, 84003769

Stribley, Charles W., House, Kaukauna MRA, 705 W. Wisconsin Ave., Kaukauna, 3/29/84, C, 84003770

Temple Zion and School, 320 N. Durkee St. and 309 E. Harris St., Appleton, 9/18/78, A, B, C, 78000123

Tompkins, James, House, 523 S. State St., Appleton, 4/03/86, C, 86000623

Washington School, 818 W. Loran St., Appleton, 6/07/84, C, 84003772

Whorton, John Hart, House, 315 W. Prospect Ave., Appleton, 11/19/74 B, C, 74000114

Zion Lutheran Church, 912 N. Oneida St., Appleton, 6/13/86, C, a, 86001309

OZAUKEE COUNTY

Bolens, Harry W., House, 824 W. Grand Ave., Port Washington, 8/25/83, B, g. 83003407

Cedarburg Mill 215 E. Columbia Ave., Cedarburg, 5/18/74, C, 74000115

Cedarburg Woolen Co. Worsted Mill, Mills of Grafton TR, 1350 14th Ave., Grafton, 6/30/83, A, 83003408

Clark, Jonathan, House, 13615 N. Cedarburg Rd., Mequon, 6/02/82, C, 82000692

Concordia Mill, 252 Green Bay Rd., Cedarburg vicinity, 4/26/74, C, 74000116

Covered Bridge, 1 mi. N of Five Corners over Cedar Creek, Cedarburg vicinity, 3/14/73, A, C, 73000092

Dodge, Edward, House, 126 E. Grand Ave., Port Washington, 7/24/75, C, b, 75000074

Grafton Flour Mill, Mills of Grafton TR ,1300 14th Ave., Grafton, 6/30/83, A, C, 83003409

Hamilton Historic District, Hamilton and Green Bay Rds., Cedarburg, 7/01/76, A, C, D, 76000070

Hilgen and Wittenberg Woolen Mill, N70 W6340 Bridge Rd., Cedarburg, 12/22/78, A, C, 78000124

Hoffman House Hotel, 200 W. Grand Ave., Port Washington, 3/01/84, A, 84003773

Old Ozaukee County Courthouse, County Courthouses of Wisconsin TR (AD), 109 W. Main St., Port Washington, 12/12/76, C, 76000071

Payne Hotel, 310 E. Green Bay Ave., Saukville, 3/14/91, A, B. 91000220

Reichert, John, Farmhouse, 14053 N. Wauwatosa Rd., Mequon. 7/01/82, C, 82000693

St. Mary's Roman Catholic Church, 430 N. Johnson St., Port Washington, 12/12/77, A, C, a, 77000042

Stony Hill School, NE of Waubeka on SR 1, Waubeka vicinity, 10/08/76, A, B, 76000072

Washington Avenue Historic District, Roughly bounded by Elm St., Cedar Creek, Hamilton Rd., and Washington Ave., Cedarburg, 1/17/86, A, B, C, 86000218

Wayside House, W61 N430 Washington Ave., Cedarburg, 3/17/82, C, 82000694

PEPIN COUNTY

Durand Free Library, 315 W. 2nd Ave., Durand, 2/20/80, C, 80000173

Pepin County Courthouse and Jail, County Courthouses of Wisconsin TR, 307 W. Madison, Durand, 3/09/82, A, C, 82000695

PIERCE COUNTY

Diamond Bluff Site-Mero Mound Group, Address Restricted, Diamond Bluff vicinity, 8/01/75, D, 75000075

Mero Archeological District (Boundary Increase), Address Restricted, Diamond Bluff, 6/04/92, D, 92000590

North Hall-River Falls State Normal School, University of Wisconsin, River Falls, 4/03/86, A, C, 86000627

Pierce County Courthouse, County Courthouses of Wisconsin TR, 411 W. Main St., Ellsworth, 3/09/82, C, 82000696
Smith, Daniel, House, 331 N. Lake St., Prescott, 3/15/84, B, 84003775
South Hall, River Falls State Normal School, 320 E. Cascade Ave., River Falls, 11/07/76, A, 76000073

POLK COUNTY

Dalles Bluff Site, Address Restricted, St. Croix Falls vicinity, 9/05/81, D, 81000054
Geiger Building-Old Polk County Courthouse, 201 Cascade St., Osceola, 12/02/85, A, 85003030
Heald, Alvah A., House, 202 Sixth Ave., Osceola, 12/02/85, B, C, 85003097
Lamar Community Center, NE of St. Croix Falls, St. Croix Falls vicinity, 3/01/82, A, 82001860
Polk County Courthouse, County Courthouses of Wisconsin TR, Main St. Balsam Lake, 3/09/82, C, 82000697
Seven Pines Lodge, SE of Lewis of WI 35, Lewis vicinity, 12/08/78, B, C, 8000125
Thompson, Thomas Henry, House, 205 N. Adams St., St. Croix Falls, 3/08/84 B, C, 84003777

PORTAGE COUNTY

Folding Furniture Works Building, 1020 First St., Stevens Point, 7/23/93, A, C, 33000666
Fox Theater, 1116-1128 Main St., Stevens Point, 7/26/82, A, B, C, 820006981
Hatch, Seneca W. & Bertha, House, Ernest Flagg Stone Masonry Houses of Milwaukee County TR, 382 N. Prospect Ave., Shorewood, 9/12/85, C, 85002028
Hotel Whiting, 1408 Strongs Ave., Stevens Point, 9/13/90, A, C, 90001457
Jensen, J. L., House, 1103 Brawley St., Stevens Point, 7/28/88, C, 88001151
Kuhl, Christina, House, 1416 Main St., Stevens Point, 1/09/78, C, 78000126

Mathias Mitchell Public Square-Main Street Historic District, Roughly Main St. from Strongs Ave. to Second St., Stevens Point, 8/13/86, A, C, 86001513
McMillan, David, House, 1924 Pine St., Stevens Point, 12/16/74, C, 74000117
Morgan, J. H., House, 1308 Madison Ave., Plover, 10/01/74, C, 74000118
Old Plover Methodist Church, Madison Ave., Plover 3/27/80, C, 80000393
Stevens Point State Normal School, 2100 Main St., Stevens Point, 12/12/76, A, 76000074

PRICE COUNTY

Bloom's Tavern, Store and House, 396 S. Avon Ave., Phillips 3/07/85, A, 85000490
Fifield Town Hall, Pine St. and Flambeau Ave., Fifield, 2/17/78, A, 78000339
Flambeau Paper Company Office Building, 200 N. First Ave., Park Falls, 9/12/85, A, C, 85002331
Johnson, Albin, Log House, E. of Ogema, Ogema vicinity, 1/20/78, A, C, 78000127
Johnson, Matt, Log House, S. of Brantwood off U.S. 8, Brantwood vicinity, 12/08/78, A, C, 78000128
Prentice Co-operative Creamery Company, 700 Main St., Prentice, 9/12/85, A, 85002329
Round Lake Logging Dam, NE of Fifield, Fifield vicinity, 9/17/81, A, C, 81000055

RACINE COUNTY

Badger Building, 610 Main St., Racine, 12/03/80, C, 8000014
Beardsley, Elam, Farmhouse, 5601 Northwest Hwy., Waterford vicinity, 3/01/82, C, 82000639
Collins, John, House, 6409 Nicholson Rd., Caledonia 11/20/74, C, 74000119
Cooley, Eli R., House, 1135 S. Main St., Racine, 4/11/73, C, 73000273
First Presbyterian Church, 716 College Ave., Racine, 3/20/73, C, a, 73000093

Hall, Chauncey, Building, 338-340 Main St., Racine, 10/10/80, C, 80000175

Hall, Chauncey, House, 1235 S. Main St., Racine, 1/02/76, C, 76000075

Hansen House, 1221 N. Main St., Racine, 6/06/79, C, 79000103

Hardy, Thomas P., House, 1319 S. Main St., Racine, 12/03/74, C, 74000120

Hazelo, Franklyn, House, 34108 Oak Knoll Rd., Burlington vicinity, 12/30/74, C, 74000121

Historic Sixth Street Business District, Roughly bounded by Water St. and Fifth St., Main Seventh St., and Grand Ave., Racine, 3/24/88, A, C, a, 88000263

Johnson, Herbert F., House, 33 E. Four Mile Rd., Wind Point vicinity, 1/08/75, C, g, NHL, 75000076

Johnson, Peter, House, 1601 State St., Racine, 1/06/86, C, 86000053

Johnson, S. C., and Son Administration Building and Research Tower, 1525 Howe St., Racine, 12/27/74, C, NHL, 74002275

Jonas, Karel, House, 1337 N. Erie St., Racine, 3/01/82, B, f, 82000700

Kaiser's, 218 6th St., Racine, 11/25/80, C, 80000176

McClurg Building, 245 Main St., Racine, 7/13/77, A, C, 77000044

Memorial Hall, 72 7th St., Racine, 4/10/80, A, C, 80000177

Murray, George, House, 2219 Washington Ave., Racine, 6/06/79, C, a, 70000104

No. 4 Engine House, 1339 Lincoln St., Racine, 0/27/79, A, C, 79000102

Norwegian Buildings at Heg Park, NE of Waterford on Heg Park Rd, Waterford vicinity, 7/17/80, A, B, a, b, f, 80000178

Old Main Street Historic District, Roughly bounded by Second St., Lake Ave., Fifth St., and Wisconsin Ave., Racine, 8/11/87, A, B, C, 87000431

Racine College, 600 21st St., Racine, 12/12/76, A, C, A, 76000076

Racine County Courthouse, 730 Wisconsin Ave., Racine, 7/28/80, A, C, 80000179

Racine Depot, 1402 Liberty St., Racine, 10/10/80, C, 80000180

Racine Elks Club, Lodge No. 252, 601 Lake Ave., Racine, 9/07/84, C, 84003778

Racine Harbor Lighthouse and Life Saving Station, Racine Harbor North Pier, Racine, 3/09/79, A, 75006077

Racine Public Library, 701 S. Main St., Racine, 3/20/81, C, 81090056

Rickeman Grocery Building, 415 6th St., Racine, 3/01/82, C, 82000701

Shoop Building, 215 State St., Racine, 4/26/78, A, C, 78000129

Southside Historic District, Roughly bounded by Lake Michigan, DeKoven Ave., Villa and Eighth Sts., Racine, 10/18/77, C, 77000147

St. Luke's Episcopal Church, Chapel, Guildhall, and Rectory, 614 S. Main St., Racine, 7/27/73, C, a, 79000105

St. Patrick's Roman Catholic Church, 1100 Erie St., Racine, 7/05/79, C, a, 79000106

US Post Office—Racine Main, 603 Main St., Racine, 5/08/85, C, 85000989

United Laymen Bible Student Tabernacle, 924 Center St., Racine, 12/08/83, C, 83004318

Uptown Theater, 1426-1430 Washington Ave., Racine, 3/01/82, C, 82000702

Whitman-Belden House, 108 N. State St., Rochester, 1/17/80, B, C, 80000181

Windpoint Light Station, U.S. Coast Guard Lighthouses and Light Stations on the Great Lakes TR, Windridge Dr. at Lake Michigan, Racine, 7/19/84, A, C, 84003780

Young Men's Christian Association Building, 314-320 6th St., Racine, 3/01/82, C, 82000703

RICHLAND COUNTY

A. D. German Warehouse, 316 S. Church St., Richland Center, 12/31/74, C, 74000122

Court Street Commercial Historic District, Roughly bounded by Mill Church, Haseltine, and Main Sts., Richland Center, 11/13/89, A, C, 89001955

Fiedler, Henry, House, Putnam and Washington Sts., Muscoda vicinity, 12/29/86, C, 86003515

Richland Center City Auditorium, 182 N. Central Ave., Richland Center, 8/18/80, A, 80000182

ROCK COUNTY

Alexander, John, Wheat Warehouse, Grout Buildings in Milton TR, 304 S. Janesville St., Milton, 9/13/78, A, B, C, 78003383

Allen, Abram, House, Grout Buildings in Milton TR, 205 E. Madison Ave., Milton, 9/13/78, C, 78003386

Armory, The, 10 S. High St., Janesville, 11/21/78, A, 78000130

Bartlett Memorial Historical Museum, 2149 St. Lawrence Ave., Beloit, 4/11/77, A, C, 77000048

Beloit Water Tower, Beloit MRA, 1005 Pleasant St., Beloit, 1/07/83, A, C, 83003410

Blodgett, Selvy, House, 417 Bluff St., Beloit, 5/23/80, A, C, 80000183

Bluff Street Historic District, Beloit MRA, Roughly both sides of Bluff St. from Shirland Ave, to Merrill St., Beloit, 1/07/83, A, C, 83003411

Brasstown Cottage, Beloit MRA, 1701 Colby Rd., Beloit, 3/04/83, C, b, 83003412

Church of St. Thomas the Apostle, Beloit MRA, 822 E. Grand Ave., Beloit, 1/07/83, C, a, 83003413

Citizens Bank, Clinton MRA, Front & Allen Sts., Clinton, 8/01/85, C, 85001661

City of Beloit Waterworks and Pump Station, 1005 Pleasant St., Beloit, 9/13/90, A, 90001460

Clark-Brown House, Cobblestone Buildings of Rock County TR, 3457 Riverside Dr., Beloit, 9/13/85, C, 85002126

Clinton Village Hall, Clinton MRA, 301 Cross St., Clinton, 8/01/85, C, 85001660

Clinton Water Tower, Water Works Structures of Rock County-19th Century TR, High St., Clinton, 3/07/85, A, 85000493

Conrad Cottages Historic District, 235-330 Milton Ave., Janesville, 3/11/93, C, 93000157

Cooksville Cheese Factory, Cooksville MRA, SR 1, Evansville vicinity, 9/17/80, A, 80000395

Cooksville Historic District, Both sides of streets bordering the Public Sq. and Rock St., Cooksville, 10/25/73, A, C, 73000254

Cooksville Mill and Mill Pond Site, Cooksville MRA, SR 1, Evansville, 9/17/80, A, D, 80000394

Cooper-Gillies House, Cooksville MRA, SR 1, Evansville vicinity, 9/17/80, C, 80000397

Court Street Methodist Church, 36 S. Main St., Janesville, 11/17/77 A, C, a, 77000045

Courthouse Hill Historic District, Roughly bounded by E. Milwaukee, St., Garfield and Oakland Aves., S. Main St., and E. Court St. and Milton Ave., Janesville, 1/17/86, B, C, 86000205

Crist, J, W., House, Beloit MRA, 2601 Afton Rd., Beloit, 1/07/83, C, 83003414

Crosby Block, Clinton MRA, 102 Allen St., Clinton, 8/01/85, C, 85001658

Culton, Charles L., House, 708 Washington St., Edgerton, 8/22/77, A, C, 77000046

De Jean House, Grout Buildings in Milton TR, 27 Third St., Milton, 9/13/78, C, 78003388

DeLong, Homer B., House, Clinton MRA, 500 Milwaukee Rd., Clinton, 8/01/85, C, 85001659

Dean, Erastus, Farmstead, E. of Janesville on U.S. 14, Janesville vicinity, 12/04/78, B, b, 78000131

Dougan Round Barn, Centric Barns in Rock County TR, 444 West Colley Rd., Beloit, 6/04/79, A, C, 79000108

Dow, J. B., House and Carpenter Douglas Barn, Beloit MRA, Cobblestone Buildings of Rock County TR (AD), 910 Board St., Beloit, 1/07/83, C, 83003415

Dow, John T., House, Cooksville MRA, SR 1, Evansville vicinity, 9/17/80, B, C, 80000396

Eager Free Public Library, 39 W. Main St., Evansville, 8/16/77, C, 77000047

East Milwaukee Street Historic District, N. Parker Dr. and E. Milwaukee St., Janesville, 2/08/80,A, C, 80000184

Edgerton Public Grade Schools, 116 N. Swift St., Edgerton, 1/14/87, A, C, 86003568

Emerson Hall, Beloit College campus, Beloit, 11/20/79, A, C, 79000109

Evansville Historic District, Roughly bounded by Allens Creek, Liberty, 4th and Garfield Sts., Evansville, 11/16/78, A, C, 78000132

Fairbanks Flats, Beloit MRA, 205, 215 Birch Ave. and 206, 216 Carpenter Ave., Beloit, 1/07/83,A, 83003416

First Congregational Church, 801 Bushnell St., Beloit, 1/23/75, C, a, 75000078

Footville Condensery, Footville MRA, Beloit St., Footville, 9/07/82, A, C, 82000704

Footville State Bank, Footville MRA, 158 Depot St., Footville, 5/07/82, A, C, 82000705

Fredendall Block, 33-39 S. Main St., Janesville, 3/25/82, C, 82000706

Fulton Congregational Church, Fulton St., Fulton, 6/07/76, A, C, a, 76000077

Gempeler Round Barn, Centric Barns in Rock County TR, SW of Orfordville, Orfordville vicinity, 6/04/79, A, C, 70000110

Gifford House, Grout Buildings in Milton TR, 308 Vernal, Milton, 9/13/78, C, 781103387

Gilley-Tofsland Octagonal Barn, Centric Barns in Rock County TR, NW of Edgerton, Edgerton vicinity, 6/04/79, A, C, 79000111

Goodrich Blacksmith Shop, Grout Buildings in Milton TR, 28 S. Janesville St., Milton, 9/13/78, B, C, 78003382

Goodrich House and Log Cabin, Grout Buildings in Milton TR (AD), 18 S. Janesville St., Milton, 2/01/72, A, B, C, 72000065

Goodrich-Buten House, Grout Buildings in Milton TR, 528 E. Madison St., Milton, 9/13/78, B, C, 78003385

Hanchett Block, 307 State St., Beloit, 3/20/80, A, 80000185

How-Beckman Mill, Address Restricted, Beloit vicinity, 9/07/77, A, g, NHL, 77000049

Janesville Cotton Mill, 220 N. Franklin St., Janesville, 7/16/80, A, 80000186

Janesville Public Library, 64 S, Main St., Janesville, 7/01/81, A, C, 81000057

Janesville Pumping Station, Water Works Structures of Rock County-19th Century TR, 500 Blk. River St., Janesville, 4/07/85, A, 85000494

Jones, Samuel S., Cobblestone House, Cobblestone Buildings of Rock County TR (AD), E. of Clinton on Milwaukee Rd., Clinton vicinity, 2/23/78, C, 78000133

Kinney Farmstead-Tay-e-he-Dah Site, Address Restricted, Edgerton vicinity, 2/17/78, A, C, D, 78000134

LaPrairie Grange Hall No. 79, SE of Janesville on Town Hall Rd., Janesville vicinity, 4/11/77, A, 77000050

Lappin-Hayes Block, 20 E. Milwaukee St., Janesville, 11/07/76, A, C, 76000224

Lathrop-Munn Cobblestone House, Cobblestone Buildings of Rock County TR (AD), 524 Bluff St., Beloit, 8/22/77, C, 77000051

Leedle Mill Truss Bridge, Cooksville MRA, SR 1, Evansville, 9/17/80, A, 80000398

Look West Historic District, Roughly bounded by Mineral Point Ave., N. Franklin and Race Sts., Laurel Ave., and N. Chatham St., Janesville, 3/26/87, A, C, 87000506

Look West Historic District (Boundary Increase), Roughly bounded by Laurel Ave, and N. Madison. W. Court and N. Palm Sts., Janesville, 12/10/93, C, 93001429

Lovejoy and Merrill-Nowlan Houses, 220 and 202 St., Lawrence Ave., Janesville, 1/21/81, A, C, 80000187

McEwan, Peter, Warehouse, Grout Buildings in Milton TR, 711 E. High St., Milton, 9/13/78, C, 78003384

Merrill Avenue Historic District, 103, 107, 111, 115 Merrill Ave., Beloit, 2/19/93, A, C, 93000028

Miller House, Cooksville MRA, SR 1, Evansville vicinity, 9/17/80, C, 80000399

Milton College Historic District, College St., Milton, 5/27/80, A, B, C, 80000188

Moran's Saloon, Beloit MRA, 312 Slate St., Beloit, 1/07/83, C, 83003417

Mouth of the Yahara Archeological District, Address Restricted, Fulton vicinity, 4/28/75, D, c, 75000079

Murray-George House, Cobblestone Buildings of Rock County TR, SR P, Beloit, 9/13/85, C, 85002125

Myers, Peter, Pork Packing Plant and Willard Coleman Building, 117-123 N. Main St., Janesville, 7/07/83, A, C, 83003418

Myers-Newhoff House, 121 N. Parker Dr., Janesville, 5/18/79, A, C, 79000277

Near East Side Historic District, Beloit MRA, Roughly bounded by Pleasant, Clary Sts., Wisconsin and E. Grand Aves., Beloit, 1/07/83, A, C, 83003419

Neese, Elbert, House, Beloit MRA, 1302 Bushnell St., Beloit, 1/07/83, B, C, 83003420

North Main Street Historic District, N. Main St. and N. Parker Dr., Janesville, 2/08/80, A, C, 80000189

Nye, Clark, House, Beloit MRA, 2501 Spring Creek Rd., Beloit, 1/07/83, C, 83003422

Old Fourth Ward Historic District, Roughly bounded by Washington St., Center Ave. Court St., Franklin St., and Monterey Park, Janesville, 5/30/90, A, C, 90000789

Orfordville Depot, Beloit St., Orfordville, 10/13/88, A, C, b, 88002004

Owen, William J., Store, Footville MRA, 220 Depot St., Footville, 5/07/82, A, C, b, 82000707

Pangborn, J. L., House, Clinton MRA, 300 Allen St., Clinton, 8/01/85, C, 85001664

Payne-Craig House, 2200 W. Memorial Dr., Janesville, 7/02/87, B, C, 87000990

Pearsons Hall of Science, Beloit College campus, Beloit, 6/30/80, A, C, 80000190

Porter, J. K., Farmstead, Cooksville MRA, SR 1, Evansville vicinity, 9/17/80, A, b, 80000400

Prospect Hill Historic District, Roughly bounded by Eisenhower, Prospect and Atwood Aves., Milwaukee St., Parker Dr. and Centerway, Janesville, 11/05/92, C, 92001558

Randall, Brewster, House, 1412 Ruger Ave., Janesville, 3/01/84, C, 84003782

Rasey House, 517 Prospect St., Beloit, 12/27/74, A, C, 74000123

Rau, Charles, House, Beloit MRA, 757 Euclid Ave., Beloit, 1/07/83, C, 83003423

Richardson Grout House, Cooksville MRA, SR 1, Evansville vicinity, 9/17/80, C, 80000102

Richardson, Hamilton, House, 429 Prospect Ave., Janesville, 7/17/78, B, C, 78000135

Richardson-Brinkman Cobblestone House, Cobblestone Buildings of Rock County TR (AD), 607 W. Milwaukee Rd., Clinton, 7/28/77, C, 77000052

Rindfleisch Building, Beloit MRA, 512 E. Grand Ave., Beloit, 1/07/83, C, 83003424

Risum Round Barn, Centric Barns in Rock County TR, SW of Orfordville, Orfordville vicinity, 6/04/79, A, C, 79000112

Shopiere Congregational Church, Buss Rd., near Shopiere Rd., Shopiere vicinity, 8/13/76, A, C, a, 76000078

Slaymaker, Stephen, House, Beloit MRA, 348 Euclid Ave., Beloit, 1/07/83, C, 83003425

Smiley, Samuel, House, SE of Orfordville on WI 213. Orfordville vicinity, 10/21/82, C, 82001849

Smith, John, House, Clinton MRA, 312 Pleasant St., Clinton, 8/01/85, C, 85001663

South Main Street Historic District, Roughly S. Main St. from Milwaukee St. to Rock Co, Courthouse grounds and E. Court St. from Parker Dr. to Rock R., Janesville, 6/01/90, A, C, 90000820

St. Paul's Episcopal Church, 212 W. Grand Ave., Beloit, 4/04/78, C, A, 78000136

Stark-Clint House, Cobblestone Buildings of Rock County TR, Creek Rd., Tiffany, 9/13/85, C, 85002124

Stebbins, Harrison, House, Cooksville MRA, SR 1, Evansville vicinity, 9/17/80, B, C, 80000401

Strang, Soloman J., House, Footville MRA, 231 North Gilbert, Footville, 5/07/82, C, 82000708

Strong Building, Beloit MRA, 400-408 E. Grand Ave., Beloit, 1/07/83, C, 83003426

Tallman House, 440 N. Jackson St., Janesville, 10/15/70, B, C, 70000085

Taylor, A. E., House, Clinton MRA, 318 Durand St., Clinton, 8/01/85, C, 85001662

Turtleville Iron Bridge, N of Beloit on Lathers Rd., Beloit vicinity, 9/15/77, A, C, 77000053

West Luther Valley Lutheran Church, SW of Orfordville on W. Church Rd., Orfordville vicinity, 5/27/80, A, B, a, 80000191

West Milwaukee Street Historic District, Roughly bounded by Wall, River, Court, and Academy Sts., Janesville, 5/17/90, A, C, 90000790

Willard, Frances, Schoolhouse, Craig Ave., Janesville, 10/05/77, B, b, 77000054

Wyman-Rye Farmstead, N of Clinton on Wyman-Rye Dr., Clinton vicinity, 11/07/77, A, C, 77000055

Yates, Florence, House, Beloit MRA, 1614 Emerson St., Beloit, 1/07/83, C, 83003427

RUSK COUNTY

Flambeau Mission Church, W. of Ladysmith, Ladysmith vicinity, 8/07/79, A, C, a, 79000113

State Bank of Ladysmith, 102 W. 2nd St., Ladysmith, 1/17/80, A, C, 80000192

SAUK COUNTY

Baraboo Public Library, 230 4th Ave., Baraboo, 9/14/81, C, 81000058

Chicago and North Western Depot, Reedsburg MRA, Railroad St., Reedsburg, 12/26/84, A, C, 84000639

City Hotel, Reedsburg MRA, 125 Main St., Reedsburg, 12/26/84, C, 84000642

Clark, William, House, 320 Walnut St., Baraboo, 4/08/80, C, 80000193

Derleth, August W., House, S10431a Lueders Rd., Sauk City vicinity, 4/30/91, B, g, 91000468

Durst-Bloedau Site, N. of Leland, Leland vicinity, 12/19/78, D; 78000137

Freethinkers Hall, 309 Polk St., Sauk City, 3/31/88, A, B, C, a, 88000237

Hackett, Edward M., House, Reedsburg MRA, 612 E. Main St., Reedsburg, 12/26/84, C, 81000644

Harris, Abner L., House, Reedsburg MRA, 226 N. Pine St., Reedsburg, 12/26/84, B, C, 840000649

Honey Creek Swiss Rural Historic District, SE of Prairie du Sac, Prairie du Sac vicinity, 4/06/90, A, C, d, 89000484

Hulbun Creek Garden Beds, Address Restricted, Delton, 8/08/91, D, 91000958

Leopold, Aldo, Shack, Central Wisconsin, Columbus vicinity, 7/14/78, A, B, g, 78000082

Main Street Commercial Historic District, Reedsburg MRA, Roughly bounded by N. Park, S. Park, N. Walnut, and S. Walnut Sts. on Main, Reedsburg, 12/26/84, A, C, 84000654

Man Mound, E of Baraboo off WI 33, Baraboo vicinity, 11/30/78, D, c, 78000138

Manchester Street Bridge, Ochsner Park, Baraboo, 10/13/88, C, b, 88002005

Our Lady of Loretto Roman Catholic Church and Cemetery, Co. Hwy. C, 1 mi. W. of Denzer, Honey Creek, 3/09/90, C, a, d, 90000378

Park Street Historic District, Reedsburg MRA, On N. Park St. roughly bounded by 6th, Locust, N. Pine and Main Sts., Reedsburg, 12/26/84, C, 84000656

Peterson, Seth, Cottage, Dell Ave., Lake Delton vicinity, 11/09/81, C, g, 81000059

Raddatz Rockshelter, Address Restricted, Leland vicinity, 12/18/78, D, 78000139

Reedsburg Brewery, Reedsburg MRA, 401 N. Walnut St., Reedsburg, 12/26/84, A, C, 84000661

Reedsburg Woolen Mill Office, Reedsburg MRA, 26 Main St., Reedsburg, 12/26/84, A, 84000664

Riggert, William, House, Reedsburg MRA, 547 S. Park St., Reedsburg, 12/26/84, C, 84000666

Ringling Brothers Circus Headquarters, Bounded roughly by Water, Brian, Lynn, and East Sts., Baraboo, 8/04/69, A, NHL, 69000032

Ringling, Al, Theatre, 136 4th Ave., Baraboo, 5/17/76, B, C, 76000202

Ringling, Albrecht C., House, 623 Broadway, Baraboo, 5/17/76, B, C, 76000079

Salem Evangelical Church, Jct. of CR PF and Church Rd., Plain vicinity, 3129/88, A, C, a, 86003576

Sauk City High School, 713 Madison St., Sauk City, 2123/89, A, C, 89000071

Sauk County Courthouse, County Courthouses of Wisconsin TR, 515 Oak St., Baraboo, 3/09/82, C, 82000711

Seven Gables, 215 6th St., Baraboo, 1/20/78, C, 78000140

Stolte, William, Jr., House, Reedsburg MRA, 432 S. Walnut St., Reedsburg, 12126/84, C, 84000667

Stolte, William, Sr., House, Reedsburg MRA, 444 S. Walnut St., Reedsburg, 12/26/84, C, 84000670

Tripp Memorial Library and Hall, 565 Water St., Prairie du Sac, 9/14/81, B, 81000060

Tuttle, A. G., Estate, N. Elizabeth St., Baraboo, 11/06/80, B, C, 80000194

SAWYER COUNTY

Hall-Raynor Stopping Place, N. of Ojibwa on WI G, Ojibwa vicinity, 8/14/79, A, C, 79000115

North Wisconsin Lumber Company Office, Florida Ave., Hayward, 5107/80, A, B, 80000403

Ojibwa Courier Press Building, E of Raddison at 110 Ojibwa Mall, Raddison vicinity, 3/01/82, A, B, 82000712

SHAWANO COUNTY

Lutheran Indian Mission, NE of Gresham on WI G, Gresham vicinity, 10/22/80, A, a, 80000195

SHEBOYGAN COUNTY

American Club, High St., Kohler, 5/22/78, A, 78000141

Cole Historic District, 501 and 517 Monroe St. and 504, 508, and 516-518 Water St., Sheboygan Falls, 12/01/88, A, B, b, 58002606

Downtown Historic District, Roughly bounded by Broadway, Monroe, Pine, and Buffalo Sts., and the Sheboygan River, Sheboygan Fall, 12/27/84, A, C, 84000691

Franklin Feed Mill, 19th Century Grist and Flouring Mills of Sheboygan County TR, Franklin Rd., Franklin, 4/11/85, A, 85000792

Friendship House, 721 Ontario Ave., Sheboygan, 7/10/74, A, C, 74000331

Glenbeulah Mill/Grist Mill, 19th Century Grist and Flouring Mills of Sheboygan County TR, Gardner St., Glenbeulah, 12/27/81, A, 84000678

Gooseville Mill/Grist Mill, 19th Century Grist and Flouring Mills of Sheboygan County TR, Silver Creek-Cascade Rd., Adell, 12/27/84, A, 81000673

Hotel Laack, 52 Stafford St., Plymouth, 12/02/85, A, C, 85003095

Huson, Henry H., House and Water Tower, 408 Collins St., Plymouth, 11/28/80, B, C, 80000196

Jung Carriage Factory, 829-835 Pennsylvania Ave., Sheboygan, 7/10/74, A, C, 74000125

Jung Shoe Manufacturing Company Factory, 620 S. Eighth St., Sheboygan, 1/22/92, C, 91001993

Kletzien Mound Group (47SB61), Address Restricted, Sheboygan vicinity, 7/23/81, D, 81000061

Kohler, John Michael, House, 608 New York Ave., Sheboygan, 11/30/82, A, B, C, 82001850

Mission House Historic District, County Trunk M, Town Herman, 12/20/84, A, C, a, 84001221

Onion River Flouring Mill/Grist Mill, 19th Century Grist and Flouring Mills of Sheboygan County TR, Hwy. 57, Waldo, 12/27/84, A, 84000679

Riverbend, Lower Falls Rd., Kohler, 12/04/80, B, C, 80000197

Robinson, Charles, House, Center St., Old Wade House State Park, Greenbush, 12/20/84, B, C, 84001125

Robinson-Herrling Sawmill, Old Wade House State Park, Greenbush, 12/27/84, D, 84000685

Sheboygan County Courthouse, County Courthouses of Wisconsin TR, 615 N. 6th St., Sheboygan, 3/12/82, A, C, g, 82000713

St. Patrick's Roman Catholic Church, WI 1, Adell vicinity, 9/08/83, C, a, 83003428

Taylor David, House, 3110 Erie Ave., Sheboygan, 1/02/76, B, 76000080

Third Ward School, 1208 S. 8th St., Sheboygan, 9/03/81, A, C, 81000062

Thomas, I. C., Drug Store, 632 N. 8th St., Sheboygan, 7/10/74, A, C, 74000126

Villa Laun, 402 Lake Side Park Dr., Elkhart Lake, 1/28/82, C, 82000714

Villa Von Baumbach, 754 Elkhart Lake Dr., Elkhart Lake, 11/30/82, C, b, 82001851

Wade, Sylvanus, House, At jct. of WI 23 and Kettle Maraine Dr. in Old Wade House State Park, Greenbush, 10/26/71, A, C, 71000041

Windway, CTH Y, N of CTH 0, Sheboygan, 7/28/88, C, 88001149

ST. CROIX COUNTY

Bell, Marcus Sears, Farm, New Richmond MRA, 1100 Heritage Dr., New Richmond, 5/31/88, C, b, 88000614

Bernd, William J., House, New Richmond MRA, 210 Second St., E, New Richmond, 5/31/88, C, 88000615

Bernd, William A., House, New Richmond MRA, 143 Arch Ave., N, New Richmond, 5/31/88, C, 88000616

Chicago, St. Paul, Minneapolis and Omaha Railroad Car Shop Historic District, Hudson and North Hudson MRA, Roughly bounded by Gallahad Rd., Sommer, 4th and St. Croix Sts., North Hudson, 10/04/84, A, C, 84000072

Darling, Frederick L., House, Hudson and North Hudson MRA, 617 3rd St., Hudson, 10/114/84, C, 84000060

Dwelley, William, House, Hudson and North Hudson MRA, 1002 4th St., Hudson, 10/04/84, C, 84000061

Epley, Dr. Frank W., Office, New Richmond MRA, 137 Third St., E, New Richmond, 5/31/88, B, 88000617

First English Lutheran Church, New Richmond MRA, 354 Third St., N., New Richmond, 5/31/88, A, a, 88000618

Glover, Ezra, Jr., House, New Richmond MRA, 415 Second St., E, New Richmond, 5/31/88, A, C, 88000619

Hudson Public Library, Hudson and North Hudson MRA, 304 Locust St., Hudson, 10/04/84, A, C, 81000062

Humphrey, Herman L., House, Hudson and North Hudson MRA, 803 Orange St., Hudson, 10/04/84, B, C, 84000063

Johnson, August, House, Hudson and North Hudson MRA, 427 St. Croix St., Hudson, 10/01/14, C, 84000064

Johnson, Dr. Samuel C., House, Hudson and North Hudson MRA, 405 Locust St., Hudson, 10/04/84, B, C, 84000065

Kell, William H., House, New Richmond MRA, 215 Green Ave., S, New Richmond, 5/31/88, C, 88000620

Lewis Farmhouse, Farm Dr., Boardman vicinity, 3/19/82, C, 82000709

Lewis-Williams House, Hudson and North Hudson MRA, 101 3rd St., Hudson, 1/02/85, B, C, 85000050

Merritt, Samuel T., House, Hudson and North Hudson MRA, 904 7th St., Hudson, 10/04/84, B, 84000066

Mielke, Joseph, House, New Richmond MRA, 326 Second St., W. New Richmond, 5/31/88, C, 88000621

Moffat, John S., House, 1004 3rd St., Hudson, 7/18/74, C, 74000124

New Richmond News Building, New Richmond MRA, 145 Second St., W, New Richmond, 5/31/88, A, 88000625

New Richmond Roller Mills Co., New Richmond MRA, 201 Knowles Ave., N. New Richmond, 5/31/88, A, 88000622

New Richmond West Side Historic District, New Richmond MRA, Roughly bounded by Willow River, Minnesota Ave., W. Second St., S. Washington Ave., New Richmond, 5/31/88, A, B, C, 88000626

Opera Hall Block, 516 2nd St., Hudson, 3/07/79, A, 79000114

Phipps, William H., House, 1005 Third St., Hudson, 6/18/87, B, C, 87000991

Second Street Commercial District, Hudson and North Hudson MRA, Roughly 1st, 2nd, Walnut, and Locust Sts., Hudson, 10/04/84, A, C, 84000067

Historic Places

Sixth Street Historic District, Hudson and North Hudson MRA, Roughly 6th St. between Myrtle and Vine Sts., Hudson, 10/04/84, C, 84000060

Soo Line Depot, New Richmond MRA, 120 High St., New Richmond, 5/31/88, A, 85000623

Soo Line High Bridge, Washington County MRA (AD), Address Restricted, Somerset vicinity, 8/22/77, A, C, NPS, 77000056

St. Croix County Courthouse, County Courthouses of Wisconsin TR, 904 3rd St., Hudson, 3/09/82, C, 82000710

Thompson, Erick J., House, New Richmond MRA, 350 Second St., W, New Richmond, 5/31/88, C, 88000624

Williams, T. E., Block, Hudson and North Hudson MRA, 321 2nd St., Hudson, 10/04/84, C, 84000070

TAYLOR COUNTY

Benn, J. W., Building, 202-204 S. Main St., Medford, 12/22/83, C, 83004320

Big Indian Farms, Address Restricted, Perkinstown vicinity, 7/11/88, D, 87001827

Jump River Town Hall, S. of WI 73, Jump River, 3/28/74, C, 74000127

Medford Free Public Library, Public Library Facilities of Wisconsin MPS, 104 E. Perkins St., Medford, 4/01/93, A, C, 93000259

Mondeaux Dam Recreation Area, Roughly bounded by Mondeaux River and Forest Rd., Westboro vicinity, 8/21/84, A, C, 84003784

Taylor County Courthouse, 224 S. 2nd, Courthouse Sq., Medford, 5/14/80, A, C, 80000198

TREMPEALEAU COUNTY

Arnold, Capt. Alexander A., Farm, N. of Galesville off U.S. 53, Galesville vicinity, 3/21/78, B, C, 78000142

Bartlett Blacksmith Shop-Scandinavian Hotel, Galesville MRA, 218 E. Mill Rd., Galesville, 9/18/84, C, 84003786

Bohrnstedt, John, House, Galesville MRA, 830 Clark St., Galesville, 9/18/84, C, 84003788

Cance, John, F., House, Galesville MRA, 807 W. Ridge Ave., Galesville, 9/18/84, B, C, 84003790

Coman House, Trempealeau MRA, 581 3rd St., Trempealeau, 11/15/84, C, 84000747

Downtown Historic District, Galesville MRA, Roughly Gale Ave., Main and Davis Sts., Galesville, 9/18/84, A, C, 84003791

Jensen, Tollef, House, Galesville MRA, 806 W. Gale Ave., Galesville, 9/18/84, C, 84003793

Main Street Historic District, Trempealeau MRA, Roughly Main St. between 1st and 3rd Sts., Trempealeau, 11/15/84, A, C, 84000763

Melchoir Hotel and Brewery Ruins, Trempealeau MRA, Address Restricted, Trempealeau vicinity, 11/15/84, A, D, 84000769

Ridge Avenue Historic District, Galesville MRA, Roughly Ridge Ave. from 4th to 6th Sts., Galesville, 9/18/84, C, 84003792

Schwert Mound Group, Trempealeau vicinity, 11/01/74, D, 74000128

Trempealeau Platform Mounds Site, Address Restricted, Trempealeau, 12/23/91, D, c, 91001822

VERNON COUNTY

B. Lawrence Site I, Address Restricted, Rockton vicinity, 6/30/75, B, 75000080

Cade Archeological District, Address Restricted, Newton vicinity, 11/03/88, D, 88002176

Goose Island Archeological Site Ve-502, Address Restricted, Stoddard vicinity, 7/17/80, B, 80000199

Hanson Petroglyphs, Viola vicinity, 12/31/74, D, 74000129

Hay Valley Archeological District, Ontario vicinity, 12/31/74, D, 74000130

Larson Cave, Address Restricted, Westby vicinity, 1/06/88, A, B, 87002240

Markee Site, Address Restricted, Rockton vicinity, 8/22/75, D, 75000081

Norwegian Evangelic Lutheran Church and Cemetery, Coon Prairie and E. Coon Prairie Rds., Westby vicinity, 7/14/86, C, a, d, 86001719

Rockton Archeological District, Ontario vicinity, 12/31/74, D, 74000131

Skumsrud, Nils, House, SE of jct. of SR 162 and U.S. 14/61, Coon Valley vicinity, 7/11/90, A, C, 90000571

Vernon County Courthouse, N. Dunlap Ave., Viroqua, 1/08/80, A, C, 80000200

Viola Rockshelter (47VE640), Address Restricted, Kickapoo Center vicinity, 12/10/87, D, 87002081

VILAS COUNTY

Strawberry Island Site, Address Restricted, Lac du Flambeau vicinity, 3/08/78, A, D, 78000340

WALWORTH COUNTY

Allyn, A, H., House, 511 E. Walworth Ave., Walworth, 9/05/85, C, 85001950

Bonnie Brae, 78 Snake Rd., Linn, 4/03/86, B, C, 86900614

Buena Vista House, 2090 Church St., East Troy, 1/18/78, C, 78000143

Davidson Hall, 550 S. Shore Dr., Lake Geneva, 7/02/87, B, C, 87000443

Douglass-Stevenson House, Main and Mill Sts., Fontana, 4/03/86, B, C, 86000615

East Wing (Old Main), University of Wisconsin, Whitewater, 12/13/84, A, C, 84000609

Elderkin, Edward, House, 127 S. Lincoln St., Elkhorn, 5/03/74, C, 74000132

Grace and Pearl Historic District, Roughly bounded by Pearl, Park, Dougall, Grace and Martin Sts., Sharon, 8/05/93, C, 93000810

Halverson Log Cabin, University of Wisconsin–Whitewater Campus, Whitewater, 1/08/85, A, b, 85000070

Heart Prairie Lutheran Church, S. of Whitewater on Town Line Rd., Whitewater vicinity, 12/27/74, A, C, a, 74000133

Johnson, A. P., House, 3455 S. Shore Dr., Delavan, 7/09/82, C, 82000715

Jones, Fred B., Estate, 3335 S. Shore Dr., Delavan Lake vicinity, 12/27/74, C, 74000134

Loomis, Horace, House, 2.4 mi. S. of East Troy, East Troy vicinity, 2/03/74, C, 74000357

Main Street Historic District, Roughly W. Main St./US 12 from Prairie St. to Fremont St. and Church St. from Forest Ave. to W. Main St., Whitewater, 12/21/89, A, C, 89002116

Maples Mound Group, Late Woodland Stage in Archeological Region 8 MPS, Address restricted, Whitewater, 6/07/91, B, 91000671

Metropolitan Block, 772 Main St., Lake Geneva, 4/19/90, C, 90000559

Meyerhofer Cobblestone House, 15 of lake Geneva on Townline Rd., Lake Geneva vicinity, 12/08/80, C, 80000202

Mile Long Site, Address Restricted, Delavan vicinity, 6/23/77, B, 77000057

Phoenix Hall–Wisconsin Institute for the Education of the Deaf and Dumb, 309 W. Walworth St., Delavan, 3/19/87, A, 87000492

Redwood Cottage, 327 Wrigley Dr., lake Geneva, 9/07/84, A, C, 84003796

Reynolds-Weed House, 12 N. Church St., Elkhorn, 3/31/83., C, 83003429

Riviera, The, 810 Wrigley Dr., Lake Geneva, 4/03/86, A, C, 86000616

Smith and Meadows Store Buildings, 2888-2890 Main St., East Troy, 3/12/93, C, 93000067

Smith, T. C., House, 865 Main St., Lake Geneva, 11/30/82, A, B, C, 82001852

Stowell, Israel, Temperance House, 61-65 E. Walworth Ave., Delavan, 8/11/78, A, 78000145

Strang, James Jesse, House, W. of Burlington on WI 11, Burlington vicinity, 1/24/74, B, C, 74000135

Webster, Joseph P., House, 9 E. Rockwell St., Elkhorn, 2/23/72, B, 72000066

Younglands, 880 Lake Shore Dr., Lake Geneva, 9/18/79, B, C, 70000116

WASHBURN COUNTY

Polson, Mrs. Richard, House, N. of Spooner, Spooner vicinity, 2/08/84, C, 84003798

Siegner, George V., House, 513 Dale St., Spooner, 3/01/82, B, C, 82000716

WASHINGTON COUNTY

Barton Historic District, Roughly bounded by Harrison and Jefferson Sts., Barton Ave., Salisbury Rd., Monroe St. and the Milwaukee R., West Bend, 3/05/92, A, C, a, 92000109

Christ Evangelical Church, W188 N12808 Fond du Lac Avenue, Germantown vicinity, 11/09/83, A, C, 83004324

Frisby, Leander F., House, 304 S. Main St., West Bend, 6/19/85, B, C, 85001363

Gadow's Mill, 1784 Barton Ave., West Bend, 12/24/74, A, 74000136

Holy Hill, 1525 Cannel Rd., Erin, 3/12/92, A, C, a, d, 92000139

Kissel's Addition Historic District, Kissel, Louis, & Sons of Hartford TR, Rural St. and W. Root Ave., Hartford, 11/03/88, A, 85002071

Kissel's Wheelock Addition Historic District, Kissel, Louis, & Sons of Hartford TR, Roughly bounded by Church St., Wheelock and Linden Aves., Branch St., and Teddy Ave., Hartford, 11/03188, A, 88002072

Kissel, George A., House, Kissel, Louis, & Sons of Hartford TR, 215 E. Sumner, Hartford, 11/03/88, B, 88002075

Kissel, Louis, House, Kissel, Louis, & Sons of Hartford TR, 407 E. Sumner, Hartford, 11/03/88, B, 88002077

Kissel, William L., House, Kissel, Louis, & Sons of Hartford TR, 67 South St., Hartford, 11/03/88, B, 88002073

Lizard Mound State Park, NE of West Bend, West Bend vicinity, 10/15/70, D, 70000038

Ritger Wagonmaking and Blacksmith Shop, 1928 WI 175, Hartford vicinity, 6/01/82, A, C, 82000717

Schunk, Jacob, Farmhouse, Donges Bay Rd., Germantown vicinity, 12/08/83, C, 83004325

St. Augustine Catholic Church and Cemetery, Co. Hwy. Y 3 mi. S of jct. of Co. Hwy. Y and SR 33, Trenton, 5/03/90, C, a, d, 90000638

St. John of God Roman Catholic Church, Convent, and School, E of Kewaskum at 1488 Highland Dr., Kewaskum vicinity, 8/09/79, A, C, a, 79000117

St. Peter's Church, 1010 Newark Dr., West Bend vicinity, 6/30/83, C, a, 83003431

Washington County Courthouse and Jail, County Courthouses of Wisconsin TR, 320 S. 5th Ave., West Bend, 3/09/82, C, 82000718

WAUKESHA COUNTY

Andrews, Sewall, House, 103 Main St., Mukwonago, 7/07/81, B, C, 81000063

Arcadian Bottling Works, Waukesha MRA, 900 N. Hartwell Ave., Waukesha, 10/28/83, A, 83004326

Arlington Apartments, Waukesha MRA, 309 Arlington St., Waukesha, 1/21/87, C, 86003651

Baer, Albert R., House, Menomonee Falls MRA, W166 N8990 Grand Ave., Menomonee Falls, 9/21/88, C, 88001645

Bailie, Ralph C., House, Hartland MRA, 530 North Ave., Hartland, 12/05/86, C, 86003407

Bank of Hartland, Hartland MRA, 1121E. Capitol Dr., Hartland, 4/21/88, C, 86003415

Barfoth-Blood Mound Group (47WK63), Address Restricted, Mukwonago vicinity, 9/02/82, D, d, 82000720

Barnes, Andrew, House, Menomonee Falls MRA, N89 W16840 Appleton Ave., Menomonee Falls, 9/21/88, C, 88001652

Beaumont Hop House, Address Restricted, Hartland vicinity, 11/23/77, A, 77000058

Big Bend Mound Group No. 2, S. of Big Bend, Big Bend vicinity, 12/19/78, D, 78000146

Bishopstead, 153 W. Oakwood Dr., Delafield, 3/01/84, B, 84003803

Blair, Sen. William, House, Waukesha MRA, 434 Madison St., Waukesha, 10/28/83, B, C, 83004327

Booth, J. C., House, About 1 mi. SW of Saylesville on Saylesville Rd., Saylesville vicinity, 1/25/73, C, 73000094

Buckley, Patrick J., House, 1101 Buckley St., Waukesha, 2/28/91, C, 91000075

Burr Oak Tavern, Hartland MRA, 315-317 E. Capitol Dr., Hartland, 12/28/88, A, B, C, g, 86003403

Camp, Thomas, Farmhouse, Menomonee Falls MRA, W204 N8151 Lannon Rd., Menomonee Falls, 9/21/88, C, 88001670

Caples' Park Historic District, Waukesha MRA, Roughly bounded by E. Newhall Ave., S, Hartwell Ave., Windsor Dr. and Oxford Rd., and S. East Ave., Waukesha, 3/17/88, C, 88000219

Chandler, Walter S., House, 151 W. College Ave., Waukesha, 12/27/74, C, 74000137

Chapel of St. Mary the Virgin, 2 mi. SW of Nashotah on Nashotah House Rd., Nashotah vicinity, 2/23/72, A, C, a, 72000067

Cobb, George N., House, S. of Oconomowoc at 1505 N. Golden Lake Rd., Oconomowoc vicinity, 3/02/82, C, 82000719

College Avenue Historic District, Waukesha MRA, Fountain St., S. East and College Aves., Waukesha, 10/28/83, A, C, 83004328

Cook, Alexander, House, Waukesha MRA, 600 E. North St., Waukesha, 10/28/83, B, 83004329

Cutler Mound Group, Address Restricted, Waukesha vicinity, 11/03/88, B, 88002184

Cutler, Morris, House, 401 Central Ave., Waukesha MRA, 10/28/83 B C, 83004330

Dansk Evangelical Lutheran Kirke, Hartland MRA, 400 W. Capitol Dr., Hartland, 4/21/88,A, C, a, 86003422

Davis, Cyrus, Farmstead, Menomonee Falls MRA, W204 N7776 Lannon Rd., Menomonee Falls, 3/15/89, C, 88001674

Davis, Cyrus-Davis Brothers Farmhouse, Menomonee Falls MRA, W204 N7818 Lannon Rd., Menomonee Falls, 9/21/88, C, 88001672

Delafield Fish Hatchery, Main St., Delafield, 5/13/81, A, C, 81000064

Dewey Mound Group, Address Restricted, Big Bend vicinity, 12/19/78, D, 78000147

Dousman Inn, 15670 Blue Mound Rd., Brookfield, 1/15/79, A, C, 79000118

Downtown Historic District, Waukesha MRA, Roughly bounded by Broadway, Grand Ave., Clinton and South Sts., Waukesha, 10/28/83, A, C, 83004331

Dwinnell, George, House, Waukesha MRA, 442 W. College Ave., Waukesha, 10/28/83, C, 83004332

East Capitol Drive Historic District, Hartland MRA, 337-702 E. Capitol Dr., Hartland, 9/11/86, C, 86002319

Elliot, Dr. F. C., House, Waukesha MRA, 501 Dunbar Ave., Waukesha, 10/28/83, C, 83004333

First Baptist Church, Waukesha MRA, 247 Wisconsin Ave., Waukesha, 10/28/83, C, a, 83004334

First Congregational Church, Hartland MRA, 214 E. Capitol Dr., Hartland, 12/08/86, C, a, 86003405

First German Reformed Church, 413 Wisconsin Ave., Waukesha, 9/13/91, C, a, 91001390

First Methodist Church, Waukesha MRA, 121 Wisconsin Ave., Waukesha, 12/01/83, C, a, 83004335

Frame, Andrew, House, Waukesha MRA, 507 N. Grand Ave., Waukesha, 10/28/83, B, C, 83004337

Friederich Farmstead Historic District, Menomonee Falls MRA, N96 W15009 County Line Rd., Menomonee Falls, 9/21/88, A, C, 88001631

Genesee Town Hall, Genesee St., Genesee Depot, 6/25/81, A, 81000065

Goodwin-McBean Site (47WK184), Address Restricted, Big Bend vicinity, 9/17/82, D, 82000721

Grace, Perry, House, Waukesha MRA, 307 N. West Ave., Waukesha, 10/28/83, C, 83004339

Grand View Health Resort, Waukesha MRA, 500 Riverview Ave., Waukesha, 1/31/84, A, g, 84003805

Gredler-Gramins House, 20190 Davidson Rd., Brookfield vicinity, 11/24/80, C, 80000203

Hadfield Company Lime Kilns, Lime Kilns of Waukesha County TR, N of Waukesha, Waukesha vicinity, 3/12/82, A, C, 82000722

Hartland Railroad Depot, Hartland MRA, 301 Pawling Ave,. Hartland, 4/21/88, A, C, b, 86003417

Haseltine Cobblestone House, N of Big Bend on Big Bend Dr., Big Bend vicinity, 1/15/80, C, 80000204

Hawks Inn, 428 Wells St., Delafield, 2/23/72, A, *C,* b, 72000068

Hemlock, David J., House, Waukesha MRA, 234 Carroll St., Waukesha, 12/01/83, C, 83004340

Henze, LeRoy A., House, Menomonee Falls MRA, N89 W15781 Main St., Menomonee Falls, 9/21/88, C, 88001638

Hinkley, Ahira R., House, NE of Eagle off WI 59, Eagle vicinity, 1/21/74, C, 74000138

Hoeltz, Herbert, House, Menomonee Falls MRA, N87 W15714 Kenwood Blvd., Menomonee Falls, 9/21/88, C, 88001636

Hoos, Elizabeth, House, Menomonee Falls MRA, W164 N9010 Water St., Menomonee Falls, 9/21/88, C, 88001640

Hoos-Rowell House, Menomonee Falls MRA, W164 N8953 Water St., Menomonee Falls, 9/21/88, C, 88001644

Hornburg, Harold, House, Hartland MRA, 213 Warren Ave., Hartland, 12/08/86, C, 86003431

Howitt, John, House, Waukesha MRA, 407 N. Grand Ave., Waukesha, 10/28/83, C, 83004341

Jackson House, Hartland MRA, 235 North Ave., Hartland, 12/08/86, C, 86003409

Johnston, William, Lime Kiln, Lime Kilns of Waukesha County TR, E. of Genesse Depot, Saylesville vicinity, 3/12/82, A, C, 82000723

Jones, Robert O., House, Waukesha MRA, 501 W. College Ave., Waukesha, 10/28/83, C, 83004342

Koehler, Frank, House and Office, Menomonee Falls MRA, N88 W16623 Appleton Ave., Menomonee Falls, 9/21/88, B, C, 88001669

Koepsel House, Old World Wisconsin, off WI 59, Eagle vicinity, 10/25/73, C, b, e, 73000095

Laflin Avenue Historic District, Waukesha MRA, W. Laflin and Garfield Aves., Waukesha, 10/28/83, A, C, 83004343

Lain-Estburg House, 229 Wisconsin Ave., Waukesha, 12/27/74, B, C, 74000139

Mace, Garwin A., House, Menomonee Falls MRA, W166 N8941 Grand Ave., Menomonee Falls, 9/21/88, C, 88001650

Mace, Garwin, Lime Kilns, Lime Kilns of Waukesha County TR, Lime Kiln Park, Menomonee Falls, 3/12/82, A, C, 82000724

Madison Street Historic District, jct. of Madison, Randall, and Third Sts., Waukesha, 3/22/90, C, 90000489

Main Street Historic District, Menomonee Falls MRA, Main and Appleton Sts., Menomonee Falls, 9/21/88, A, C, 88001629

Mann, William G., House, Waukesha MRA, 346 Maple Ave., Waukesha, 10/28/83, A, C, 83004349

McCall Street Historic District, Waukesha MRA, McCall and James Sts., and N. East and Hartwell Aves., Waukesha, 2/01/83, B, C, 83004348

McCall Street Historic District (Boundary Increase), Waukesha MRA, Roughly Charles and James Sts. from College Ave. to McCall St., and Hartwell Ave. from College to Grove St., Waukesha, 3/29/93, C, 93000154

Menomonee Falls City Hall, Menomonee Falls MRA, N88 W16631 Appleton Ave., Menomonee Falls, 9/21/88, A, C, 88001667

Menomonee Golf Club, Menomonee Falls MRA, N73 W13430 Appleton Ave., Menomonee Falls, 9/21/88, C, 88001663

Miller-Davidson House, On County Line Rd., E. of U.S. 41, Menomonee Falls, 4/24/73, C, 73000096

Moore, Dr. Volney L., House, Waukesha MRA, 307 E. Main St., Waukesha, 10/28/83, C, 83004350

National Guard Armory 127th Regiment Infantry Company G, 103 E. Jefferson at Main St., Oconomowoc, 12/06/84, A, 84000709

National Hotel, Waukesha MRA, 235 W. Main St., Waukesha, 10/28/83, A, 83004344

Nelson, Charles E., Sr., House, 520 N, Grand Ave., Waukesha, 4/05/90, C, 90000560

Nickell, William A., House, Waukesha MRA, 511 Lake St., Waukesha, 10/28/83, C, 83004346

Oconomowoc City Hall, 174 E. Wisconsin Ave., Oconomowoc, 4/10/80. A, C, 80000205

Oconomowoc Depot, 115 Collins St., Oconomowoc, 1/29/80, A, C, 80000206

Okauchee House, 34880 Lake Dr., Okauchee, 8/11/78, A, C, 78000149

Old Waukesha County Courthouse, 101 W. Main St., Waukesha, 3/27/75, C, D, 75000082

Pabst, Gustave, Estate, 36100 Genesee Lake Rd., Summit, 11/27/89, C, a, 89002033

Peck, Clarence, Residence, 430 and 434 N. Lake Rd., Oconomowoc, 1/28/88, B, C, 87002569

Peck, Walter L., House, 38928 Islandale Dr., Oconomowoc, 4/10/86, C, 86000715

Peterson Site (47WK199), Address Restricted, Big Bend vicinity, 9/02/82, D, 82000726

Pokrandt Blacksmith Shop, Waukesha MRA, 128 E. St. Paul Ave., Waukesha, 10/28/83, A, 83004351

Pratt, Hannah, House, Waukesha MRA, 501 Barney St., Waukesha, 10/28/83, C, 83004352

Pratt, John A., House, Menomonee Falls MRA, N88 W15634 Park Blvd., Menomonee Falls, 9/21/88, C, 88001634

Putney Block, 301 W. Main St., 816 and 802 Grand Ave., Waukesha, 9/23/82, C, 82000727

Putney, Frank H., House, Waukesha MRA, 223 Wisconsin Ave., Waukesha, 10/28/83, C, 83004353

Resthaven Hotel, Waukesha MRA, 915 N. Hartwell Ave., Waukesha, 10/28/83, A, C, 83004354

Sanger, Casper M., House, Waukesha MRA, 507 E. College Ave., Waukesha, 10/28/83, A, C, a, 83004357

Schuttler, Henry and Mary, House, 371 E. Lisbon Rd., Oconomowoc, 7/16/87, C, 87001122

Sign of the Willows, Hartland MRA, 122 E. Capitol Dr., Hartland, 12/08/86, C, 86003428

Silurian Mineral Springhouse, Waukesha MRA, Post Office Circle, Waukesha, 1/31/84, A, C, 84003814

Sloan, William P., House, Waukesha MRA, 912 N. Barstow St., Waukesha, 10/28/83, C, b, 83004368

Smith, Camillia, House, Waukesha MRA, 603 N. West Ave., Waukesha, 10/28/83, C, 83004358

St. John Chrysostom Church, 1111 Genesee St., Delafield, 2/23/72, C, A, 72000069

St. John's Military Academy, Genesee St., Delafield, 10/28/77, A, B, C, g, 77000059

St. Joseph's Catholic Church Complex, Waukesha MRA, 818 N. East Ave., Waukesha, 10/28/83, A, C, a, 83004355

St. Matthias Episcopal Church, Waukesha MRA, 111 E. Main St., Waukesha, 10/28/83, C, A, 83004356

Statesan Historic District, Boys School Rd., Wales vicinity, 4/21/88, A, a, 88000454

Third Street Bridge, Menomonee Falls MRA, Roosevelt Dr., Menomonee Falls, 9/21/88, C, 88001647

Totten-Butterfield House, Waukesha MRA, 515 N. Grand Ave., Waukesha, 1/31/84, C, b, 84003816

Trapp Filling Station, Hartland MRA, 252-256 W. Capitol Dr., Hartland, 12/08/86, C, 86003419

Turck, Christian, House, Off WI 59 in Old World Wisconsin, Eagle vicinity, 10/25/73, C, b, e, 73000097

United Unitarian and Universalist Church, 216 Main St., Mukwonago, 10/01/87, A, C, a, 87001759

Van Buren, Sarah Belle, House, Hartland MRA, 128 Hill St., Hartland, 12/08/86, C, 86003426

Village Park Bandstand, Menomonee Falls MRA, Village Park on Garfield Dr., Menomonee Falls, 9/21/88, A, 88001653

Ward District No. 3 Schoolhouse, WI 67 and Betts Rd., Eagle vicinity, 7/07/81, A, C, 81000066

Warren, Stephen, House, Hartland MRA, 235 E. Capitol Dr., Hartland, 12/08/86, B, C, 86003432

Waukesha Post Office, Waukesha MRA, 235 W. Broadway Ave., Waukesha, 10/28/83, C, 83004359

Waukesha Pure Food Company, Waukesha MRA, 550 Elizabeth St., Waukesha, 10/28/83, A, C, 83004360

Welch, C. A., House, Waukesha MRA, 616 White Rock Ave., Waukesha, 10/28/83, A, C, 83004361

West, Deacon, Octagon House, 370 High St., Pewaukee, 5/12/75, C, 75000083

Wick, Michael, Farmhouse and Barn, Menomonee Falls MRA, N72 W13449 Good Hope Rd., Menomonee Falls, 9/21/88, C, 88001665

Wisconsin Avenue Historic District, Waukesha MRA, Wisconsin, Waukesha, 10/28/83, C, 83004362

Wisconsin Industrial School for Boys, Waukesha MRA, 621 and 627 W. College Ave., Waukesha, 1/21/87, A, C, 86003652

Yanke, Louis, Saloon, Waukesha MRA, 200 Madison Ave., Waukesha, 10/28/83, C, 83004363

Zimmer, Johann, Farmhouse, Menomonee Falls MRA, W156 N9390 Pilgrim Rd., Menomonee Falls, 9/21/88, C, 88001632

Zion Evangelical Lutheran Church, Hartland MRA, 403 W. Capitol Dr., Hartland, 12/08/86, C, a, 86003423

WAUPACA COUNTY

Browne Law Office, 202 E. Union St., Waupaca, 8/18/80, A, B, 80000208

Commandant's Residence Home, Wisconsin Home for Veterans TR, Off WI 22, King, 6/19/85, A, C, 85001364

Crescent Roller Mills, 213 Oborn St., Waupaca, 12/20/78, A, 78000150

Danes Hall, 303 N. Main St., Waupaca, 1/17/80, A, 80000209

Halfway House, Potts Ave., King vicinity, 3/01/82, A, B, 8200728

Kasper, Philip H., Cheese Factory, W of Bear Creek on WI 22, Bear Creek vicinity, 8/27/76, A, B, 76000081

Old Hospital, Wisconsin Home for Veterans TR, Off WI 22, King, 6/19/85, A, C, 85001365

Rural on the Crystal Historic District, Roughly bounded by Arbor St., Rapley, St., Rural Rd., and Cleghorn St., Rural, 4/12/89, A, C, 89000231

Sanders Site (47WP26 and 47WP70), Address Restricted, Fremont vicinity 2/09/84, D, 84003819

Shearer-Cristy House, 315 E. Lake St., Waupaca, 12/22/83, C, 83004364

Historic Places

Veterans Cottages Historic District, Wisconsin Home for Veterans TR, Off WI 22, King, 6/19/85, A, C, 85001367
Veterans Home Chapel, Wisconsin Home for Veterans TR, Off WI 22, King, 6/19/85, A, C, a, 85001366
Wipf, J. & C., Mills, 280 N. Main St., Iola, 12/08/87, A, b, 87002108

WAUSHARA COUNTY

Kimball, Alanson M., House, 204 Middleton St., Pine River 10/20/88, C, 88002023
Waushara County Courthouse, Waushara County Sheriff's Residence and Jail, County Courthouses of Wisconsin TR, 209 St. Marie St., Wautoma 3/09/82, C, 82000729

WINNEBAGO COUNTY

Algoma Boulevard Methodist Church, 1171 Algoma Blvd., Oshkosh, 12/03/74, C, a, 74000140
Augustin, Gustav, Block, 68 Racine St. Menasha, 5/30/86, C, 86001181
Babcock, Havilah, House, 537 E. Wisconsin Ave., Neenah, 8/07/74, B, C, 74000141
Black Oak School, 5028 S. Green Bay Rd., Nekimi, 6/25/87, C, b, 87001062
Bowen, Abraham Briggs, House, 1010 Bayshore Dr., Oshkosh, 4/22/82, C, 82000731
Brainerd Site, Address Restricted, Neenah vicinity, 9/07/84, D, 84003823
Brin Building, 1 Main St., Menasha, 7/10/86, A, 86001541
Buckstaff Observatory, 2119 N. Main St., Oshkosh, 5/17/79, A, B, 79000119
Carpenter Site (47WN246), Address Restricted, Eureka vicinity, 4/07/82, D, 82000725
Cole Watch Tower, W. of Omro on WI 21, Omro vicinity, 6/09/78, A, g, 78000148
Daily Northwestern Building, 224 State St., Oshkosh, 5/13/82, A, C, 82000732
Doty Island (47WN30), Address Restricted, Menasha vicinity, 6/20/85, D, 85001368

157

Eureka Lock and Lock Tender's House, S of Eureka on Fox River, Eureka vicinity, 9/29/76, A, 76000082
First Presbyterian Church, 110 Church Ave., Oshkosh, 12/27/74, C, a, 74000142
Frontenac, 132-140 High St. and 9 Brown St., Oshkosh, 4/22/82, C, 82000733
Gram, Hans, House, 345 E. Wisconsin Ave., Neenah, 7/02/87, C, 87001123
Grand Loggery, Doty Park (Lincoln St.), Neenah, 3/22/74, B, b, e, 74000143
Grignon, Augustin, Hotel, SE corner of Main and Washington Sts., Butte des Morts, 1/14/75, A, C, 75000084
Guenther, Richard, House, 1200 Washington Ave., Oshkosh, 3/01/84, A, B, C, 81003824
Hooper, Jessie Jack, House, 1149 Algoma Blvd., Oshkosh, 12/18/78, B, C, 78000151
Kamrath Site, Address Restricted, Winneconne vicinity, 5/06/75, D, 750001185
Koch, Carl, Block, 2 Tayco St., Menasha, 7/10/86, A, C, 80001539
Larson Brothers Airport, WI 150, Clayton, 1/05/84, A, C, 84003825
Lasley's Point Site, Address Restricted, Winneconne vicinity, 9/06/79, D, 79000120
Lutz, Robert, House, 1440 Knapp St., Oshkosh, 5/27/82 B, C, 82000734
Metzig Garden Site (47WN283), Address Restricted Wolf vicinity, 12/29/88, D, 88003470
Morgan, John R., House, 234 Church Ave., Oshkosh, 10/14/83, B, C, 83004365
Neenah United States Post Office, 307 S. Commercial St., Neenah, 11/08/90, C, 90001743
Omro High School, Annex and Webster Manual Training School, 515 S. Webster St., Omro, 6/19/85, A, C, 85001369
Orville Beach Memorial Manual Training School, 240 Algoma Blvd., Oshkosh, 9/12/85, A, C, 85002334
Oshkosh Grand Opera House, 100 High Ave., Oshkosh, 9/21/74, A, 74000144
Oshkosh State Normal School Historic District, Buildings at 800, 842, and 912 Algoma Blvd., and 845 Elmwood Ave., Oshkosh, 12/06/84, A, C, 84000722
Overton Archeological District, Address Restricted, Oshkosh vicinity, 5/02/75, D, 75000086

Oviatt House, 842 Algoma Blvd., Oshkosh, 8/27/79, A, B, C, 79000121

Paepke, Henry, House, 251 E. Doty Ave., Neenah, 3/13/87, C, 87000462

Paine Art Center and Arboretum, 1410 Algoma Blvd., Oshkosh, 12/01/78, B, C, 78000152

Paine Lumber Company Historic District, Off Congress Ave. roughly between High, New York, and Summit Aves., and Paine Lumber Access Rd., Oshkosh, 6/26/86, A, C, 86001392

Pollock, William E., Residence, 765 Algoma Blvd., Oshkosh, 12/06/84, C, 81000728

Read School, 1120 Algoma Blvd., Oshkosh, 2/11/93, C, 93000025

Shattuck, Franklyn C., House, 547 E. Wisconsin Ave., Neenah, 12/04/78, B, C, 78000153

Smith, Charles R., House, 824 E. Forest Ave., Neenah, 7/16/79, A, B, 79000122

Smith, Henry Spencer, House 706 E. Forest Ave., Neenah, 6/25/82, B, 82000735

Tayco Street Bridge, Tayco and Water Sts., Menasha, 5/30/86, C, 86001182

Trinity Episcopal Church, 203 Algoma Blvd., Oshkosh, 12/30/74, C, a, 74000145

US Post Office–Menasha, 84 Racine St., Menasha, 8/22/86, C, 86001518

Upper Main Street Historic District, 63-240 Main, 3 Mill, 56 Racine and 408 Water Sts., Menasha, 12/06/84, A, C, 84000714

Vining, Gorham P., House, 1590 Oakridge Rd., Neenah, 12/08/83, C, 83004366

Wall, Thomas R., Residence, 751 Algoma Blvd., Oshkosh, 12/06/84, C, 84000732

Washington Avenue Historic District, Roughly bounded by Merritt Ave., Linde and Lampert Sts., Washington Ave., Bowen and Evan Sts., Oshkosh, 5/22/86, C, 86001129

Washington Street Historic District, 214-216 Washington St., Menasha, 5/30/86, C, a, 86001180

Winnebago County Courthouse, County Courthouses of Wisconsin TR, 415 Jackson St., Oshkosh, 6/23/82, C, g, 82000736

Wisconsin Avenue Historic District, 106-226 W. Wisconsin Ave., 110 Church St., Neenah, 6/14/84, A, C, 84003817

Wisconsin National Life Insurance Building, 220 Washington Ave., Oshkosh, 4/29/82, C, 82000737

WOOD COUNTY

Upham, Gov. William H., House, 212 W. 3rd St., Marshfield, 12/12/76, B, 76000083
Wakeley's Tavern, W. end of Wakeley Rd., Nekoosa, 12/27/74, A, 74000146

WISCONSIN CONSTITUTION

TABLE OF CONTENTS

The Encyclopedia of Wisconsin

Constitution

We, the people of Wisconsin, grateful to Almighty God for our freedom, in order to secure its blessings, form a more perfect government, insure domestic tranquility and promote the general welfare, do establish this constitution.

ARTICLE I.
DECLARATION OF RIGHTS

Equality; inherent rights. SECTION 1. *[As amended April 1986]* All people are born equally free and independent, and have certain inherent rights; among these are life, liberty and the pursuit of happiness; to secure these rights, governments are instituted, deriving their just powers from the consent of the governed. *[1983 AJR–9; 1985 AJR–9]*

Slavery prohibited. SECTION 2. There shall be neither slavery, nor involuntary servitude in this state, otherwise than for the punishment of crime, whereof the party shall have been duly convicted.

Free speech; libel. SECTION 3. Every person may freely speak, write and publish his sentiments on all subjects, being responsible for the abuse of that right, and no laws shall be passed to restrain or abridge the liberty of speech or of the press. In all criminal prosecutions or indictments for libel, the truth may be given in evidence, and if it shall appear to the jury that the matter charged as libelous be true, and was published with good motives and for justifiable ends, the party shall be acquitted; and the jury shall have the right to determine the law and the fact.

Right to assemble and petition. SECTION 4. The right of the people peaceably to assemble, to consult for the common good, and to petition the government, or any department thereof, shall never be abridged.

Trial by jury; verdict in civil cases. SECTION 5. *[As amended November 1922]* The right of trial by jury shall remain inviolate, and shall extend to all cases at law without regard to the amount in controversy; but a jury trial may be waived by the parties in all cases in the manner prescribed by law. Provided, however, that the legislature may, from time to time, by statute provide that a valid verdict, in civil cases, may be based on the votes of a specified number of the jury, not less than five-sixths thereof. *[1919 AJR–26; 1921 AJR–14; 1921 c. 504]*

Excessive bail; cruel punishments. SECTION 6. Excessive bail shall not be required nor shall excessive fines be imposed, nor cruel and unusual punishments inflicted.

Rights of accused. SECTION 7. In all criminal prosecutions the accused shall enjoy the right to be heard by himself and counsel; to demand the nature and cause of the accusation against him; to meet the witnesses face to face; to have compulsory process to compel the attendance of witnesses in his behalf; and in prosecution by indictment, or information, to a speedy public trial by an impartial jury of the county or district wherein the offense shall have been committed; which county or district shall have been previously ascertained by law.

Prosecutions; double jeopardy; self-incrimination; bail; habeas corpus. SECTION 8. *[As amended per certification of the Board of State Canvassers dated April 7, 1982]* (1) No person may be held to answer for a criminal offense without due process of law, and no person for the same offense may be put twice in jeopardy of punishment, nor may be compelled in any criminal case to be a witness against himself or herself.

(2) All persons, before conviction, shall be eligible for release under reasonable conditions designed to assure their appearance in court, protect members of the community from serious bodily harm or prevent the intimidation of witnesses. Monetary conditions of release may be imposed at or after the initial appearance only upon a finding that there is a reasonable basis to believe that the conditions are necessary to assure appearance in court. The legislature may authorize, by law, courts to revoke a person's release for a violation of a condition of release.

(3) The legislature may by law authorize, but may not require, circuit courts to deny release for a period not to exceed 10 days prior to the hearing required under this subsection to a person who is accused of committing a murder punishable by life imprisonment or a sexual assault punishable by a maximum imprisonment of 20 years, or who is accused of committing or attempting to commit a felony involving serious bodily harm to another or the threat of serious bodily harm to another and who has a previous conviction for committing or attempting to commit a felony involving serious bodily harm to another or the threat of serious bodily harm to another. The legislature may authorize by law, but may not require, circuit courts to continue to deny release to those accused persons for an additional period not to exceed 60 days following the hearing required under this subsection, if there is a requirement that there be a finding by the court based on clear and convincing evidence presented at a hearing that the accused committed the felony and a requirement that there be a finding by the court that available conditions of release will not adequately protect members of the community from serious bodily harm or prevent intimidation of witnesses. Any law enacted under this subsection shall be specific, limited and reasonable. In determining the 10-day and 60-day periods, the court shall omit any period of time found by the court to result from a delay caused by the defendant or a continuance granted which was initiated by the defendant.

(4) The privilege of the writ of habeas corpus shall not be suspended unless, in cases of rebellion or invasion, the public safety requires it. [*June 1980 Spec.Sess. AJR–9; 1981 AJR–5*]

Remedy for wrongs. SECTION 9. Every person is entitled to a certain remedy in the laws for all injuries, or wrongs which he may receive in his person, property, or character; he ought to obtain justice freely, and without being obliged to purchase it, completely and without denial, promptly and without delay, conformably to the laws.

Treason. SECTION 10. Treason against the state shall consist only in levying war against the same, or in adhering to its enemies, giving them aid and comfort. No person shall be convicted of treason unless on the testimony of two witnesses to the same overt act, or on confession in open court.

Searches and seizures. SECTION 11. The right of the people to be secure in their persons, houses, papers, and effects against unreasonable searches and seizures shall not be violated; and no warrant shall issue but upon probable cause, supported by oath or affirmation, and particularly describing the place to be searched and the persons or things to be seized.

Attainder; ex post facto; contracts. SECTION 12. No bill of attainder, ex post facto law, nor any law impairing the obligation of contracts, shall ever be passed, and no conviction shall work corruption of blood or forfeiture of estate.

Private property for public use. SECTION 13. The property of no person shall be taken for public use without just compensation therefor.

Feudal tenures; leases; alienation. SECTION 14. All lands within the state are declared to be allodial, and feudal tenures are prohibited. Leases and grants of agricultural land for a longer term than fifteen years in which rent or service of any kind shall be reserved, and all fines and like restraints upon alienation reserved in any grant of land, hereafter made, are declared to be void.

Equal property rights for aliens and citizens. SECTION 15. No distinction shall ever be made by law between resident aliens and citizens, in reference to the possession, enjoyment or descent of property.

Imprisonment for debt. SECTION 16. No person shall be imprisoned for debt arising out of or founded on a contract, expressed or implied.

Exemption of property of debtors. SECTION 17. The privilege of the debtor to enjoy the necessary comforts of life shall be recognized by wholesome laws, exempting a reasonable amount of property from seizure or sale for the payment of any debt or liability hereafter contracted.

Freedom of worship; liberty of conscience; state religion; public funds. SECTION 18. *[As amended November 1982]* The right of every person to worship Almighty God according to the dictates of conscience shall never be infringed; nor shall any person be compelled to attend, erect or support any place of worship, or to maintain any ministry, without consent; nor shall any control of, or interference with, the rights of conscience be permitted, or any preference be given by law to any religious establishments or modes of worship; nor shall any money be drawn from the treasury for the benefit of religious societies, or religious or theological seminaries. *[1979 AJR–76; 1981 AJR–35; submit: May'82 Spec.Sess. AJR–1]*

Religious tests prohibited. SECTION 19. No religious tests shall ever be required as a qualification for any office of public trust under the state, and no person shall be rendered incompetent to give evidence in any court of law or equity in consequence of his opinions on the subject of religion.

Military subordinate to civil power. SECTION 20. The military shall be in strict subordination to the civil power.

Rights of suitors. SECTION 21. *[As amended April 1977]* (1) Writs of error shall never be prohibited, and shall be issued by such courts as the legislature designates by law.

(2) In any court of this state, any suitor may prosecute or defend his suit either in his own proper person or by an attorney of the suitor's choice. *[1975 AJR–11; 1977 SJR–9]*

Maintenance of free government. SECTION 22. The blessings of a free government can only be maintained by a firm adherence to justice, moderation, temperance, frugality and virtue, and by frequent recurrence to fundamental principles.

Transportation of school children. SECTION 23. *[As created April 1967]* Nothing in this constitution shall prohibit the legislature from providing for the safety and welfare of children by providing for the transportation of children to and from any parochial or private school or institution of learning. *[1965 AJR–70; 1967 AJR–7]*

Use of school buildings. SECTION 24. *[As created April 1972]* Nothing in this constitution shall prohibit the legislature from authorizing, by law, the use of public school buildings by civic, religious or charitable organizations during nonschool hours upon payment by the organization to the school district of reasonable compensation for such use. *[1969 AJR–74; 1971 AJR–10]*

ARTICLE II.
BOUNDARIES

State boundary. SECTION 1. It is hereby ordained and declared that the state of Wisconsin doth consent and accept of the boundaries prescribed in the act of congress entitled "An act to enable the people of Wisconsin territory to form a constitution and state government, and for the admission of such state into the Union," approved August sixth, one thousand eight hundred and forty-six, to wit: Beginning at the northeast corner of the state of Illinois — that is to say, at a point in the center of Lake Michigan where the line of forty-two degrees and thirty minutes of north latitude crosses the same; thence running with the boundary line of the state of Michigan, through Lake Michigan, Green Bay, to the mouth of the Menominee river; thence up the channel of the said river to the Brule river; thence up said last-mentioned river to Lake Brule; thence along the southern shore of Lake Brule in a direct line to the center of the channel between Middle and South Islands, in the Lake of the Desert; thence in a direct line to the head waters of the Montreal river, as marked upon the survey made by Captain Cram; thence down the main channel of the Montreal river to the middle of Lake Superior; thence through the center of Lake Superior to the mouth of the St. Louis river; thence up the main channel of said river to the first rapids in the same, above the Indian village, according to Nicollet's map; thence due south to the main branch of the river St. Croix; thence down the main channel of said river to the Mississippi; thence down the center of the main channel of that river to the northwest corner of the state of Illinois; thence due east with the northern boundary of the state of Illinois to the place of beginning, as established by "An act to enable the people of the Illinois territory to form a constitution and state government, and for the admission of such state into the Union on an equal footing with the original states," approved April 18th, 1818.

Enabling act accepted. SECTION 2. *[As amended April 1951]* The propositions contained in the act of congress are hereby accepted, ratified and confirmed, and shall remain irrevocable without the consent of the United States; and it is hereby ordained that this state shall never interfere with the primary disposal of the soil within the same by the United States, nor with any regulations congress may find necessary for securing the title in such soil to bona fide purchasers thereof; and in no case shall nonresident proprietors be taxed higher than residents. Provided, that nothing in this constitution, or in the act of congress aforesaid, shall in any manner prejudice or affect the right of the state of Wisconsin to 500,000 acres of land granted to said state, and to be hereafter selected and located and under the act of congress entitled "An act to appropriate the proceeds of the sales of the public lands, and grant pre-emption rights," approved September fourth, one thousand eight hundred and forty-one. *[1949 AJR–64; 1951 AJR–7]*

ARTICLE III.
SUFFRAGE

Electors. SECTION 1. *[As created April 1986]* Every United States citizen age 18 or older who is a resident of an election district in this state is a qualified elector of that district. *[1983 AJR–33; 1985 AJR–3]*

Implementation. SECTION 2. *[As created April 1986]* Laws may be enacted:

(1) Defining residency.

(2) Providing for registration of electors.

(3) Providing for absentee voting.

(4) Excluding from the right of suffrage persons:

(a) Convicted of a felony, unless restored to civil rights.

(b) Adjudged by a court to be incompetent or partially incompetent, unless the judgment specifies that the person is capable of understanding the objective of the elective process or the judgment is set aside.

(5) Subject to ratification by the people at a general election, extending the right of suffrage to additional classes. *[1983 AJR–33; 1985 AJR–3]*

Secret ballot. SECTION 3. *[As created April 1986]* All votes shall be by secret ballot. *[1983 AJR–33; 1985 AJR–3]*

ARTICLE IV.
LEGISLATIVE

Legislative power. SECTION 1. The legislative power shall be vested in a senate and assembly.

Legislature, how constituted. SECTION 2. The number of the members of the assembly shall never be less than fifty-four nor more than one hundred. The senate shall consist of a number not more than one-third nor less than one-fourth of the number of the members of the assembly.

Apportionment. SECTION 3. *[As amended November 1982]* At its first session after each enumeration made by the authority of the United States, the legislature shall apportion and district anew the members of the senate and assembly, according to the number of inhabitants. *[1979 AJR–76; 1981 AJR–35; submit: May'82 Spec.Sess. AJR–1]*

Representatives to the assembly, how chosen. SECTION 4. *[As amended November 1982]* The members of the assembly shall be chosen biennially, by single districts, on the Tuesday succeeding the first Monday of November in even-numbered years, by the qualified electors of the several districts, such districts to be bounded by county, precinct, town or ward lines, to consist of contiguous territory and be in as compact form as practicable. *[1979 AJR–76; 1981 AJR–35; submit: May'82 Spec.Sess. AJR–1]*

Senators, how chosen. SECTION 5. *[As amended November 1982]* The senators shall be elected by single districts of convenient contiguous territory, at the same time and in the same manner as members of the assembly are required to be chosen; and no assembly district shall be divided in the formation of a senate district. The senate districts shall be numbered in the regular series, and the senators shall be chosen alternately from the odd and even-numbered districts for the term of 4 years. *[1979 AJR–76; 1981 AJR–35; submit: May'82 Spec.Sess. AJR–1]*

Constitution

Qualifications of legislators. SECTION 6. No person shall be eligible to the legislature who shall not have resided one year within the state, and be a qualified elector in the district which he may be chosen to represent.

Organization of legislature; quorum; compulsory attendance. SECTION 7. Each house shall be the judge of the elections, returns and qualifications of its own members; and a majority of each shall constitute a quorum to do business, but a smaller number may adjourn from day to day, and may compel the attendance of absent members in such manner under such penalties as each house may provide.

Rules; contempts; expulsion. SECTION 8. Each house may determine the rules of its own proceedings, punish for contempt and disorderly behavior, and with the concurrence of two-thirds of all the members elected, expel a member; but no member shall be expelled a second time for the same cause.

Officers. SECTION 9. [*As amended April 1979*] Each house shall choose its presiding officers from its own members. [*1977 SJR-51; 1979 SJR-1*]

Journals; open doors; adjournments. SECTION 10. Each house shall keep a journal of its proceedings and publish the same, except such parts as require secrecy. The doors of each house shall be kept open except when the public welfare shall require secrecy. Neither house shall, without consent of the other, adjourn for more than three days.

Meeting of legislature. SECTION 11. [*As amended April 1968*] The legislature shall meet at the seat of government at such time as shall be provided by law, unless convened by the governor in special session, and when so convened no business shall be transacted except as shall be necessary to accomplish the special purposes for which it was convened. [*1965 AJR-5; 1967 AJR-15*]

Ineligibility of legislators to office. SECTION 12. No member of the legislature shall, during the term for which he was elected, be appointed or elected to any civil office in the state, which shall have been created, or the emoluments of which shall have been increased, during the term for which he was elected.

Ineligibility of federal officers. SECTION 13. [*As amended April 1966*] No person being a member of congress, or holding any military or civil office under the United States, shall be eligible to a seat in the legislature; and if any person shall, after his election as a member of the legislature, be elected to congress, or be appointed to any office, civil or military, under the government of the United States, his acceptance thereof shall vacate his seat. This restriction shall not prohibit a legislator from accepting short periods of active duty as a member of the reserve or from serving in the armed forces during any emergency declared by the executive. [*1963 SJR-24; 1965 SJR-15*]

Filling vacancies. SECTION 14. The governor shall issue writs of election to fill such vacancies as may occur in either house of the legislature.

Exemption from arrest and civil process. SECTION 15. Members of the legislature shall in all cases, except treason, felony and breach of the peace, be privileged from arrest; nor shall they be subject to any civil process, during the session of the legislature, nor for fifteen days next before the commencement and after the termination of each session.

Privilege in debate. SECTION 16. No member of the legislature shall be liable in any civil action, or criminal prosecution whatever, for words spoken in debate.

Enactment of laws. SECTION 17. [*As amended April 1977*] (1) The style of all laws of the state shall be "The people of the state of Wisconsin, represented in senate and assembly, do enact as follows:".

(2) No law shall be enacted except by bill. No law shall be in force until published.

(3) The legislature shall provide by law for the speedy publication of all laws. [*1975 AJR-11; 1977 SJR-9*]

Title of private bills. SECTION 18. No private or local bill which may be passed by the legislature shall embrace more than one subject, and that shall be expressed in the title.

Origin of bills. SECTION 19. Any bill may originate in either house of the legislature, and a bill passed by one house may be amended by the other.

Yeas and nays. SECTION 20. The yeas and nays of the members of either house on any question shall, at the request of one-sixth of those present, be entered on the journal.

SECTION 21. [*Repealed. 1927 SJR-61; 1929 SJR-7; vote April 1929*]

167

Powers of county boards. SECTION 22. The legislature may confer upon the boards of supervisors of the several counties of the state such powers of a local, legislative and administrative character as they shall from time to time prescribe.

Town and county government. SECTION 23. [As amended April 1972] The legislature shall establish but one system of town government, which shall be as nearly uniform as practicable, but the legislature may provide for the election at large once in every 4 years of a chief executive officer in any county with such powers of an administrative character as they may from time to time prescribe in accordance with this section and shall establish one or more systems of county government. [1969 SJR-58; 1971 SJR-4]

Chief executive officer to approve or veto resolutions or ordinances; proceedings on veto. SECTION 23a. [As amended April 1969] Every resolution or ordinance passed by the county board in any county shall, before it becomes effective, be presented to the chief executive officer. If he approves, he shall sign it; if not, he shall return it with his objections, which objections shall be entered at large upon the journal and the board shall proceed to reconsider the matter. Appropriations may be approved in whole or in part by the chief executive officer and the part approved shall become law, and the part objected to shall be returned in the same manner as provided for in other resolutions or ordinances. If, after such reconsideration, two-thirds of the members-elect of the county board agree to pass the resolution or ordinance or the part of the resolution or ordinance objected to, it shall become effective on the date prescribed but not earlier than the date of passage following reconsideration. In all such cases, the votes of the members of the county board shall be determined by ayes and noes and the names of the members voting for or against the resolution or ordinance or the part thereof objected to shall be entered on the journal. If any resolution or ordinance is not returned by the chief executive officer to the county board at its first meeting occurring not less than 6 days, Sundays excepted, after it has been presented to him, it shall become effective unless the county board has recessed or adjourned for a period in excess of 60 days, in which case it shall not be effective without his approval. [1967 AJR-18; 1969 SJR-8]

Lotteries and divorces. SECTION 24. [As amended April 1987] (1) Except as provided in this section, the legislature shall never authorize any lottery or grant any divorce.

(2) Except as otherwise provided by law, the following activities do not constitute consideration as an element of a lottery:

(a) To listen to or watch a television or radio program.

(b) To fill out a coupon or entry blank, whether or not proof of purchase is required.

(c) To visit a mercantile establishment or other place without being required to make a purchase or pay an admittance fee.

(3) The legislature may authorize the following bingo games licensed by the state, but all profits shall accrue to the licensed organization and no salaries, fees or profits may be paid to any other organization or person: bingo games operated by religious, charitable, service, fraternal or veterans' organizations or those to which contributions are deductible for federal or state income tax purposes.

(4) The legislature may authorize the following raffle games licensed by the state, but all profits shall accrue to the licensed local organization and no salaries, fees or profits may be paid to any other organization or person: raffle games operated by local religious, charitable, service, fraternal or veterans' organizations or those to which contributions are deductible for federal or state income tax purposes. The legislature shall limit the number of raffles conducted by any such organization.

(5) This section shall not prohibit pari-mutuel on-track betting as provided by law. The state may not own or operate any facility or enterprise for pari-mutuel betting, or lease any state-owned land to any other owner or operator for such purposes.

(6) The legislature may authorize the creation of a lottery to be operated by the state as provided by law. The expenditure of public funds or of revenues derived from lottery operations to engage in promotional advertising of the Wisconsin state lottery is prohibited. Any advertising of the state lottery shall indicate the odds of a specific lottery ticket to be selected as the winning ticket for each prize amount offered. The net proceeds of the state lottery shall be deposited in the treasury of the state, to be used for property tax relief as provided by law. [Pari-mutuel: 1985 AJR-45; 1987 AJR-2. State lottery: 1985 SJR-1; 1987 AJR-3.]

Constitution

Stationery and printing. SECTION 25. The legislature shall provide by law that all stationery required for the use of the state, and all printing authorized and required by them to be done for their use, or for the state, shall be let by contract to the lowest bidder, but the legislature may establish a maximum price; no member of the legislature or other state officer shall be interested, either directly or indirectly, in any such contract.

Extra compensation; salary change. SECTION 26. [*As amended April 1977*] The legislature shall never grant any extra compensation to any public officer, agent, servant or contractor, after the services shall have been rendered or the contract entered into; nor shall the compensation of any public officer be increased or diminished during his term of office except that when any increase or decrease provided by the legislature in the compensation of the justices of the supreme court or judges of any court of record shall become effective as to any such justice or judge, it shall be effective from such date as to each of such justices or judges. This section shall not apply to increased benefits for persons who have been or shall be granted benefits of any kind under a retirement system when such increased benefits are provided by a legislative act passed on a call of ayes and noes by a three-fourths vote of all the members elected to both houses of the legislature, which act shall provide for sufficient state funds to cover the costs of the increased benefits. [*1975 AJR-11; 1977 SJR-9*]

Suits against state. SECTION 27. The legislature shall direct by law in what manner and in what courts suits may be brought against the state.

Oath of office. SECTION 28. Members of the legislature, and all officers, executive and judicial, except such inferior officers as may be by law exempted, shall before they enter upon the duties of their respective offices, take and subscribe an oath or affirmation to support the constitution of the United States and the constitution of the state of Wisconsin, and faithfully to discharge the duties of their respective offices to the best of their ability.

Militia. SECTION 29. The legislature shall determine what persons shall constitute the militia of the state, and may provide for organizing and disciplining the same in such manner as shall be prescribed by law.

Elections by legislature. SECTION 30. [*As amended November 1982*] All elections made by the legislature shall be by roll call vote entered in the journals. [*1979 AJR-76; 1981 AJR-35; submit: May'82 Spec.Sess. AJR-1*]

Special and private laws prohibited. SECTION 31. [*As amended November 1892*] The legislature is prohibited from enacting any special or private laws in the following cases:

1st. For changing the name of persons or constituting one person the heir at law of another.

2d. For laying out, opening or altering highways, except in cases of state roads extending into more than one county, and military roads to aid in the construction of which lands may be granted by congress.

3d. For authorizing persons to keep ferries across streams at points wholly within this state.

4th. For authorizing the sale or mortgage of real or personal property of minors or others under disability.

5th. For locating or changing any county seat.

6th. For assessment or collection of taxes or for extending the time for the collection thereof.

7th. For granting corporate powers or privileges, except to cities.

8th. For authorizing the apportionment of any part of the school fund.

9th. For incorporating any city, town or village, or to amend the charter thereof. [*1889 SJR-13; 1891 SJR-13; 1891 c. 362*]

General laws on enumerated subjects. SECTION 32. [*Created November 1871*] The legislature shall provide general laws for the transaction of any business that may be prohibited by section thirty-one of this article, and all such laws shall be uniform in their operation throughout the state. [*1870 SJR-14; 1871 AJR-29; 1871 c. 122*]

Auditing of state accounts. SECTION 33. [*Created November 1946*] The legislature shall provide for the auditing of state accounts and may establish such offices and prescribe such duties for the same as it shall deem necessary. [*1943 SJR-35; 1945 SJR-24*]

Continuity of civil government. SECTION 34. *[Created April 1961]* The legislature, in order to ensure continuity of state and local governmental operations in periods of emergency resulting from enemy action in the form of an attack, shall (1) forthwith provide for prompt and temporary succession to the powers and duties of public offices, of whatever nature and whether filled by election or appointment, the incumbents of which may become unavailable for carrying on the powers and duties of such offices, and (2) adopt such other measures as may be necessary and proper for attaining the objectives of the section. *[1959 AJR–48; 1961 SJR–1]*

ARTICLE V.
EXECUTIVE

Governor; lieutenant governor; term. SECTION 1. *[As amended April 1979]* The executive power shall be vested in a governor who shall hold office for 4 years; a lieutenant governor shall be elected at the same time and for the same term. *[1977 SJR–51; 1979 SJR–1]*

SECTION 1m. *[Repealed. 1977 SJR–51; 1979 SJR–1; vote April 1979]*

SECTION 1n. *[Repealed. 1977 SJR–51; 1979 SJR–1; vote April 1979]*

Eligibility. SECTION 2. No person except a citizen of the United States and a qualified elector of the state shall be eligible to the office of governor or lieutenant governor.

Election. SECTION 3. *[As amended April 1967]* The governor and lieutenant governor shall be elected by the qualified electors of the state at the times and places of choosing members of the legislature. They shall be chosen jointly, by the casting by each voter of a single vote applicable to both offices beginning with the general election in 1970. The persons respectively having the highest number of votes cast jointly for them for governor and lieutenant governor shall be elected; but in case two or more slates shall have an equal and the highest number of votes for governor and lieutenant governor, the two houses of the legislature, at its next annual session shall forthwith, by joint ballot, choose one of the slates so having an equal and the highest number of votes for governor and lieutenant governor. The returns of election for governor and lieutenant governor shall be made in such manner as shall be provided by law. *[1965 AJR–3; 1967 AJR–8 and SJR–11]*

Powers and duties. SECTION 4. The governor shall be commander in chief of the military and naval forces of the state. He shall have power to convene the legislature on extraordinary occasions, and in case of invasion, or danger from the prevalence of contagious disease at the seat of government, he may convene them at any other suitable place within the state. He shall communicate to the legislature, at every session, the condition of the state, and recommend such matters to them for their consideration as he may deem expedient. He shall transact all necessary business with the officers of the government, civil and military. He shall expedite all such measures as may be resolved upon by the legislature, and shall take care that the laws be faithfully executed.

SECTION 5. *[Repealed. 1929 SJR–81; 1931 SJR–6; vote November 1932]*

Pardoning power. SECTION 6. The governor shall have power to grant reprieves, commutations and pardons, after conviction, for all offenses, except treason and cases of impeachment, upon such conditions and with such restrictions and limitations as he may think proper, subject to such regulations as may be provided by law relative to the manner of applying for pardons. Upon conviction for treason he shall have the power to suspend the execution of the sentence until the case shall be reported to the legislature at its next meeting, when the legislature shall either pardon, or commute the sentence, direct the execution of the sentence, or grant a further reprieve. He shall annually communicate to the legislature each case of reprieve, commutation or pardon granted, stating the name of the convict, the crime of which he was convicted, the sentence and its date, and the date of the commutation, pardon or reprieve with his reasons for granting the same.

Lieutenant governor, when governor. SECTION 7. *[As amended April 1979]* (1) Upon the governor's death, resignation or removal from office, the lieutenant governor shall become governor for the balance of the unexpired term.

Constitution

(2) If the governor is absent from this state, impeached, or from mental or physical disease, becomes incapable of performing the duties of the office, the lieutenant governor shall serve as acting governor for the balance of the unexpired term or until the governor returns, the disability ceases or the impeachment is vacated. But when the governor, with the consent of the legislature, shall be out of this state in time of war at the head of the state's military force, the governor shall continue as commander in chief of the military force. *[1977 SJR–51; 1979 SJR–1]*

Secretary of state, when governor. SECTION 8. *[As amended April 1979]* (1) If there is a vacancy in the office of lieutenant governor and the governor dies, resigns or is removed from office, the secretary of state shall become governor for the balance of the unexpired term.

(2) If there is a vacancy in the office of lieutenant governor and the governor is absent from this state, impeached, or from mental or physical disease becomes incapable of performing the duties of the office, the secretary of state shall serve as acting governor for the balance of the unexpired term or until the governor returns, the disability ceases or the impeachment is vacated. *[1977 SJR–51; 1979 SJR–1]*

SECTION 9. *[Repealed. 1929 SJR–82; 1931 SJR–7; vote November 1932]*

Governor to approve or veto bills; proceedings on veto. SECTION 10. *[As amended November 1930]* Every bill which shall have passed the legislature shall, before it becomes a law, be presented to the governor; if he approve, he shall sign it, but if not, he shall return it, with his objections, to that house in which it shall have originated, who shall enter the objections at large upon the journal and proceed to reconsider it. Appropriation bills may be approved in whole or in part by the governor, and the part approved shall become law, and the part objected to shall be returned in the same manner as provided for other bills. If, after such reconsideration, two-thirds of the members present shall agree to pass the bill, or the part of the bill objected to, it shall be sent, together with the objections, to the other house, by which it shall likewise be reconsidered, and if approved by two-thirds of the members present it shall become a law. But in all such cases the votes of both houses shall be determined by yeas and nays, and the names of the members voting for or against the bill or the part of the bill objected to, shall be entered on the journal of each house respectively. If any bill shall not be returned by the governor within six days (Sundays excepted) after it shall have been presented to him, the same shall be a law unless the legislature shall, by their adjournment, prevent its return, in which case it shall not be a law. *[1927 SJR–35; 1929 SJR–40]*

ARTICLE VI.
ADMINISTRATIVE

Election of secretary of state, treasurer and attorney general; term. SECTION 1. *[As amended April 1979]* The qualified electors of this state, at the times and places of choosing the members of the legislature, shall in 1970 and every 4 years thereafter elect a secretary of state, treasurer and attorney general who shall hold their offices for 4 years. *[1977 SJR–51; 1979 SJR–1]*

SECTION 1m. *[Repealed. 1977 SJR–51; 1979 SJR–1; vote April 1979]*

SECTION 1n. *[Repealed. 1977 SJR–51; 1979 SJR–1; vote April 1979]*

SECTION 1p. *[Repealed. 1977 SJR–51; 1979 SJR–1; vote April 1979]*

Secretary of state; duties, compensation. SECTION 2. *[As amended November 1946]* The secretary of state shall keep a fair record of the official acts of the legislature and executive department of the state, and shall, when required, lay the same and all matters relative thereto before either branch of the legislature. He shall perform such other duties as shall be assigned him by law. He shall receive as a compensation for his services yearly such sum as shall be provided by law, and shall keep his office at the seat of government. *[1943 SJR–35; 1945 SJR–24]*

Treasurer and attorney general; duties, compensation. SECTION 3. The powers, duties and compensation of the treasurer and attorney general shall be prescribed by law.

County officers; election, terms, removal; vacancies. SECTION 4. *[As amended April 1982]* (1) Sheriffs, coroners, registers of deeds, district attorneys, and all other elected county officers except judicial officers and chief executive officers, shall be chosen by the electors of the respective counties once in every 2 years.

(2) The offices of coroner and surveyor in counties having a population of 500,000 or more are abolished. Counties not having a population of 500,000 shall have the option of retaining the elective office of coroner or instituting a medical examiner system. Two or more counties may institute a joint medical examiner system.

(3) Sheriffs shall hold no other office. Sheriffs may be required by law to renew their security from time to time, and in default of giving such new security their office shall be deemed vacant.

(4) The governor may remove any elected county officer mentioned in this section, giving to the officer a copy of the charges and an opportunity of being heard.

(5) All vacancies in the offices of sheriff, coroner, register of deeds or district attorney shall be filled by appointment. The person appointed to fill a vacancy shall hold office only for the unexpired portion of the term to which appointed and until a successor shall be elected and qualified. [1979 AJR-99; 1981 AJR-7]

ARTICLE VII.
JUDICIARY

Impeachment; trial. SECTION 1. [As amended November 1932] The court for the trial of impeachments shall be composed of the senate. The assembly shall have the power of impeaching all civil officers of this state for corrupt conduct in office, or for crimes and misdemeanors; but a majority of all the members elected shall concur in an impeachment. On the trial of an impeachment against the governor, the lieutenant governor shall not act as a member of the court. No judicial officer shall exercise his office, after he shall have been impeached, until his acquittal. Before the trial of an impeachment the members of the court shall take an oath or affirmation truly and impartially to try the impeachment according to evidence; and no person shall be convicted without the concurrence of two-thirds of the members present. Judgment in cases of impeachment shall not extend further than to removal from office, or removal from office and disqualification to hold any office of honor, profit or trust under the state; but the party impeached shall be liable to indictment, trial and punishment according to law. [1929 SJR-103; 1931 SJR-8]

Court system. SECTION 2. [As amended April 1977] The judicial power of this state shall be vested in a unified court system consisting of one supreme court, a court of appeals, a circuit court, such trial courts of general uniform statewide jurisdiction as the legislature may create by law, and a municipal court if authorized by the legislature under section 14. [1975 AJR-11; 1977 SJR-9]

Supreme court: jurisdiction. SECTION 3. [As amended April 1977] (1) The supreme court shall have superintending and administrative authority over all courts.

(2) The supreme court has appellate jurisdiction over all courts and may hear original actions and proceedings. The supreme court may issue all writs necessary in aid of its jurisdiction.

(3) The supreme court may review judgments and orders of the court of appeals, may remove cases from the court of appeals and may accept cases on certification by the court of appeals. [1975 AJR-11; 1977 SJR-9]

Supreme court: election, chief justice, court system administration. SECTION 4. [As amended April 1977] (1) The supreme court shall have 7 members who shall be known as justices of the supreme court. Justices shall be elected for 10-year terms of office commencing with the August 1 next succeeding the election. Only one justice may be elected in any year. Any 4 justices shall constitute a quorum for the conduct of the court's business.

(2) The justice having been longest a continuous member of said court, or in case 2 or more such justices shall have served for the same length of time, the justice whose term first expires, shall be the chief justice. The justice so designated as chief justice may, irrevocably, decline to serve as chief justice or resign as chief justice but continue to serve as a justice of the supreme court.

(3) The chief justice of the supreme court shall be the administrative head of the judicial system and shall exercise this administrative authority pursuant to procedures adopted by the supreme court. The chief justice may assign any judge of a court of record to aid in the proper disposition of judicial business in any court of record except the supreme court. [1975 AJR-11; 1977 SJR-9]

SECTION 5. *[Repealed. 1975 AJR-11; 1977 SJR-9; vote April 1977]*

Court of appeals. SECTION 5. *[Created April 1977]* [1] The legislature shall by law combine the judicial circuits of the state into one or more districts for the court of appeals and shall designate in each district the locations where the appeals court shall sit for the convenience of litigants.

(2) For each district of the appeals court there shall be chosen by the qualified electors of the district one or more appeals judges as prescribed by law, who shall sit as prescribed by law. Appeals judges shall be elected for 6-year terms and shall reside in the district from which elected. No alteration of district or circuit boundaries shall have the effect of removing an appeals judge from office during the judge's term. In case of an increase in the number of appeals judges, the first judge or judges shall be elected for full terms unless the legislature prescribes a shorter initial term for staggering of terms.

(3) The appeals court shall have such appellate jurisdiction in the district, including jurisdiction to review administrative proceedings, as the legislature may provide by law, but shall have no original jurisdiction other than by prerogative writ. The appeals court may issue all writs necessary in aid of its jurisdiction and shall have supervisory authority over all actions and proceedings in the courts in the district. *[1975 AJR-11; 1977 SJR-9]*

Circuit court: boundaries. SECTION 6. *[As amended April 1977]* The legislature shall prescribe by law the number of judicial circuits, making them as compact and convenient as practicable, and bounding them by county lines. No alteration of circuit boundaries shall have the effect of removing a circuit judge from office during the judge's term. In case of an increase of circuits, the first judge or judges shall be elected. *[1975 AJR-11; 1977 SJR-9]*

Circuit court: election. SECTION 7. *[As amended April 1977]* For each circuit there shall be chosen by the qualified electors thereof one or more circuit judges as prescribed by law. Circuit judges shall be elected for 6-year terms and shall reside in the circuit from which elected. *[1975 AJR-11; 1977 SJR-9]*

Circuit court: jurisdiction. SECTION 8. *[As amended April 1977]* Except as otherwise provided by law, the circuit court shall have original jurisdiction in all matters civil and criminal within this state and such appellate jurisdiction in the circuit as the legislature may prescribe by law. The circuit court may issue all writs necessary in aid of its jurisdiction. *[1975 AJR-11; 1977 SJR-9]*

Judicial elections, vacancies. SECTION 9. *[As amended April 1977]* When a vacancy occurs in the office of justice of the supreme court or judge of any court of record, the vacancy shall be filled by appointment by the governor, which shall continue until a successor is elected and qualified. There shall be no election for a justice or judge at the partisan general election for state or county officers, nor within 30 days either before or after such election. *[1975 AJR-11; 1977 SJR-9]*

Judges: eligibility to office. SECTION 10. *[As amended April 1977]* (1) No justice of the supreme court or judge of any court of record shall hold any other office of public trust, except a judicial office, during the term for which elected. No person shall be eligible to the office of judge who shall not, at the time of election or appointment, be a qualified elector within the jurisdiction for which chosen.

(2) Justices of the supreme court and judges of the courts of record shall receive such compensation as the legislature may authorize by law, but may not receive fees of office. *[1975 AJR-11; 1977 SJR-9]*

SECTION 11. *[Repealed. 1975 AJR-11; 1977 SJR-9; vote April 1977]*

Disciplinary proceedings. SECTION 11. *[Created April 1977]* Each justice or judge shall be subject to reprimand, censure, suspension, removal for cause or for disability, by the supreme court pursuant to procedures established by the legislature by law. No justice or judge removed for cause shall be eligible for reappointment or temporary service. This section is alternative to, and cumulative with, the methods of removal provided in sections 1 and 13 of this article and section 12 of article XIII. *[1975 AJR-11; 1977 SJR-9]*

Clerks of circuit and supreme courts. SECTION 12. *[As amended November 1882]* There shall be a clerk of the circuit court chosen in each county organized for judicial purposes by the qualified electors thereof, who shall hold his office for two years, subject to removal as shall be provided by law; in case of a vacancy, the judge of the circuit court shall have power to appoint a clerk until the vacancy shall be filled by an election; the clerk thus elected or appointed shall give such security as the legislature may require. The supreme court shall appoint its own clerk, and a clerk of the circuit court may be appointed a clerk of the supreme court. *[1881 AJR-16; 1882 SJR-20; 1882 c. 290]*

Justices and judges: removal by address. SECTION 13. *[As amended April 1977]* Any justice or judge may be removed from office by address of both houses of the legislature, if two-thirds of all the members elected to each house concur therein, but no removal shall be made by virtue of this section unless the justice or judge complained of is served with a copy of the charges, as the ground of address, and has had an opportunity of being heard. On the question of removal, the ayes and noes shall be entered on the journals. *[1975 AJR-11; 1977 SJR-9]*

Municipal court. SECTION 14. *[As amended April 1977]* The legislature by law may authorize each city, village and town to establish a municipal court. All municipal courts shall have uniform jurisdiction limited to actions and proceedings arising under ordinances of the municipality in which established. Judges of municipal courts may receive such compensation as provided by the municipality in which established, but may not receive fees of office. *[1975 AJR-11; 1977 SJR-9]*

SECTION 15. *[Repealed. 1963 SJR-32; 1965 SJR-26; vote April 1966]*

SECTION 16. *[Repealed. 1975 AJR-11; 1977 SJR-9; vote April 1977]*

SECTION 17. *[Repealed. 1975 AJR-11; 1977 SJR-9; vote April 1977]*

SECTION 18. *[Repealed. 1975 AJR-11; 1977 SJR-9; vote April 1977]*

SECTION 19. *[Repealed. 1975 AJR-11; 1977 SJR-9; vote April 1977]*

SECTION 20. *[Repealed. 1975 AJR-11; 1977 SJR-9; vote April 1977]* See Art. I, sec. 21.

SECTION 21. *[Repealed. 1975 AJR-11; 1977 SJR-9; vote April 1977]* See Art. IV, sec. 17.

SECTION 22. *[Repealed. 1975 AJR-11; 1977 SJR-9; vote April 1977]*

SECTION 23. *[Repealed. 1975 AJR-11; 1977 SJR-9; vote April 1977]*

Justices and judges: eligibility for office; retirement. SECTION 24. *[As amended April 1977]* (1) To be eligible for the office of supreme court justice or judge of any court of record, a person must be an attorney licensed to practice law in this state and have been so licensed for 5 years immediately prior to election or appointment.

(2) Unless assigned temporary service under subsection (3), no person may serve as a supreme court justice or judge of a court of record beyond the July 31 following the date on which such person attains that age, of not less than 70 years, which the legislature shall prescribe by law.

(3) A person who has served as a supreme court justice or judge of a court of record may, as provided by law, serve as a judge of any court of record except the supreme court on a temporary basis if assigned by the chief justice of the supreme court. *[1975 AJR-11; 1977 SJR-9]*

ARTICLE VIII.

FINANCE

Rule of taxation uniform; income, privilege and occupation taxes. SECTION 1. *[As amended April 1974]* The rule of taxation shall be uniform but the legislature may empower cities, villages or towns to collect and return taxes on real estate located therein by optional methods. Taxes shall be levied upon such property with such classifications as to forests and minerals including or separate or severed from the land, as the legislature shall prescribe. Taxation of agricultural land and undeveloped land, both as defined by law, need not be uniform with the taxation of each other nor with the taxation of other real property. Taxation of merchants' stock-in-trade, manufacturers' materials and finished products, and livestock need not be uniform with the taxation of real property and other personal property, but the taxation of all such merchants' stock-in-trade, manufacturers' materials and finished products and livestock shall be uniform, except that the

Constitution

legislature may provide that the value thereof shall be determined on an average basis. Taxes may also be imposed on incomes, privileges and occupations, which taxes may be graduated and progressive, and reasonable exemptions may be provided. *[1971 AJR-2; 1973 AJR-1]*

Appropriations; limitation. SECTION 2. *[As amended November 1877]* No money shall be paid out of the treasury except in pursuance of an appropriation by law. No appropriation shall be made for the payment of any claim against the state except claims of the United States and judgments, unless filed within six years after the claim accrued. *[1876 SJR-14; 1877 SJR-5; 1877 c. 158]*

Credit of state. SECTION 3. *[As amended April 1975]* Except as provided in s. 7 (2) (a), the credit of the state shall never be given, or loaned, in aid of any individual, association or corporation. *[1973 AJR-145; 1975 AJR-1]*

Contracting state debts. SECTION 4. The state shall never contract any public debt except in the cases and manner herein provided.

Annual tax levy to equal expenses. SECTION 5. The legislature shall provide for an annual tax sufficient to defray the estimated expenses of the state for each year; and whenever the expenses of any year shall exceed the income, the legislature shall provide for levying a tax for the ensuing year, sufficient, with other sources of income, to pay the deficiency as well as the estimated expenses of such ensuing year.

Public debt for extraordinary expense; taxation. SECTION 6. For the purpose of defraying extraordinary expenditures the state may contract public debts (but such debts shall never in the aggregate exceed one hundred thousand dollars). Every such debt shall be authorized by law, for some purpose or purposes to be distinctly specified therein; and the vote of a majority of all the members elected to each house, to be taken by yeas and nays, shall be necessary to the passage of such law; and every such law shall provide for levying an annual tax sufficient to pay the annual interest of such debt and the principal within five years from the passage of such law, and shall specially appropriate the proceeds of such taxes to the payment of such principal and interest; and such appropriation shall not be repealed, nor the taxes be postponed or diminished, until the principal and interest of such public debt shall have been wholly paid.

Public debt for public defense; bonding for public purposes. SECTION 7. *[As amended April 1975]* (1) The legislature may also borrow money to repel invasion, suppress insurrection, or defend the state in time of war; but the money thus raised shall be applied exclusively to the object for which the loan was authorized, or to the repayment of the debt thereby created.

(2) Any other provision of this constitution to the contrary notwithstanding:

(a) The state may contract public debt and pledges to the payment thereof its full faith, credit and taxing power:

1. To acquire, construct, develop, extend, enlarge or improve land, waters, property, highways, buildings, equipment or facilities for public purposes.

2. To make funds available for veterans' housing loans.

(b) The aggregate public debt contracted by the state in any calendar year pursuant to paragraph (a) shall not exceed an amount equal to the lesser of:

1. Three-fourths of one per centum of the aggregate value of all taxable property in the state; or

2. Five per centum of the aggregate value of all taxable property in the state less the sum of: a. the aggregate public debt of the state contracted pursuant to this section outstanding as of January 1 of such calendar year after subtracting therefrom the amount of sinking funds on hand on January 1 of such calendar year which are applicable exclusively to repayment of such outstanding public debt and, b. the outstanding indebtedness as of January 1 of such calendar year of any entity of the type described in paragraph (d) to the extent that such indebtedness is supported by or payable from payments out of the treasury of the state.

(c) The state may contract public debt, without limit, to fund or refund the whole or any part of any public debt contracted pursuant to paragraph (a), including any premium payable with respect thereto and any interest to accrue thereon, or to fund or refund the whole or any part of any indebtedness incurred prior to January 1, 1972, by any entity of the type described in paragraph (d), including any premium payable with respect thereto and any interest to accrue thereon.

(d) No money shall be paid out of the treasury, with respect to any lease, sublease or other agreement entered into after January 1, 1971, to the Wisconsin State Agencies Building Corporation, Wisconsin State Colleges Building Corporation, Wisconsin State Public Building Corporation, Wisconsin University Building Corporation or any similar entity existing or operating for similar purposes pursuant to which such nonprofit corporation or such other entity undertakes to finance or provide a facility for use or occupancy by the state or an agency, department or instrumentality thereof.

(e) The legislature shall prescribe all matters relating to the contracting of public debt pursuant to paragraph (a), including: the public purposes for which public debt may be contracted; by vote of a majority of the members elected to each of the 2 houses of the legislature, the amount of public debt which may be contracted for any class of such purposes; the public debt or other indebtedness which may be funded or refunded; the kinds of notes, bonds or other evidence of public debt which may be issued by the state; and the manner in which the aggregate value of all taxable property in the state shall be determined.

(f) The full faith, credit and taxing power of the state are pledged to the payment of all public debt created on behalf of the state pursuant to this section and the legislature shall provide by appropriation for the payment of the interest upon and instalments of principal of all such public debt as the same falls due, but, in any event, suit may be brought against the state to compel such payment.

(g) At any time after January 1, 1972, by vote of a majority of the members elected to each of the 2 houses of the legislature, the legislature may declare that an emergency exists and submit to the people a proposal to authorize the state to contract a specific amount of public debt for a purpose specified in such proposal, without regard to the limit provided in paragraph (b). Any such authorization shall be effective if approved by a majority of the electors voting thereon. Public debt contracted pursuant to such authorization shall thereafter be deemed to have been contracted pursuant to paragraph (a), but neither such public debt nor any public debt contracted to fund or refund such public debt shall be considered in computing the debt limit provided in paragraph (b). Not more than one such authorization shall be thus made in any 2-year period. [*1973 AJR–145; 1975 AJR–1*]

Vote on fiscal bills; quorum. SECTION 8. On the passage in either house of the legislature of any law which imposes, continues or renews a tax, or creates a debt or charge, or makes, continues or renews an appropriation of public or trust money, or releases, discharges or commutes a claim or demand of the state, the question shall be taken by yeas and nays, which shall be duly entered on the journal; and three-fifths of all the members elected to such house shall in all such cases be required to constitute a quorum therein.

Evidences of public debt. SECTION 9. No scrip, certificate, or other evidence of state debt, whatsoever, shall be issued, except for such debts as are authorized by the sixth and seventh sections of this article.

Internal improvements. SECTION 10. [*As amended April 1968*] The state shall never contract any debt for works of internal improvement, or be a party in carrying on such works; but whenever grants of land or other property shall have been made to the state, especially dedicated by the grant to particular works of internal improvement, the state may carry on such particular works and shall devote thereto the avails of such grants, and may pledge or appropriate the revenues derived from such works in aid of their completion. Provided, that the state may appropriate money in the treasury or to be thereafter raised by taxation for the construction or improvement of public highways or the development, improvement and construction of airports or other aeronautical projects or the acquisition, improvement or construction of veterans' housing or the improvement of port facilities. Provided, that the state may appropriate moneys for the purpose of acquiring, preserving and developing the forests of the state; but of the moneys appropriated under the authority of this section in any one year an amount not to exceed two-tenths of one mill of the taxable property of the state as determined by the last preceding state assessment may be raised by a tax on property. [*1965 SJR–28; 1967 SJR–18*]

Constitution

ARTICLE IX.
EMINENT DOMAIN AND PROPERTY OF THE STATE

Jurisdiction on rivers and lakes; navigable waters. SECTION 1. The state shall have concurrent jurisdiction on all rivers and lakes bordering on this state so far as such rivers or lakes shall form a common boundary to the state and any other state or territory now or hereafter to be formed, and bounded by the same; and the river Mississippi and the navigable waters leading into the Mississippi and St. Lawrence, and the carrying places between the same, shall be common highways and forever free, as well to the inhabitants of the state as to the citizens of the United States, without any tax, impost or duty therefor.

Territorial property. SECTION 2. The title to all lands and other property which have accrued to the territory of Wisconsin by grant, gift, purchase, forfeiture, escheat or otherwise shall vest in the state of Wisconsin.

Ultimate property in lands; escheats. SECTION 3. The people of the state, in their right of sovereignty, are declared to possess the ultimate property, in and to all lands within the jurisdiction of the state; and all lands the title to which shall fall from a defect of heirs shall revert or escheat to the people.

ARTICLE X.
EDUCATION

Superintendent of public instruction. SECTION 1. [As amended November 1982] The supervision of public instruction shall be vested in a state superintendent and such other officers as the legislature shall direct; and their qualifications, powers, duties and compensation shall be prescribed by law. The state superintendent shall be chosen by the qualified electors of the state at the same time and in the same manner as members of the supreme court, and shall hold office for 4 years from the succeeding first Monday in July. The term of office, time and manner of electing or appointing all other officers of supervision of public instruction shall be fixed by law. [1979 AJR-76; 1981 AJR-35; submit: May'82 Spec.Sess. AJR-1]

School fund created; income applied. SECTION 2. [As amended November 1982] The proceeds of all lands that have been or hereafter may be granted by the United States to this state for educational purposes (except the lands heretofore granted for the purpose of a university) and all moneys and the clear proceeds of all property that may accrue to the state by forfeiture or escheat; and the clear proceeds of all fines collected in the several counties for any breach of the penal laws, and all moneys arising from any grant to the state where the purposes of such grant are not specified, and the 500,000 acres of land to which the state is entitled by the provisions of an act of congress, entitled "An act to appropriate the proceeds of the sales of the public lands and to grant pre-emption rights," approved September 4, 1841; and also the 5 percent of the net proceeds of the public lands to which the state shall become entitled on admission into the union (if congress shall consent to such appropriation of the 2 grants last mentioned) shall be set apart as a separate fund to be called "the school fund," the interest of which and all other revenues derived from the school lands shall be exclusively applied to the following objects, to wit:

(1) To the support and maintenance of common schools, in each school district, and the purchase of suitable libraries and apparatus therefor.

(2) The residue shall be appropriated to the support and maintenance of academies and normal schools, and suitable libraries and apparatus therefor. [1979 AJR-76; 1981 AJR-35; submit: May'82 Spec.Sess. AJR-1]

District schools; tuition; sectarian instruction; released time. SECTION 3. [As amended April 1972] The legislature shall provide by law for the establishment of district schools, which shall be as nearly uniform as practicable; and such schools shall be free and without charge for tuition to all children between the ages of 4 and 20 years; and no sectarian instruction shall be allowed therein; but the legislature by law may, for the purpose of religious instruction outside the district schools, authorize the release of students during regular school hours. [1969 AJR-41; 1971 AJR-17]

Annual school tax. SECTION 4. Each town and city shall be required to raise by tax, annually, for the support of common schools therein, a sum not less than one-half the amount received by such town or city respectively for school purposes from the income of the school fund.

Income of school fund. SECTION 5. Provision shall be made by law for the distribution of the income of the school fund among the several towns and cities of the state for the support of common schools therein, in some just proportion to the number of children and youth resident therein between the ages of four and twenty years, and no appropriation shall be made from the school fund to any city or town for the year in which said city or town shall fail to raise such tax; nor to any school district for the year in which a school shall not be maintained at least three months.

State university; support. SECTION 6. Provision shall be made by law for the establishment of a state university at or near the seat of state government, and for connecting with the same, from time to time, such colleges in different parts of the state as the interests of education may require. The proceeds of all lands that have been or may hereafter be granted by the United States to the state for the support of a university shall be and remain a perpetual fund to be called "the university fund," the interest of which shall be appropriated to the support of the state university, and no sectarian instruction shall be allowed in such university.

Commissioners of public lands. SECTION 7. The secretary of state, treasurer and attorney general, shall constitute a board of commissioners for the sale of the school and university lands and for the investment of the funds arising therefrom. Any two of said commissioners shall be a quorum for the transaction of all business pertaining to the duties of their office.

Sale of public lands. SECTION 8. Provision shall be made by law for the sale of all school and university lands after they shall have been appraised; and when any portion of such lands shall be sold and the purchase money shall not be paid at the time of the sale, the commissioners shall take security by mortgage upon the lands sold for the sum remaining unpaid, with seven per cent interest thereon, payable annually at the office of the treasurer. The commissioners shall be authorized to execute a good and sufficient conveyance to all purchasers of such lands, and to discharge any mortgages taken as security, when the sum due thereon shall have been paid. The commissioners shall have power to withhold from sale any portion of such lands when they shall deem it expedient, and shall invest all moneys arising from the sale of such lands, as well as all other university and school funds, in such manner as the legislature shall provide, and shall give such security for the faithful performance of their duties as may be required by law.

ARTICLE XI.
CORPORATIONS

Corporations; how formed. SECTION 1. [As amended April 1981] Corporations without banking powers or privileges may be formed under general laws, but shall not be created by special act, except for municipal purposes. All general laws or special acts enacted under the provisions of this section may be altered or repealed by the legislature at any time after their passage. [1979 AJR–53; 1981 AJR–13]

Property taken by municipality. SECTION 2. [As amended April 1961] No municipal corporation shall take private property for public use, against the consent of the owner, without the necessity thereof being first established in the manner prescribed by the legislature. [1959 AJR–22; 1961 SJR–8]

Municipal home rule; debt limit; tax to pay debt. SECTION 3. [As amended April 1981] (1) Cities and villages organized pursuant to state law may determine their local affairs and government, subject only to this constitution and to such enactments of the legislature of statewide concern as with uniformity shall affect every city or every village. The method of such determination shall be prescribed by the legislature.

(2) No county, city, town, village, school district, sewerage district or other municipal corporation may become indebted in an amount that exceeds an allowable percentage of the taxable property located therein equalized for state purposes as provided by the legislature. In all cases the allowable percentage shall be 5 percent except as specified in pars. (a) and (b).

(a) For any city authorized to issue bonds for school purposes, an additional 10 percent shall be permitted for school purposes only, and in such cases the territory attached to the city for school purposes shall be included in the total taxable property supporting the bonds issued for school purposes.

(b) For any school district which offers no less than grades one to 12 and which at the time of incurring such debt is eligible for the highest level of school aids, 10 percent shall be permitted.

Constitution

(3) Any county, city, town, village, school district, sewerage district or other municipal corporation incurring any indebtedness under sub. (2) shall, before or at the time of doing so, provide for the collection of a direct annual tax sufficient to pay the interest on such debt as it falls due, and also to pay and discharge the principal thereof within 20 years from the time of contracting the same.

(4) When indebtedness under sub. (2) is incurred in the acquisition of lands by cities, or by counties or sewerage districts having a population of 150,000 or over, for public, municipal purposes, or for the permanent improvement thereof, or to purchase, acquire, construct, extend, add to or improve a sewage collection or treatment system which services all or a part of such city or county, the city, county or sewerage district incurring the indebtedness shall, before or at the time of so doing, provide for the collection of a direct annual tax sufficient to pay the interest on such debt as it falls due, and also to pay and discharge the principal thereof within a period not exceeding 50 years from the time of contracting the same.

(5) An indebtedness created for the purpose of purchasing, acquiring, leasing, constructing, extending, adding to, improving, conducting, controlling, operating or managing a public utility of a town, village, city or special district, and secured solely by the property or income of such public utility, and whereby no municipal liability is created, shall not be considered an indebtedness of such town, village, city or special district, and shall not be included in arriving at the debt limitation under sub. (2). [1979 SJR–28; 1981 SJR–5]

Acquisition of lands by state and subdivisions; sale of excess. SECTION 3a. [As amended April 3, 1956] The state or any of its counties, cities, towns or villages may acquire by gift, dedication, purchase, or condemnation lands for establishing, laying out, widening, enlarging, extending, and maintaining memorial grounds, streets, highways, squares, parkways, boulevards, parks, playgrounds, sites for public buildings, and reservations in and about and along and leading to any or all of the same; and after the establishment, layout, and completion of such improvements, may convey any such real estate thus acquired and not necessary for such improvements, with reservations concerning the future use and occupation of such real estate, so as to protect such public works and improvements, and their environs, and to preserve the view, appearance, light, air, and usefulness of such public works. If the governing body of a county, city, town or village elects to accept a gift or dedication of land made on condition that the land be devoted to a special purpose and the condition subsequently becomes impossible or impracticable, such governing body may by resolution or ordinance enacted by a two-thirds vote of its members elect either to grant the land back to the donor or dedicator or his heirs or accept from the donor or dedicator or his heirs a grant relieving the county, city, town or village of the condition; however, if the donor or dedicator or his heirs are unknown or cannot be found, such resolution or ordinance may provide for the commencement of proceedings in the manner and in the courts as the legislature shall designate for the purpose of relieving the county, city, town or village from the condition of the gift or dedication. [1953 SJR–29; 1955 SJR–9]

General banking law. SECTION 4. [As amended April 1981] The legislature may enact a general banking law for the creation of banks, and for the regulation and supervision of the banking business. [1979 AJR–53; 1981 AJR–13]

ARTICLE XII.
AMENDMENTS

Constitutional amendments. SECTION 1. Any amendment or amendments to this constitution may be proposed in either house of the legislature, and if the same shall be agreed to by a majority of the members elected to each of the two houses, such proposed amendment or amendments shall be entered on their journals, with the yeas and nays taken thereon, and referred to the legislature to be chosen at the next general election, and shall be published for three months previous to the time of holding such election; and if, in the legislature so next chosen, such proposed amendment or amendments shall be agreed to by a majority of all the members elected to each house, then it shall be the duty of the legislature to submit such proposed amendment or amendments to the people in such manner and at such time as the legislature shall prescribe; and if the people shall approve and ratify such amendment or amendments by a majority of the electors voting thereon, such amendment or amendments shall become part of the constitution;

179

provided that if more than one amendment be submitted, they shall be submitted in such manner that the people may vote for or against such amendment separately.

Constitutional conventions. SECTION 2. If at any time a majority of the senate and assembly shall deem it necessary to call a convention to revise or change this constitution, they shall recommend to the electors to vote for or against a convention at the next election for members of the legislature. And if it shall appear that a majority of the electors voting thereon have voted for a convention, the legislature shall, at its next session, provide for calling such convention.

ARTICLE XIII.
MISCELLANEOUS PROVISIONS

Political year; elections. SECTION 1. [*As amended April 1986*] The political year for this state shall commence on the first Monday of January in each year, and the general election shall be held on the Tuesday next succeeding the first Monday of November in even-numbered years. [*1983 AJR-33; 1985 AJR-3*]

SECTION 2. [*Repealed. 1973 SJR-6; 1975 SJR-4; vote April 1975*]

Eligibility to office. SECTION 3. No member of congress, nor any person holding any office of profit or trust under the United States (postmasters excepted) or under any foreign power; no person convicted of any infamous crime in any court within the United States; and no person being a defaulter to the United States or to this state, or to any county or town therein, or to any state or territory within the United States, shall be eligible to any office of trust, profit or honor in this state.

Great seal. SECTION 4. It shall be the duty of the legislature to provide a great seal for the state, which shall be kept by the secretary of state, and all official acts of the governor, his approbation of the laws excepted, shall be thereby authenticated.

SECTION 5. [*Repealed. 1983 AJR-33; 1985 SJR-3; vote April 1986*]

Legislative officers. SECTION 6. The elective officers of the legislature, other than the presiding officers, shall be a chief clerk and a sergeant at arms, to be elected by each house.

Division of counties. SECTION 7. No county with an area of nine hundred square miles or less shall be divided or have any part stricken therefrom, without submitting the question to a vote of the people of the county, nor unless a majority of all the legal voters of the county voting on the question shall vote for the same.

Removal of county seats. SECTION 8. No county seat shall be removed until the point to which it is proposed to be removed shall be fixed by law, and a majority of the voters of the county voting on the question shall have voted in favor of its removal to such point.

Election or appointment of statutory officers. SECTION 9. All county officers whose election or appointment is not provided for by this constitution shall be elected by the electors of the respective counties, or appointed by the boards of supervisors, or other county authorities, as the legislature shall direct. All city, town and village officers whose election or appointment is not provided for by this constitution shall be elected by the electors of such cities, towns and villages, or of some division thereof, or appointed by such authorities thereof as the legislature shall designate for that purpose. All other officers whose election or appointment is not provided for by this constitution, and all officers whose offices may hereafter be created by law, shall be elected by the people or appointed, as the legislature may direct.

Vacancies in office. SECTION 10. [*As amended April 1979*] (1) The legislature may declare the cases in which any office shall be deemed vacant, and also the manner of filling the vacancy, where no provision is made for that purpose in this constitution.

(2) Whenever there is a vacancy in the office of lieutenant governor, the governor shall nominate a successor to serve for the balance of the unexpired term, who shall take office after confirmation by the senate and by the assembly. [*1977 SJR-51; 1979 SJR-1*]

Passes, franks and privileges. SECTION 11. [*As amended November 1936*] No person, association, copartnership, or corporation, shall promise, offer or give, for any purpose, to any political committee, or any member or employe thereof, to any candidate for, or incumbent of any office or position under the constitution or laws, or under any ordinance of any town or municipality, of this state, or to any person at the request or for the advantage of all or any of them, any free pass or frank, or any privilege withheld from any person, for the traveling accommodation or transportation of any person or property, or the transmission of any message or communication.

No political committee, and no member or employe thereof, no candidate for and no incumbent of any office or position under the constitution or laws, or under any ordinance of any town or municipality of this state, shall ask for, or accept, from any person, association, copartnership, or corporation, or use, in any manner, or for any purpose, any free pass or frank, or any privilege withheld from any person, for the traveling accommodation or transportation of any person or property, or the transmission of any message or communication.

Any violation of any of the above provisions shall be bribery and punished as provided by law, and if any officer or any member of the legislature be guilty thereof, his office shall become vacant.

No person within the purview of this act shall be privileged from testifying in relation to anything therein prohibited; and no person having so testified shall be liable to any prosecution or punishment for any offense concerning which he was required to give his testimony or produce any documentary evidence.

Notaries public and regular employes of a railroad or other public utilities who are candidates for or hold public offices for which the annual compensation is not more than three hundred dollars to whom no passes or privileges are extended beyond those which are extended to other regular employes of such corporations are excepted from the provisions of this section. [1933 AJR–50; 1935 AJR–67]

Recall of elective officers. SECTION 12. [*As amended April 1981*] The qualified electors of the state, of any congressional, judicial or legislative district or of any county may petition for the recall of any incumbent elective officer after the first year of the term for which the incumbent was elected, by filing a petition with the filing officer with whom the nomination petition to the office in the primary is filed, demanding the recall of the incumbent.

(1) The recall petition shall be signed by electors equaling at least twenty-five percent of the vote cast for the office of governor at the last preceding election, in the state, county or district which the incumbent represents.

(2) The filing officer with whom the recall petition is filed shall call a recall election for the Tuesday of the 6th week after the date of filing the petition or, if that Tuesday is a legal holiday, on the first day after that Tuesday which is not a legal holiday.

(3) The incumbent shall continue to perform the duties of the office until the recall election results are officially declared.

(4) Unless the incumbent declines within 10 days after the filing of the petition, the incumbent shall without filing be deemed to have filed for the recall election. Other candidates may file for the office in the manner provided by law for special elections. For the purpose of conducting elections under this section:

(a) When more than 2 persons compete for a nonpartisan office, a recall primary shall be held. The 2 persons receiving the highest number of votes in the recall primary shall be the 2 candidates in the recall election, except that if any candidate receives a majority of the total number of votes cast in the recall primary, that candidate shall assume the office for the remainder of the term and a recall election shall not be held.

(b) For any partisan office, a recall primary shall be held for each political party which is by law entitled to a separate ballot and from which more than one candidate competes for the party's nomination in the recall election. The person receiving the highest number of votes in the recall primary for each political party shall be that party's candidate in the recall election. Independent candidates and candidates representing political parties not entitled by law to a separate ballot shall be shown on the ballot for the recall election only.

(c) When a recall primary is required, the date specified under sub. (2) shall be the date of the recall primary and the recall election shall be held on the Tuesday of the 4th week after the recall primary or, if that Tuesday is a legal holiday, on the first day after that Tuesday which is not a legal holiday.

(5) The person who receives the highest number of votes in the recall election shall be elected for the remainder of the term.

(6) After one such petition and recall election, no further recall petition shall be filed against the same officer during the term for which he was elected.

(7) This section shall be self-executing and mandatory. Laws may be enacted to facilitate its operation but no law shall be enacted to hamper, restrict or impair the right of recall. [*1979 SJR–5; 1981 SJR–2*]

Article XIV.
Schedule

Effect of change from territory to state. Section 1. That no inconvenience may arise by reason of a change from a territorial to a permanent state government, it is declared that all rights, actions, prosecutions, judgments, claims and contracts, as well of individuals as of bodies corporate, shall continue as if no such change had taken place; and all process which may be issued under the authority of the territory of Wisconsin previous to its admission into the union of the United States shall be as valid as if issued in the name of the state.

Territorial laws continued. Section 2. All laws now in force in the territory of Wisconsin which are not repugnant to this constitution shall remain in force until they expire by their own limitation or be altered or repealed by the legislature.

Section 3. [*Repealed. 1979 AJR–76; 1981 AJR–35; submit: May'82 Spec.Sess. AJR–1; vote November 1982*]

Section 4. [*Repealed. 1979 AJR–76; 1981 AJR–35; submit: May'82 Spec.Sess. AJR–1; vote November 1982*]

Section 5. [*Repealed. 1979 AJR–76; 1981 AJR–35; submit: May'82 Spec.Sess. AJR–1; vote November 1982*]

Section 6. [*Repealed. 1979 AJR–76; 1981 AJR–35; submit: May'82 Spec.Sess. AJR–1; vote November 1982*]

Section 7. [*Repealed. 1979 AJR–76; 1981 AJR–35; submit: May'82 Spec.Sess. AJR–1; vote November 1982*]

Section 8. [*Repealed. 1979 AJR–76; 1981 AJR–35; submit: May'82 Spec.Sess. AJR–1; vote November 1982*]

Section 9. [*Repealed. 1979 AJR–76; 1981 AJR–35; submit: May'82 Spec.Sess. AJR–1; vote November 1982*]

Section 10. [*Repealed. 1979 AJR–76; 1981 AJR–35; submit: May'82 Spec.Sess. AJR–1; vote November 1982*]

Section 11. [*Repealed. 1979 AJR–76; 1981 AJR–35; submit: May'82 Spec.Sess. AJR–1; vote November 1982*]

Section 12. [*Repealed. 1979 AJR–76; 1981 AJR–35; submit: May'82 Spec.Sess. AJR–1; vote November 1982*]

Common law continued in force. Section 13. Such parts of the common law as are now in force in the territory of Wisconsin, not inconsistent with this constitution, shall be and continue part of the law of this state until altered or suspended by the legislature.

Section 14. [*Repealed. 1979 AJR–76; 1981 AJR–35; submit: May'82 Spec.Sess. AJR–1; vote November 1982*]

Section 15. [*Repealed. 1979 AJR–76; 1981 AJR–35; submit: May'82 Spec.Sess. AJR–1; vote November 1982*]

Implementing revised structure of judicial branch. Section 16. [*As affected November 1982*] (1), (2), (3) and (5) [*Repealed*]

(4) [*Amended*] The terms of office of justices of the supreme court serving on August 1, 1978, shall expire on the July 31 next preceding the first Monday in January on which such terms would otherwise have expired, but such advancement of the date of term expiration shall not impair any retirement rights vested in any such justice if the term had expired on the first Monday in January. [*1979 AJR–76; 1981 AJR–35; submit: May'82 Spec.Sess. AJR–1*]

Note: For attached resolutions and signatures see end of Constitution as printed in the *Revised Statutes* of 1849 and 1858.

BOOKS ABOUT WISCONSIN

—A Select Bibliography

Algire, Tom. *Wisconsin.* Portland, Oregon, Graphic Arts Center Publishing Co., 1981.

Alphonsa, Sister Mary. *The Story of Father van den Broek.* Chicago, 1907.

Anderson, Rasmus Bjorn. *Life Story of Rasmus B. Anderson.* Madison, The Author, 1915.

Apps, Jerry. *Breweries of Wisconsin.* 1992.

Bartlett, William W. *History, Tradition and Adventure in the Chippewa Valley.* Chippewa Falls, Wis., The Author, 1929.

Bennett, P. S. *History of Methodism in Wisconsin.* Cincinnati, Cranston & Stowe, 1890.

Berger, Victor L. *Voice and Pen of Victor L. Berger.* Milwaukee, The Milwaukee *Leader*, 1929.

Bhatia, Shyam Sunder. *Age and Sex Structure of Wisconsin Villages, 1970.* Oshkosh, Wis., Dept. of Geography, University of Wisconsin - Oshkosh, 1974.

Black Hawk. *Life of Black Hawk; Ma-ka-tai-me-she-kia-kiak.* Iowa City, Iowa State Historical Society, 1932.

Blair, Emma Helen, ed. *The Indian Tribes of the Upper Mississippi Valley and the Region of the Great Lakes.* Cleveland. The Arthur H. Clark Co., 1911.

Borst, Charlotte G. *Catching Babies: The Professionalization of Childbirth, 1870-1920.* 1996.

Bradford, Mary Lemira (Davidson). *Memoirs of Mary D. Bradford.* Evansville, Wis., 1932.

Breck, Charles, comp. *The Life of the Reverend James Lloyd Breck, D.D.* New York, E. & J.B. Young, 1883.

Bruce, Wm. George. *A Short History of Milwaukee.* Milwaukee, Bruce Pub. Co., 1936.

Bryant. Benjamin F., ed. *Memoirs of La Crosse Country.* Madison, 1907.

Butts, Porter. *Art in Wisconsin.* Madison, Madison Art Association, 1936.

Campbell, Henry Colin. *Wisconsin in Three Centuries, 1634-1905.* New York, The Century History Co., 1906.

Carver, Jonathan. *Travels through the Interior Parts of North America in the Years 1766, 1767, and 1768.* London, Printed for the Author, 1778.

The Catholic Hal. Milwaukee. *Commemorating 300 years of Catholic History in Wisconsin.* Milwaukee, 1934.

Chamberlin, Thomas Chrowder, and others. *Geology of Wisconsin.* Madison, 1877-83. 4 v. and atlas. (Wisconsin Geological and Natural History Survey.)

Clemens, Samuel Langhorne (Mark Twain). *Life on the Mississippi.* Boston, J. R. Osgood and Co., 1883 (and in numerous later editions).

Clohisy, Matt. *Wisconsin Trees.* Milwaukee, the Milwaukee *Journal*, 1927.

Cole, Harry Ellsworth. *Stagecoach and Tavern Tales of the Old Northwest,* ed. by Louis Phelps Kellogg. Cleveland, The Arthur H. Clark Co., 1930.

Commons, John Rogers. *Myself.* New York, Macmillan, 1934.

Conard, Howard L., ed. *History of Milwaukee from its First Settlement to the Year 1895.* Chicago and New York, Am. Biographical Pub. Co., 1896. 2 v.

Cooper, Zachary. *Black Settlers in Rural Wisconsin.* 1994.

Current, Richard Nelson. *Wisconsin: A Bicentennial History.* New York, Norton, 1977.

Davidson, John N. *In Unnamed Wisconsin.* Milwaukee, S. Chapman, 1895.

Davis, Susan Burdick. *Wisconsin Lore for Boys and Girls.* Eau Claire, Wis., E. M. Hale & Co., 1931.

Derleth, August William, and Raymond E. F. Larsson, ed. *Poetry Out of Wisconsin.* New York, Harrison, 1937.

Dudley, Kathryn Marie. *The End of the Line: Lost Jobs, New Lives in Postindustrial America (Morality and Society).* 1994.

Duns, Olaus Fredrik. *Frontier Parsonage: Letters of Olaus Fredrik Duns, Norwegian pastor in Wisconsin, 1855-1858..* New York, Arno Press, 1979 (c. 1947).

Edwards, Everett E., comp. *The Early Writings of Frederick Jackson Turner.* Madison, The University of Wisconsin Press, 1938.

Eisinger, Peter K. *The Patterns of Interracial Politics.* New York, Academic Press, 1976.

Evans, Constance M., and Ona B. Earll. *Prairie du Chien and the Winnishiek.* Prairie du Chien, Wis., 1928.

Fassett, Norman Carter. *Spring Flora of Wisconsin.* Madison, The Author, 1931.

Featherstonhaugh, George William. *A Canoe Voyage up the Minnay Sotor.* London, R. Bentley, 1947.

Fenneman. N. M. *On the Lakes of Southeastern Wisconsin.* Madison, 1901. (Wisconsin Geological and Natural History Survey. Bulletin 8.)

Fitzpatrick, Edward A. *Wisconsin.* New York, The Bruce Pub. Co., 1931.

—. *History of Northern Wisconsin.* Chicago, Western Historical Pub. Co., 1881.

Fry, C. Luther. *The New and the Old Immigrant on the Land.* New York, George H. Doran Co., 1922.

Gale, Zona "Wisconsin, a Voice from the Middle Border." *These United States.* 1st series. New York Boni & Liveright, 1923.

Gregory, John Goadby. *History of Milwaukee, Wisconsin.* Chicago, The S. J. Clarke Pub. Co., 1931. 4 v., ill.

Haugen, Nils P. *Pioneer and Political Reminiscences.* Evansville, Wis., The Antes press, 1930.

Heming, Harry Hooper. *The Catholic Church in Wisconsin.* Milwaukee, Catholic Historical Pub. Co., 1895-1898.

Hense-Jensen, Wilhelm. *Wisconsin's Deutsch-Amerikaner.* Milwaukee, Die Deutsche Gesellschaft, 1900-02. 2 v.

Hoan, Daniel Webster. *City Government; the Record of the Milwaukee Experiment.* New York, Harcourt, Brace & Co., 1936.

Holand, Hjalmar Rued. *Old Peninsula Days; Tales and Sketches of the Door County Peninsula.* Ephraim, Wis., Pioneer Pub. Co., 1925.

Holliday, Diane Young, et al. *Digging and Discovery: Wisconsin Archaeology.* 1998.

Holmes, Frederick L. *Regulation of Railroads and Public Utilities in Wisconsin.* New York and London, D. Appleton Co., 1915.

Howe, Frederic Clemson. *Wisconsin: an Experiment in Democracy.* New York, Schribner, 1912.

Jacobson, Joanne. *Authority and Alliance in the Letters of Henry Adams (Wisconsin Studies in American Autobiography.* 1992.

Judson, Katherine Berry, ed. *Myths and Legends of the Mississippi Valley and the Great Lakes.* Chicago, A. C. McClurg, 1914.

Kearney, Luke Sylvester. *The Hodag, and Other Tales of the Logging Camps.* Wausau, Wis., The Author, 1928.

Kellogg, Louise Phelps. *The British Regime in Wisconsin and the Northwest.* Madison. Wisconsin State Historical Society, 1935.

——. *The French Regime in Wisconsin and the Northwest.* Madison. Wisconsin State Historical Society, 1925. (Wisconsin Historical Series, v. I.)

Koss, Rudolf. *Milwaukee.* Milwaukee, Milwaukee Herald, 1871.

——. *Madison, Dane County and Surrounding Towns.* Madison, William J. Park & Co., 1877.

Kumlien, L., and N. Hollister. *Birds of Wisconsin.* Milwaukee, 1903. (Wisconsin Geological and Natural History Survey.)

La Follette, Robert M. *Autobiography.* Madison, Robert M. La Follette Co., 1913.

Lacher, J. Henry A. *The German Element in Wisconsin.* America, 1925.

Leavitt, Judith Walzer. *The Healthiest City: Milwaukee and the Politics of Health Reform.* 1996.

Leonard, William Ellery. *The Locomotive-God.* New York, London, The Century Co., 1927.

Martin, Lawrence. *The Physical Geography of Wisconsin.* Madison, 1916. (Wisconsin Geological and Natural History Survey. Bulletin 36.)

McCarthy, Charles. *The Wisconsin Idea.* New York, Macmillan, 1912.

McDonald, Grace. *History of the Irish in Wisconsin in the Nineteenth Century.* New York, Arno Press, 1976, c. 1954.

McKern, Will Carleton. *A Winnebago Myth.* Year Book, Public Museum, Milwaukee, 1929, v. 9: 215-230.

McMurtrie, Douglas Crawford. *Early Printing in Wisconsin.* Seattle, Wash., McCaffrey, 1931.

Merk, Frederick. *Economic History of Wisconsin During the Civil War Decade.* Madison, Wisconsin State Historical Society, 1916.

Merrick, George B. *Old Times on the Upper Mississippi.* Cleveland, The Arthur H. Clark Co., 1909.

Muir, John. *The Story of My Boyhood and Youth.* Boston and New York, Houghton, Mifflin & Co., 1913.

Nehrling, Henry. *Our Native Birds of Song and Beauty.* Milwaukee, George Brumder, 1893. 2 v.

Bibliography

Nolen, John. *Madison: a Model City.* Boston, 1911.

Nute, Grace Lee. *The Voyageur.* New York and London, D. Appleton & Co., 1931.

Olmsted, Robert P. *Milwaukee Rails.* Woodridge, Ill., McMillan Publications, 1980.

Paul, Justus F. and Barbara D. *The Badger State.* Grand Rapids: Eerdmans, 1978. Index. A documentary history of Wisconsin.

Pederson, Jane Marie. *Between Memory and Reality: Family and Community in Rural Wisconsin, 1870-1970 (History of American Thought and Culture).* 1992.

Qualey, Carlton. *Norwegian Settlement in the United States.* Northfield, Minn., Norwegian American Historical Association, 1938.

Red River Lumber Co. *The Marvelous Exploits of Paul Bunyan.* Minneapolis, 1922.

Rockwell, Ethel Theodora. *The Centennial Cavalcade of Wisconsin. Madison, 1936.*

Roth, Filibert. *On the Forestry Conditions of Northern Wisconsin.* Madison, 1898. (Wisconsin Geological and Natural History Survey. Bulletin I.)

Rounds, Charles Ralph. *Wisconsin Authors and Their Works.* Madison, Parker Educational Co., 1918.

Sayre, Robert F. *The Examined Self: Benjamin Franklin, Henry Adams, and Henry James (Wisconsin Studies in American Autobiography.* 1998.

Scanlan, Peter Lawrence. *Prairie du Chien: French, British, American.* Menasha, Wis., Geo. Banta Pub. Co., 1937.

Schurz, Carl. *The Reminiscences of Carl Schurz.* New York, Macmillan, 1907-8.

Shaw, J. F. "Study in Wisconsin Civics." *Wisconsin Blue Book,* 1929.

Skinner, Alanson. *Material Culture of the Menomini.* New York, Museum of the American Indian, Heye Foundation, 1921.

Smith, William Rudolph. *Observations on the Wisconsin Territory.* New York, Arno Press, 1975, c. 1838.

Stearns, John William, ed. *The Columbian History of Education in Wisconsin.* Milwaukee, 1893.

Shaw, J. F "Study in Wisconsin Civics." *Wisconsin Blue Book,* 1929.

Stewart, Lillian Kimball. *A Pioneer of Old Superior.* Boston, Christopher Pub. House, 1930.

Strong, Moses McCure. *History of the Territory of Wisconsin, from 1836 to 1848.* Madison, 1885.

Thomson, Alexander McDonald. *A Political History of Wisconsin.* Milwaukee, E. C. Williams Co., 1900.

Thwaites, Reuben Gold. *The Story of Wisconsin.* Boston, Lothrop, 1980 (rev. ed. 1988).

—. *Wisconsin Magazine of History.* Madison, Wisconsin State Historical Society, 1917 to date.

Titus, William A. *History of the Fox River Valley, Lake Winnebago and the Green Bay Region.* Chicago, 1930. 3 v.

Trask, Kerry A. *Fire Within: A Civil War Narrative from Wisconsin.* 1998.

Turner, Frederick Jackson. *The Frontier in American History.* New York, Holt, 1920.

Turner, Jennie McMullin. *Wisconsin Pioneers.* Appleton C. C. Nelson Pub. Co., 1929.

Twining, Charles E. *Downriver: Orrin H. Ingram end the Empire Lumber Company.* Madison, State Historical Society of Wisconsin, 1975.

Umhoefer, Jim. *Guide to Wisconsin's Parks, Forests, Recreation Areas and Trails.* Madison, Northword, 1982.

University of Wisconsin. *The University and Conservation of Wildlife.* Madison, 1937. (Science Inquiry Publication III.)

Veitch, Jonathan. *American Superrealism: Nathanael West and the Politics of Representation in the 1930s (The Wisconsin Project on American Writers.* 1997.

Vexler, Robert I., ed. *Chronology and Documentary Handbook of the State of Wisconsin.* Dobbs Ferry, N. Y., Oceana Publications, 1978.

Wells, Robert W. *Yesterday's Milwaukee.* Miami, E. A. Seemann Pub., 1976.

Wilson, F. G. *Forest Trees of Wisconsin; How to Know Them.* Madison, 1928.

—. *Wisconsin Fish.* Milwaukee, The Milwaukee *Journal,* 1928.

Winslow, John Bradley. *The Story of a Great Court.* Chicago, Flood, 1912.

Wisconsin Executive Office. *Committee of Land Use and Forestry.* Report. Forest Land Usein Wisconsin. Madison, 1932.

Wisconsin Jewish Chronicle. *Jewish Community Blue Book of Milwaukee and Wisconsin.* Milwaukee, 1924-26. 2 v. and supplement.

Bibliography

Wisconsin State Historical Society. *Genealogical Research.* Madison, The Society, 1979.

Wisconsin. *The Wisconsin Blue Book, 1937.* Madison, 1937. Compiled by the Wisconsin Legislative Reference Library. Biennial. First pub. 1853.

Woodward, David, et al. *Cultural Map of Wisconsin: Wisconsin's History, Culture, Land & People.* 1996.

Wright, Frank Lloyd. *An Autobiography.* London, New York, etc., Longmans, Green & Co., 1932.

Ylvisaker, Erling. *Eminent Pioneers.* Minneapolis, Augsburg Pub. Co., 1934.

Young, Kimball, J. L Gillin, and C. L. Dedrick. *The Madison Community.* Madison, 1934.

Zeitlin, Richard H. and Hale, Frederick. *Germans in Wisconsin.* 1977.